ROOTS OF TM

Paul Mason learned the practice of 'Transcendental Meditation' or 'TM' in 1970 when he visited the Maharishi's *ashram* at Rishikesh after having hitch-hiked to India from Britain. This experience spurred him to dig deeper into the history of the teaching of meditation, whereupon he was commissioned to write Maharishi's lifestory. This authoritative work has been revised, expanded, and re-published as *Maharishi Mahesh Yogi: The Biography of the Man Who Gave Transcendental Meditation to the World.*

Interest in Transcendental Meditation led to research into the lifestory and teachings of Maharishi's master, 'Guru Dev', Swami Brahmananda Saraswati, Shankaracharya of Jyotirmath, the most prominent religious position in Northern India.

Guru Dev is credited for the revival of knowledge and teaching of Transcendental Meditation.

Titles by Paul Mason:

Maharishi Mahesh Yogi: The Biography of the Man Who Gave Transcendental Meditation to the World

The Beatles, Drugs, Mysticism & India:
Maharishi Mahesh Yogi - Transcendental Meditation - Jai Guru Deva OM

Roots of TM: The Transcendental Meditation of Guru Dev & Maharishi Mahesh Yogi
^
Den Transcendentala Meditationens Ursprung - Turning Pages
Swedish edition 2017

108 Discourses of Guru Dev:
The Life and Teachings of Swami Brahmananda Saraswati, Shankaracharya of Jyotirmath (1941-53) - Volume I
~
The Biography of Guru Dev:
The Life and Teachings of Swami Brahmananda Saraswati, Shankaracharya of Jyotirmath (1941-53) - Volume II
~
Guru Dev as Presented by Maharishi Mahesh Yogi:
The Life and Teachings of Swami Brahmananda Saraswati, Shankaracharya of Jyotirmath (1941-53) - Volume III

The Knack of Meditation:
The No-Nonsense Guide to Successful Meditation

Dandi Swami: The Story of the Guru's Will, Maharishi Mahesh Yogi, the Shankaracharyas of Jyotir Math & Meetings with Dandi Swami Narayanand Saraswati

Via Rishikesh: En Route to Chittavrittinirodha

Mala: A String of Unexpected Meetings

Kathy's Story

The Maharishi: The Biography of the Man Who Gave Transcendental Meditation to the World
Element Books - First English edition 1994
Evolution Books - Revised English edition 2005
Maharishi Mahesh Yogi - Aquamarin - German edition 1995
O Maharishi - Nova Era - Portuguese edition 1997

ROOTS OF TM

THE TRANSCENDENTAL MEDITATION OF GURU DEV & MAHARISHI MAHESH YOGI

by
Paul Mason

PREMANAND
www.paulmason.info
premanandpaul@yahoo.co.uk

First published by Premanand 2015
© Paul Mason 2015, 2016, 2017, 2020, 2022
ISBN 978-0-9562228-8-6

All rights reserved
No part of this book may be reproduced
or utilized, in any form or by any means
electronic or mechanical, without
permission in writing from the Publisher.

Cover design by Premanand

Photo on front cover is of Shankaracharya Swami Brahmananda Saraswati aboard mobile dais, at Old Square, near Mussoorie Library, Mussoorie, on Shankaracharya Day, 23rd September 1952

Foreword

By the mid-1960's the term *'Transcendental Meditation'* became fixed after Maharishi Mahesh Yogi spread the message of meditation far and wide across the free world. Maharishi then became very famous himself, largely due to his public association with celebrities, and in particular the world famous pop group The Beatles who in 1968 attended an advanced training course with him in India.

When I travelled to India in 1970 I did so by hitch-hiking from Britain, across many countries of the Middle East before finally finding myself in North India. Possibly because The Beatles had done so before me, I decided to visit the *ashram* of Maharishi Mahesh Yogi, just for 'a cup of cocoa and a chat about philosophy', and therefore made my way to the pilgrimage town of Rishikesh, surrounded by jungle. Having crossed the River Ganges and climbed up to Maharishi Ashram, I was introduced there to a practice referred to as 'transcendental' meditation.

The teaching of this *'Transcendental Meditation'* or *'TM'* is preceded by a short ceremony called a *puja*, conducted before a portrait of an Indian teacher, an ascetic called Swami Brahmanandaa Saraswati, known to TM meditators as 'Guru Dev'.

Surprisingly, despite the fact that Swami Brahmananda Saraswati was a prominent and influential public speaker, Maharishi's organisations share but scant information about Guru Dev's life story and disclose nothing about his teachings.

As little was known about the early life of Maharishi Mahesh Yogi, or the origins and history of the teaching of Transcendental Meditation, I set myself to uncover as much information as could be found.

In the 1990's I was commissioned by *Element Books* to write the biography of Maharishi Mahesh Yogi, which was published as *'The Maharishi: The Biography of the Man Who Gave Transcendental Meditation to the World'*.

Later, in 2007 an ambition was fulfilled when a 3-volume set of books on Guru Dev was published, all based on my translations of Hindi works on Swami Brahmananda.

Then, in 2013, I compiled a book entitled *'Dandi Swami: The Story of the Guru's Will, Maharishi Mahesh Yogi, the Shankaracharyas of Jyotir Math & Meetings With Dandi Swami Narayanand Saraswati'.*

In 2017, a monumental research project found form in the publication of *'The Beatles, Drugs, Mysticism & India'.*

In 2020, the biography Maharishi's biography was totally revised, enlarged and re-published as *'Maharishi Mahesh Yogi: The Biography of the Man Who Gave Transcendental Meditation to the World'.*

This volume, the *'Roots of TM'*, is intended to enable readers to better understand how and why Maharishi Mahesh Yogi spread the teaching of Transcendental Meditation around the world.

'Roots of TM' provides background information on Maharishi Mahesh Yogi and his master, Guru Dev, Swami Brahmananda Saraswati, and provides a source book of information about their teachings and techniques.

'Roots of TM' is not intended as a general guide to Indian philosophy, or as a study of the many ancient spiritual practices of India, nor as a *mantra* handbook.

'Roots of TM' offers information about Maharishi's 'missing years', from the time when his master passed away through to the gradual build up of his stated mission to spiritually regenerate the world; 'Why can't we spiritually regenerate the world through this technique?' he asked.

'Roots of TM' contains numerous quotations and rare transcripts of lectures by Guru Dev and by Maharishi. Furthermore, it details the course of events that would eventually find Maharishi lecturing at the Masquers Club, an actor's social club in Hollywood. It also tells how Maharishi came to adopt a businesslike attitude to money matters, and how he planned to create a headquarters high in the Himalayas where he intended to train others to teach transcendental meditation.

'Roots of TM' digs deeply into rare materials in order to give detailed profiles of the teachings of both master and disciple, thus affording readers an opportunity to make informed comparisons of both these teachers' methods and their objectives.

"Living Bridge"
Hooker's Himalayan Journals, 1855

Contents

1. The Transcendental Meditation Technique	15
2. Adi Shankara	27
3. Swami Brahmananda Saraswati	31
4. Mahesh Prasad meets Swami Brahmananda	47
5. Raj Varma meets Swami Brahmananda Saraswati	53
6. Installation of Shankaracharya of Jyotirmath	61
7. The Shankaracharya of Jyotir Math Recruits a Secretary	65
8. Vedic India	73
9. The Teachings of Swami Brahmananda Saraswati	75
10. Yoga Teachings of Swami Brahmananda	97
11. Contemporary Meditation Teachings	105
12. Swami Brahmananda & the First Presidents of India	109
13. A New Shankaracharya of Jyotirmath	127
14. Brahmachari Mahesh Ji	137
15. Maharishi Mahesh Yogi	157
16. Maharishi's First Published Discourses	165
17. In Praise of the Guru	191
18. Spiritual Regeneration Movement (SRM)	199
19. Maharishi Leaves India for the West	211
20. International Meditation Society (IMS)	231
21. Transcendental Meditation (TM)	269
22. Purity of the Teaching	273
23. The Story of the Pandit, the Brahmachari and the Guru	277
Reference Notes	285
Glossary	295

*'Om Lead Me To Light
Om Dawn In My Sight
Om Take Me To Thine
Om Make Me To Shine.'* [1]

- Mahesh Srivastava
January 1941

The Transcendental Meditation Technique

Practice

This Transcendental Meditation, or TM, is a system of meditation, which is generally practiced twice daily. A teacher introduces one to the practice of TM. After a short interview with an initiator (a teacher of TM), there follows a short ceremony to which the initiate brings flowers, fruit & fresh cotton handkerchief. During the *puja* ceremony the teacher murmurs a traditional Sanskrit composition (a version of *Acharya Vandana*) and performs a ritual set of offerings in front of a portrait of Guru Dev, a revered Indian sage. Following this ceremony the initiate is given a *mantra* and an explanation of how to use the *mantra* to good effect in meditation.

Method

During his time as Shankaracharya, Guru Dev advocated a method which involves the use of two techniques practiced simultaneously;

   1. '*japa*', the 'mental repetition of a *mantra*'

   2. '*dhyana*', is 'meditation' or 'contemplation'.

Guru Dev explained that to practice *japa* alone, the mind flits about, and by *dhyana* alone the mind becomes restrained, but by practicing a combination of the two methods, success is met with.

In the instructions as to how to practice Transcendental Meditation one is first asked to understand how effortlessly thought occurs, then one is guided as to how to repeat a *mantra*:-

   'When we close our eyes, naturally we feel some quietness,

some silence, yes? Did you have some thoughts in that silence? Did you notice that a thought comes effortlessly, spontaneously? This is how effortlessly we should think the *mantra*.'

'In this meditation, we do not concentrate; we do not try to think the *mantra* clearly. Mental repetition is not a clear pronunciation. It is just a faint idea. We don't try to make a rhythm of the *mantra*. We don't try to control thoughts. We do not wish that thoughts should not come. If a thought comes, we do not try to push it out. We don't feel sorry about it. When a thought comes, the mind is completely absorbed in the thought.'

'When we become aware that we are not thinking the *mantra*, then we quietly come back to the *mantra*. Very easily we think the *mantra* and if at any moment we feel that we are forgetting it, we should not try to persist in repeating it. Only very easily we start and take it as it comes and do not hold the *mantra* if it tends to slip away.'

'The *mantra* may change in different ways. It can get faster or slower, louder or softer, clearer or fainter. Its pronunciation may change, lengthen or shorten or even may appear to be distorted or it may not appear to change at all. In every case, we take it as it comes, neither anticipating nor resisting change, just simple innocence.'

'There is no need to try to stop thinking, because thoughts are a part of meditation. Even if the mind is filled with other thoughts while the *mantra* is going on, there is no conflict. Our concern is with the *mantra*, and if other thoughts are there along with it, we do not mind them and we don't try to remove them. We are not concerned with them, we innocently favour the *mantra*.'

'Noise is no barrier to meditation. Even in a noisy market, it is possible to be thinking thoughts and whenever we can think, we can meditate. So one can think the *mantra* comfortably even though aware of outside noises. We just innocently favour the *mantra* and do not try to resist noise in any way.'

'It is easy and simple. It is just the normal, natural process of thinking the *mantra* and taking it as it comes. Now, this is how we will meditate, easily, morning and evening.'

'One thing is very important, that we do not try to meditate. We do not try to keep the tempo of the *mantra* the same, nor do we try to change the tempo. And, we do not concentrate against thoughts we might have, or against noises we might hear. We do not resist thoughts, we do not resist noise, we do not resist the *mantra* changing or disappearing, we do not resist anything. We take it as it comes. It is a very simple, natural, innocent process. When we meditate at home, we start with half a minute sitting easily. That means, close the eyes about half a minute and then start the *mantra* easily. And when we want to end meditation then we stop thinking the *mantra* inside, but do not open the eyes for about 2 minutes. This is very important that we start with half a minute of silence and end with 2 minutes of silence.'

Importantly, all these instructions, about using the *mantra* correctly, rely on the ability of the meditator to witness, to remember, and if necessary, to adjust, his or her practice. So, Transcendental Meditation is not simply a matter of sitting quietly and mentally intoning and repeating a pleasant sound, it also relies on the ability of the meditator to bear witness to this process. If the meditator repeats the *mantra*, and is mindful of that repetition, then he is practicing *japa* and *dhyana*, and what occurs is that he/she 'transcends' quite naturally and spontaneously, and at times finds himself/herself in a state of 'restful alertness' where thought and mental action have subsided and there is a *stasis*, a suspension of mental and physical activity. So the mind is stilled and this is the state of *yoga*, as described in *Patanajali's Yoga Sutras*, in *Bhagavad Gita*, and in innumerable other texts.

There are several explanations offered as to how Transcendental Meditation works, *viz.* because it is 'effortless', 'spontaneous', and 'a simple natural innocent process'.

Further insight might be gained, about how TM works, from this exchange between a student of TM and Maharishi Mahesh Yogi:

Question - "How can we think something effortlessly when we are told to try to think it? It doesn't make sense."

Maharishi - "Right, it <u>doesn't</u> make sense. Mind is told to be effortless, and mind is also told to think this thought. Mind tries to bring together these two contradictory instructions and in this moment of struggling to do these two contradictory actions, mind slips between both instructions and there it slips inward toward the source of thought."

Effects

Subjectively, it is as if one were stepping back a pace, within, drawing one's breath and taking some moments to compose oneself. One might also say that this TM meditation is like routinely clearing one's vision or cleaning one's windscreen. But more importantly this meditation seems to perform the function of a circuit breaker, automatically ridding one of accumulated stress. In short, to many of its practitioners, Transcendental Meditation is an invaluable practice, as it seems to enable one to find solace from everyday entanglements and pressures, whilst simultaneously recharging one's batteries. The practice is held to yield these benefits without any effort; therefore one is told that it is not necessary to change one's philosophy or lifestyle. So, it is important to understand that one is not being persuaded to adopt Indian thinking or religion, but merely to practice a routine that will hopefully put a light in the eye and a spring in the step!

The principal effects of twice-daily periods of Transcendental Meditation appear to be;

1. Feeling more relaxed

2. Feeling more capable of attending to one's everyday life.

3. Sensation of well-being

4. Possibility of experiencing higher states of consciousness.

Importantly, Maharishi declared TM to be scientifically verifiable and not dependant on any attendant philosophy. Equally important is that he also claimed that TM is not a process of autosuggestion.

Background

When Maharishi Mahesh Yogi arrived in the USA in 1959, he announced:-
> 'I have brought from the land of ancient sages to the modern man of this new world a simple technique of living in peace and happiness.'[2]

Maharishi claimed the meditation practice he taught to be easy to learn, effective at improving one's life, and having the ability to produce positive life changing effects within a very short time. The proposed method requires setting aside two periods of about twenty minutes daily, to sit quietly and practice a simple mental technique.

Regarding the source of the meditation technique, Maharishi would always unhesitatingly give credit to his master, Swami Brahmananda Saraswati, to whom he referred to as 'Guru Dev'.
> 'My life truly began 16 years ago at the feet of my Master when I learned the secret of swift and deep meditation, a secret I now impart to the world.'[3]

The importance of this *guru* is reinforced by the fact that there is always a portrait of Swami Brahmananda prominently displayed when each new student learns the Transcendental Meditation technique.
> Question: Maharishi, the Press notes that each week you give all the credit, for all the knowledge that you are bestowing on the world, to your own master Guru Dev. So the Press is asking the question; "From where did Guru Dev get the knowledge?" They

had understood from things that you had said and written that he was a recluse sage in the hidden forests of the Himalayas and Central India, so how did he get all of that knowledge that he was then able to give to you and you have now given to the whole world?'

Maharishi Mahesh Yogi: "I got the knowledge from my Guru Dev. My Guru Dev got the knowledge from his Guru Dev. He got the knowledge from his Guru Dev. He got the knowledge from his Guru Dev. All the knowledge, descending down, generation after generation, that is why we give credit to the source of knowledge." [4]

In order to discover where the teachings upon which Transcendental Meditation is based came from, we need to find the source of some of the key aspects of the teaching.

Where does the 'life is bliss' philosophy come from?

For this we need to take a look at the Indian Scriptures, at a body of material called the Upanishads – *'upanishad'* means 'to sit down near'. The Upanishads are the teachings of *rishis*; *'rishi'* is a Sanskrit word meaning 'wise man'. Sometimes the *rishis* are referred to as *maharishis*, (*'maha'* means 'great', so *'maharishi'* is 'great sage'). It is of note that these *rishis* often had families who they would instruct, as is evident from the following instance, where the sage Varuna is teaching his son Bhrigu about bliss, (*'anandam'* is the Sanskrit word for bliss). The Sanskrit text is displayed along with Maharishi's translation of this teaching from the *Taittiriya Upanishad*:-

आनन्दाद्ध्येव खल्विमानि भूतानि जायन्ते ।
आनन्देन जातानि जीवन्ति ।
आनन्दं प्रयन्त्यभिसंविशन्तीति ।

'From Anandam is the whole creation born. In Anandam do the creatures live and in Anandam shall all this ultimately merge! Anandam is the one reality of the universe, ultimate and absolute. Anandam is the one reality of life eternal and absolute. Anandam is the life of every body. Anandam is the very existence of every being'[5]

For many that sounds just too good to be true! But, just supposing it was true, how would one go about discovering this '*anandam*', this 'delight' or 'bliss'?

In the *Katha Upanishad*, another Scripture, said to be about two and a half thousand years old, one can find advice on an ancient practice called '*yoga*'.

> 'When the five senses are settled
> and the mind has ceased to think
> and the intellect does not stir
> That is the highest state, they say.'

> 'Thus *"yoga"* is considered to be holding still the senses.
> Then one should be alert,
> for "*yoga*" comes and goes.'[6]

Clear guidance as to establishing the correct conditions for '*yoga*' meditation is provided in the famous Hindu Scripture *Bhagavad Gita,* the title of which literally means the 'Song of God':-

> 'In a clean spot, having set a firm seat (cushion) of his own, neither too high nor too low, made of cloth, a deerskin and *kusha*-grass, one upon the other.
> 'There, having made the mind one-pointed, with the activities of the mind and the senses controlled, let him, seated on the seat, practise *"yoga"* for self-purification.
> 'Let him steadily hold his body, keeping head and neck erect and still, directing the gaze towards the tip of the nose, without looking in any direction.'[7]

'Abandoning without reserve, all desires born of thought and imagination, and completely restraining the whole group of senses, by the mind, from all sides.
'Gradually, gradually let him attain to quietude by firmly holding the intellect; establishing the mind in the Self; let him not think even of anything.
'From whatever cause the restless and unsteady mind wanders away, from that let him restrain it and bring it under the control of the Self alone.
'For supreme happiness comes to the *yogi* whose mind is quite peaceful, whose passion is quieted...'[8]

Clearly, the *'yoga'* referred to here is not the array of physical exercises known as *'yoga asana'*, which belongs to a branch of *yoga* called *hatha yoga* (*'hatha'*, is a Sanskrit word meaning 'force' or 'effort'). In Hatha Yoga, *asanas* are performed as a preparation for *yoga* meditation.

A clear definition of the word *'yoga'* can be found in Patanjali's *'Yoga Sutras'*:-

योगश्चित्तवृत्तिनिरोधः

yogash-chitta-vritti-nirodhah
'"*yoga*" is the halting of mental activity'[9]

As this is a particularly important quotation, close examination of the original wording and context of the verse is in order:-
'Now, the teaching of *"yoga"*,
"yoga" is *"nirodha"* (restraint, stopping, halting) of the *"vritti"* (whirling, thought-waves, mental activity) of the *"chitta"* (consciousness, memory, subconscious).
Then the seer rests in his own self.
At other times he is identified with the whirling [of the mind].'[10]

If "*yoga* is the halting of mental activity" then how is this *yoga* best affected?

The 'halting of mental activity' is a state where the 'seer' rests and gains greater wakefulness. However, there is confusion and disagreement as to how to bring about this state of mind. The description in the *Bhagavad Gita* seems clear enough – to quieten down, let the mind settle, let go of thoughts, and find a state of deep relaxation. But to some this sounds difficult to do, which is why methods and techniques are suggested. Transcendental meditation is one such technique of temporarily reducing mental activity.

Maharishi Mahesh Yogi suggests that in the *Bhagavad Gita* is offered a description of the technique of Transcendental Meditation, but it is difficult to find any specific mention about using *mantras*, and a *mantra* is an essential part of the practice of Transcendental Meditation.

In India *yoga* meditation that involves use of a *mantra* is referred to as '*mantra japa*'. '*japa*' is the repetition of a '*mantra*', 'a word or words of significance or power'. There are three forms of *japa*, repetition; '*vaikhari*' – 'spoken', '*upaanshu*' – 'whispered', & '*manasa*' – 'in the mind'.

A holy man, travelling from place to place, might bless an individual by offering to teach them meditation practice, and at some quiet spot, maybe beneath a tree outside the village, he might impart a '*guru mantra*', a word or words held to be sacred, to be inwardly intoned by the recipient.

By way of illustration, the Indian Scriptures tell the tale of a highway robber who was challenged by some sages to reconsider his lifestyle, and who then learned *mantra japa* meditation. Apparently the robber was successful in his practice for he went on to compose one of India's most famous literary works, the *Ramayana*, the story of Lord Rama told in verse.

Swami Brahmananda Saraswati, the master of Maharishi Mahesh Yogi, tells the story of Valmiki's initiation into *mantra japa*:-
   '… according to the instructions of the *rishis*, he started to recite "Raama", "Raama". Sitting steadily, he became deeply immersed in chanting the name of Bhagwan (God), and white ants made an anthill over him. Afterwards, when he came out of the anthill, his name became Valmiki .[11]
   [note: '*valmika*' is a Sanskrit word for 'anthill']

The Role of the Guru.

According to custom, a *guru* is a teacher, a master, a spiritual guide, a religious instructor, and one who explains the *Shastras*, the religious texts. Before becoming a *guru* that person would have first been a *chela,* or disciple, to a *guru* himself. With dedication and devotion to his *guru* he would have undergone long training and become disciplined, taken vows of *sannyas,* and become a *swami*, a renunciate monk. Great store is set by '*gurukripa*', the 'grace of the *guru'* and Swami Brahmanandahimself stated simply; 'By *guru kripa* all is accomplished.'[12]

Generally speaking, all *swamis* belong to a *sampradaya,* or order, and interestingly in connection with the notion that one must learn meditation from a *guru*; the following line circulates, which is commonly attributed to the *Padma Purana,* but is of dubious origin:-

sampradaya-vihina ye mantras ye nishphala matah

'*Mantras* which are not received through a *sampradaya* are considered fruitless'

Adi Shankara

Adi Shankara

Adi Shankara was born at Kaladi in the Chera Kingdom of South India (situated in modern day Kerala), and at the age of 8 years old Shankara was initiated as a *sannyasi* monk.

Shankara is held to have revived and reformed the national religion of India, and is famous for debating with an advocate of ritualism, and he is said to have defeated his opponent who then became his disciple.

Shankara is also said to have set up the *Smarta* teaching, the harmonisation of the various devotional belief systems, demonstrating compatibility between them all. He is also said to have established the teaching of *Advaita* (non-dualism), which harmonises the teachings about *Brahman*, the universal spirit, and *Atman*, the individual spirit.

It is also believed that Shankara was responsible for structuring the orders of *sannyasi* (monks), which are known as *sampradayas*. One such *sampradaya* is for *danda swamis* (stick-carrying swamis), who are also known as *'dasanami swamis'*. Each *dandi swami* carries a *'danda'*, a 'stick' or 'staff', usually wrapped in cloth. Each *dandi swami* is known by two names, the first name being the name given by his *guru*, and the latter name being his *sampradaya*, which would be one of the *'dasanami'*, the 'ten names', viz. Saraswati, Tirtha, Aranya, Bharati, Asram, Giri, Parvata, Sagara, Vana, and Puri.

Shankara, or one of his successors, is said to have composed the *Brahma Sutras*, and many commentaries of the Scriptures and many devotional verses, amongst them *'Bhaja Govindam'*.

> *Bhaja Govindam bhaja Govindam*
> *Govindam bhajamudhamate.*
> *namasmaranaadanyamupaayam*
> *nahi pashyamo Bhavatarane..'*

> 'Worship Govinda (Krishna), worship Govinda,
> worship Govinda, Oh fool!
> Other than chanting the Lord's names,
> there is no other way to cross the life's ocean'

Shankara also wrote the *'Guru Stotram'*, a set of verses in praise of the *guru*, which includes the very famous verse:-

> 'Guru Brahma, Guru Vishnu, Guru Deva Maheshwara. Guru Sakshath Parambrahma, Tasmai Shri Gurave Namaha.'

> 'Guru is the creator Brahma, Guru is the preserver Vishnu, Guru is the destroyer Shiva. Guru is directly the supreme spirit
> - I offer my salutations to this Guru.'

Adi Shankara is also famous for having set up *a math*, or monastery (also known as *peeth*), known as Badarikashram or Jyotir Math. Other *peeths* were also founded, at Dwaraka in the west, Govardhan in the east, and Sringeri in the south. Shankaracharya Adi Shankara died at the age of 33.

The title 'Shankaracharya' is formed from the name 'Shankara' and the word '*acharya*' - Shankar is of course the name of the god Shiva and also the name of Adi Shankara (*'adi'* has a meaning of 'first' or 'original'), whereas *'acharya'* simply means 'teacher'. Each *'math'*, or monastery, has its own *parampara* (succession) which leads back to the time of Adi Shankara – and each one in the *parampara* of teachers is known as 'Shankaracharya'. Perhaps this is why there is confusion as to when the first Shankaracharya, Adi Shankara lived, with recorded dates of birth ranging from 44 BC - 805 AD.

Shankaracharyas of Jyotir Math

The earliest known heads of Jyotir Math (Shankaracharyas) are listed as; Acharya Trotakah (also known as Trotakacharya),

Acharya Krishnah, Kumarah, Garunah, Shukah, Vidhyah, Vishalah, Vakulah, Vamanah, Sundarah, Arunah, Sriniwasah, Sukhanandah, Vidyanandah, Shivah, Girih, Vidyadharah, Gunandah, Naryanah and Umapatih.

The Shankaracharyas of Jyotirmath for the last few centuries are listed below:-

Title/Name	Year
Acharya Balkrishna Swami	1443-1500
Acharya Hari Brahma	1500-1501
Acharya Hari Smaran	1501-1509
Acharya Vrindavan Swami	1509-1511
Acharya Anantnaryan Swami	1511-1512
Acharya Bhawanand Swami	1512-1526
Acharya Krishnanand Swami	1526-1536
Acharya Hari Narain Swami	1536-1544
Acharya Brahmanand Swami	1544-1564
Acharya Devanand Swami	1564-1579
Acharya Raghunath Swami	1579-1604
Acharya Purnadeo Swami	1604-1630
Acharya Krishnadeo Swami	1630-1639
Acharya Acharya Shivanand Swami	1639-1646
Acharya Balkrishna Swami	1646-1660
Acharya Narain Updendra Swami	1660-1693
Acharya Harishchandar Swami	1693-1706
Acharya Sadanand Swami	1706-1716
Acharya Keshav Swami	1716-1724
Acharya Narain Tirtha Swami	1724-1766
Acharya Ram Krishna Swami	1766-1776
- vacant -	1776 onwards [13]

As revealed in this list, the position of Shankaracharya of Jyotir Math was filled by a succession of *'acharayas'*, or *'gurus'*, but by the mid-18th century the lineage had lapsed and local farmers were using land formerly held by the monastery.

On April 1st 1941, after a lapse of one hundred and sixty-five years, a new Shankaracharya of Jyotir Math was appointed, an elderly *sannyasi* by the name of Swami Brahmananda Saraswati.

Swami Brahmananda Saraswati

Swami Brahmananda Saraswati

Swami Brahmananda was born in North India in 1871 and his given birth name was that of Raja Ram Mishra.

Raja Ram was very close to his grandfather, so when his grandfather died whilst Raja Ram was but a young boy, his family were naturally protective:-

> 'Due to the vigilance of those of the household, the young lad could not see the dead body of his grandfather, but when they took it out of the house, after they had gone a little way, a servant showed him all the people coming for the grandfather. The young child heard the crowd saying again and again;
>
> राम नाम सत्य है
>
> *"Ram nam satya hai"*
> 'Rama's name is truth'.
>
> The young child's eyes saw that grandfather had been covered, saw that he had gone to sleep, and his ears heard *"Ram nam satya hai"* - 'Rama's name is truth'. He considered this to be his grandfather's last instruction. In the mind of the young child he awoke to two ideas:-
>
> (1). Grandfather will not be met with now.
> (2). *"Ram nam satya hai"* - 'Rama's name is truth.'[14]

Apparently, Raja Ram began to think deeply about the transient nature of worldly life, and:-

> 'A year elapsed.
>
> Being eight years old it came to be time for the ceremony of investiture with the sacred thread. All decided on performing the initiation and then sending him for some time to Kashi (Benares, Varanasi) to study. Having become eight years old, and after the performance the ritual of the sacred thread, you

were sent to Kashi to study the wealth of the *Vedas*. On arriving there you made a special impression in the study of Sanskrit. You resolved to devote your own life in advancing spiritually.

At this age, according to the prevailing custom of the caste of Brahmans on the edge of Ayodhya, the celebrated Saryuparin/Mishra Brahmans of Gana, the time of the marriage feast came. Relatives made an effort. Some folk came to Kashi to summon the young child to go with them. It became obvious to you that they came from the house to call you for the marriage. Just now all the milk teeth had not yet fallen out and at that age thousands of young lads are dusty and dirty, in a state of ignorance playing hither and thither, wrestling and fighting with one another, and laughing, remaining wrapped up in childhood. At that very delicate age of eight to nine years old, into your ears falls the word *"vivaha"*, 'marriage'. The heart arose with a sudden start. The hairs stood up on end, - *"vivaha"?* Marriage, and a relationship with worldliness?[15]

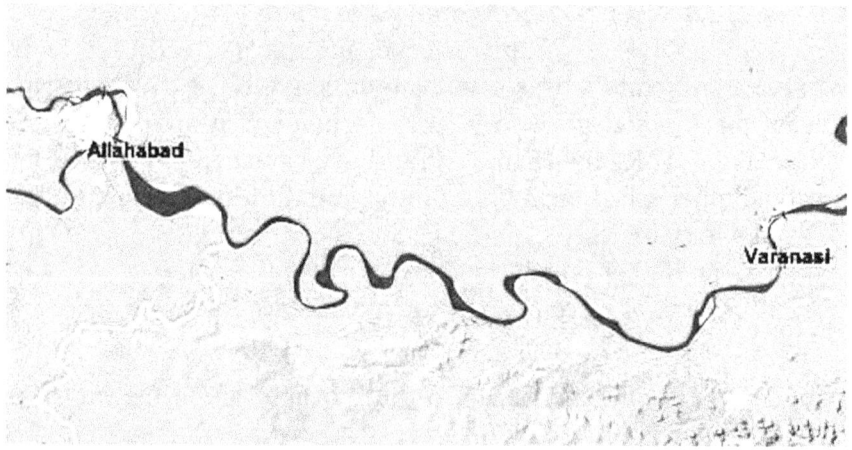

At the news of his impending marriage, Raja Ram slipped away from his school and took off on foot walking up river. Eventually he competed the distance of 125km from Benares (Varanasi) to Allahabad, quite a distance for a small lad! From there he journeyed onwards, by train, a further 700km to holy town of

Hardwar. From Hardwar he was all set to proceed to the nearby pilgrimage town of Rishikesh, where he was apprehended by a policeman, and returned to his parents.

Despite being sent back home, Raja Ram's mind was quite made up to take to a spiritual life, so on his return he spent his time in spiritual conversation with the elders of his family. His resolve to leave home did not diminish, and he set about convincing his parents, who in turn consulted the local priest. After listening and watching her son debating with the family's priest, his mother made her feelings known in this way:-

'He who is going following the upwards path this much and who the *guru* of our tribe is doing *"pranaam"* to (a respectful greeting made by putting one's palms together and often touching the feet of the person greeted), I do not think it reasonable that we take him off the elephant to cause him to sit on an ass. I cannot command him to withdraw from the *"kalyana marg"* (the way to happiness, salvation) to enter into the difficulties of the householder.'

He asked the permission to leave of his own Mata Ji. He was met with the answer;

"जाओ भजन करो"

"jao bhajan karo"
'Go do *bhajan* (sing praise).'

'But don't become a begging *sadhu,* and when you get the desire sometime for being a householder, then come home at once.'[16]

So, then, within a few days Raja Ram up and left his kith and kin and set off again for the Himalayas.

'Wandering on you arrived at Rishikesh.

This is a holy place and from ancient times it has been an important sacred place of pilgrimage. This little town has become a gateway to the area of the immense Himalayas of Northern India. Indeed, it is a pleasing place. It is especially beloved by *sadhus* (religious people), *mahatmas* (great souls), those seeking salvation and *sadhakas* (those engaged in spiritual discipline).

How many *sadhakas*, from age-to-age have been guided and have fulfilled their desire in finding a world of happiness in the beautiful jungles on all four sides of Rishikesh?

Here you discerned that by practicing *japa* (repetition of *mantra*) and practising *tapa* (austerity) of your own initiative would be against the code of conduct.

Bhagwan Adi Shankaracharya took refuge of a *guru* too, therefore it is not proper to transgress the code of conduct, but he sensed he should make a search for someone who is really a *sadguru* (good *guru*). Of what sort a person should a *sadguru* be?

"श्रोत्रियं ब्रह्मनिष्ठम!"

"Shrotriyam brahmanishtham"
'One who has studied the *Vedas* thoroughly, - a devotee of
Brahman (one possessing knowledge of the immortal Self)'
from *Manduka Upanishad* 1:2:12

To these two words he added two of his own, *"krodharahita"* – devoid of '*krodha*' ('anger', 'heat', 'fury') and *"balbrahmachari"* – 'celibacy since boyhood'.[17]

'Really, at how many *ghats* did he drink the water, indeed how much difficulties befell him? But the search was proceeding for a *guru* that was *shrotriya brahmanishtha*. He stayed near many respected *mahatmas* (high-souled people) but none appeared to exactly match the criteria. Searching and searching he arrived at Uttarkashi, situated in the Himalayas. [Uttarkashi is a town situated in a valley approximately midway on the route between Rishikesh and the head of the Ganga River at Gangotri. The Ganga River is known in this area as Bhagairathi. Uttarkashi is the northern Varanasi, *'uttari'* means 'northern'; Kashi is another name for Varanasi.]

At Uttarkashi he sought refuge from Shri 108 Dandi Swami Shri Swami Krishnananda Saraswati Ji Maharaj, a lifelong celibate *yogi* and great disciple of Shringeri Peeth. There he took initiation wholly as a monk. And Gurudeva gave you the name Brahma Chaitanya Brahmachari.

Swami Ji was an instructor of Indian *Shastras* (treatises) and a perfectly accomplished ascetic of the highest order. Really he lived by the highest principles, there was nobody who could equal or surpass him in living. He had arrived at the highest degree of knowledge of the divine, he was himself in the self of Brahman, in the presence of god Shiva, the Self of Paramatma (the Transcendental Being).'[18]

Shri 108 Shri Dandi Swami Ji Krishnananda Saraswati

'There were quite a good many disciples there, people doing practises of *yoga*, and *hatha yoga*, and *raja yoga*, and *mantra yoga*, so many people, disciples, engaged in their own practices.'[19]

Having been accepted as a student of a respected *guru*, Raja Ram Mishra was given the name Brahma Chaitanya Brahmachari. The young *brahamachari* (celibate student) stayed in his *guru's ashram* in Uttarkashi, living in the end *'kutiya'*, 'cottage'. At length his *guru*, Swami Krishnanand, instructed him to go and stay in a *gupha* (cave) some three miles away, and there he continued his *sadhana* (spiritual development) alone, returning to the *ashram* weekly, on a Thursday, to pick up fresh provisions and to offer his progress report to the *guru*.

'Shri Maharaj Ji stayed beside Guru Ji in Uttarkashi, perfecting penance, learning the *Shastra* and practising and living according to the rules of Yoga philosophy. At twenty-five years old, having become Self-realised he came down from the Himalayas. Guru Ji moved with him. For some days they stayed in Kajaliwan, near Rishikesh. This is an isolated and uninhabited place, a very dense jungle where it is commonplace for carnivorous creatures to stroll about. Thus if any *sadhu* or *mahatma* went to stop in this place for any time then it quickly became known in the villages near and far, and the inhabitants would run for his *darshan*.'[20]

After a short while Swami Krishnanand returned to Uttarkashi, leaving Brahmachari Brahma Chaitanya to follow his solitary *sadhana*,

'Years passed together with various interesting and instructive events, which are inordinately difficult to mention. Everything for the improvement of your life occurred automatically. By the grace of the Gurudeva you obtained many sorts of *yoga* and gained actions of rituals (spiritual powers). Always you remained in your own *sadhana*. Really, at the roots of trees in uninhabited forests were the places you dwelt. Wild fruits, roots, vegetables etc were really his food. Naturally the lion, tiger, deer etc came to be the fellow inhabitants of your life. Never did he beg donations but lived far away from the society of mankind, not keeping company with women. Your natural quality was to understand equality, from the blade of grass up to Kubera devoted to wealth. In this way, doing *tapasya* in Gangotri (Himalyas), at Nepal, Kashmir, the Vindhya (mountains), the Amarakantaka (the source of the Narmada River) he was experiencing *"atmananda"* (bliss of oneness with the Supreme Soul).'[21]

In 1906, at the age of 35, Brahmachari Brahma Chaitanya met with his *guru* in Allahabad, and received formal initiation into *sannyas*. He was given his *sannyasi* name, and was gifted a *danda* (a staff), *kamandalu* (water-pot) *and kaupeen* (loincloth).
'From that day on your name became Shri Swami Brahmananda Saraswati Maharaj. The *sadhus, mahatmas* and other devout people queued for your *darshan* and for your *ashirvad* (blessing).

Your habit was to wander about in uninhabited wooded places, but whenever folk got to hear where you were, they would arrive for *darshan*. At festival times you might go to the cities, to Kashi (Varanasi), Prayag (Allahabad), Ayodhya etc, then crowds would come for the benefit of *darshan*.'[22]

Swami Brahmananda later recalled instances of his time alone:-
'Back at that time I always wore a loincloth. Sometimes that was bound as a *"pagri"* (turban) on the head and sometimes it was being hung on the waist. Making a *tava* (a pan to cook flat bread) of one smallish flat stone, and kneading the *"aataa"* (flour). When the *"roti"* (round unleavened bread) was baking, and the sounds of cracking came from that stone, then the heart spontaneously generated waves of *ananda* (bliss). Having seen this sort of circumstance anybody would have said: "This is a *paramahansa"* (a *swami*), and someone else would be thinking, "This is an *avadhoota* (one who has shaken off all worldly bonds)". But no, he appeared to possess the form of *jeevanmukti*

(freedom of human life) but in the inner soul *jeevanmukti* was being enjoyed as boundless *ananda* (happiness).'[23]

'The years when we lived in the inaccessible jungles we experienced the Omniscience and Omnipotence of God. Wherever there were no arrangements for worldly needs, there necessary arrangement was made on time for devotees of God.'[24]

In his memoirs, Swami Rama recalls meeting Swami Brahmananda.
'Travelling toward the forests of Reva State, I went to the Satana forest and there met a swami who was very handsome and highly educated in the *Vedantic* and yoga tradition. He knew the scriptures and was a very brilliant *saadhaka* (spiritual practitioner). He was later nominated as Shankaracharya of Jyotirmayapitham, which is in the Himalayas on the way to Badrinath. His name was Brahmananda Saraswati.

He used to live only on germinated gram seeds mixed with a little bit of salt. He lived on a hillock in a small natural cave near a mountain pool. I was led by the villagers to that place, but I did not find anyone there and became disappointed. The next day I went again and found a few footprints on the edge of the pool made by his wooden sandals. I tried, but I could not track the footprints. Finally, on the fifth day of effort, early in the morning before sunrise, I went back to the pool and found him taking a bath. I greeted him saying, *"Namo narayan,"* which is a commonly used salutation among swamis meaning, "I bow to the divinity in you." He was observing silence so he motioned for me to follow him to his small cave and I did so gladly. This was the eighth day of his silence and I gently spoke to him about the purpose of my visit. I wanted to know how he was living and the ways and methods of his spiritual practices. During our conversation, he started talking to me about Sri Vidya, the highest of paths followed only by accomplished Sanskrit scholars in India.

'Swami Brahmananda was one of the rare *Siddhas* who had the knowledge of *Sri Vidya*. His authoritative knowledge of the Upanishads, and especially of Shankara's commentaries, was superb. He was also a very good speaker. Swami Karpatri, a renowned scholar, was the disciple who requested him to accept the prestige and dignity of Shankaracharya in the North, a seat which had been vacant for 300 years. Whenever he travelled from one city to another, people flocked in the thousands to hear him, and after his nomination as Shankaracharya, his followers increased. One thing very attractive about his way of teaching was his combination of the *bhakti* and Advaita systems. During my brief stay with him, he also talked about Madhusudana's commentary on the Bhagavad Gita.

'Shri Yantra' **made of ruby**

Swami Brahmananda had a *Sri Yantra* made out of rubies, and as he showed it to me, he explained the way he worshipped it. It is interesting to note how the great sages direct all their spiritual, mental and physical resources toward their ultimate goal. Among all the swamis of India, I only met a few who radiated such brilliance and yet lived in the public, remaining unaffected by worldly temptations and distractions. I stayed with him only a week and then left for Uttarkashi.'[25]

Swami Brahmananda's love of solitude is clearly evidenced by his preference for living in thickly forested areas, often staying in secluded caves. It is said that he had a good affinity with wild animals and that on at least one occasion rode on the back of a tiger! Many tales of miracle working and healings are told, with one telling of his advising someone with venereal disease to bathe in the Ganga River, whereupon it is said they found themselves cured.

Infrequently Swami Brahmananda would venture into a town or city.

In 1930, on a visit to the city of Allahabad in North India, he received news that his *guru,* Shri Swami Krishnanand Saraswati, was there, and so made his way to see him:-

'Maharaj Shri (Swami Brahmananda) wanted to do *pranaam* by the proper code of conduct, by the lifting of the *danda* (staff). But Guru ji did not give him *pranaam* but having taken the *danda* from the hand he brought him flat with the chest (he hugged him) and sat him on a seat nearby.

He said, 'Maharaj, it is *maryaada* (proper code of conduct), please accept my doing *pranaam.*'

Guru Ji said, 'Go sit, the *maryaada* here is really our will.'

At that time many dozens gathered about Guru Ji. Having seen this behaviour all were astonished, that Guru Ji gives so much respect to Swami Ji.

One of them said, 'Why not? Having seen that he has arrived in his own position Guru Ji will also be acting accordingly. Then it is not improper. But look then at how impatient he is for bowing to Guru Ji. He is fostering an excellent standard of decorum.'

At this time Guru Ji commanded; 'You have stayed a long time in the jungles and mountains. Stay near the towns now, so that some of the people can benefit.'

After this, he too lived near to towns. *Guru Ji respected you and honoured you so much that sometimes he was given to say,* 'He is much more fit than us then, and is learned, and is peerless in giving answers and in removing doubts.'[26]

It was just a matter of time before Swami Brahmananda would have disciples himself, and n 1926 he encountered the 19 year-old Hari Narayana Ojha and gave him *naistika diksha* (first initiation) as a *brahmachari*, bestowing the name Hariharachaitanya Brahmachari. Later, in 1931, Swami Brahmananda formally ordained this same *chela* (student), giving him *sannyas diksha* (formal initiation as a *sannyasi*) and renaming him Swami

Hariharanand Saraswati. Later still, because of this *chela's* habit of eating with his hands he was nicknamed 'Karpatri' ('He who uses his hands as a dish') and the name stuck.

In 1932, in Varanasi, Swami Karpatri engaged in his first *Shastrartha* (religious debate), on the subject of 'Should the *pranava* '*OM*' be given to the lowest castes or not?' Apparently, the young *swami* successfully explained that whilst other *mantras* could be given to these castes, the '*OM*' ought not be.

-~~~~~~-

In 1936, after the death of his *guru*, Swami Brahmananda had several buildings built in Varanasi, in the Choti Gaivi area of the city, a half hour's walk from the Dashashwamedh Ghat of the River Ganga. Three properties were created;

1. A college, Shri Brahmavidya Niketan, where students could receive free education in Sanskrit language.
2. A temple, named the Shri Brahmanandeshwar Mahadev Ji Mandir
3. An *ashram* situated in Sidhi Giri Bhag, named Shri Brahma Niwas, with numerous rooms to accommodate students.

These properties were raised up and placed under the protection of the Shri 1008 Swami Krishnanand Saraswati Trust.

After setting up his *ashram*, Swami Brahmananda, became far more accessible, and attracted quite a following of devotees, who referred to him as, *'Maharaj Shri'*; or 'Blessed Great King', *'Shri Charana'*; 'the Blessed Feet'. He was also known as *'Gurudeo'* or *'Gurudeva'*; a term used widely in India, which means 'Guru Divine', the phrase *'Jay Gurudeva'* meaning 'Success to Gurudev'.

Mahesh Prasad meets Swami Brahmananda

Maharishi Mahesh Yogi is famous for spreading Transcendental Meditation to the west. As a young man he was known as Mahesh Prasad ji and later as Brahmachari Mahesh ji. His father, Shri Ram Prasad Shrivastava, was a Revenue Inspector, and Mahesh is said to have been the third of four children, the eldest son being 'J.P' Jageshwar Prasad Srivastava.

Although Mahesh's family hail from Jabalpur in Madhya Pradesh, it has also been reported that he was born some little distance away in the village of Chichli, near Gadawara, also in Madhya Pradesh. Again it is said he was born in the Panduka region near Raipur. According to his passport, Mahesh's birthplace is given as Pounalulla, and his date of his birth as 12th January 1918. His brother JP states that Mahesh was born 12th January 1917.

Maharishi relates how it is to be brought up in an Indian family:-
> 'The children in India are told when you get up you bow down to your mother, you bow down to your father, you bow down to your elders. You go to the temple, you bow down to the Deity. You go to school, you bow down to your teacher.
>
> It provides a great shield of security and assistance from all quarters for the child to grow on right lines with great energy, with great intelligence, with great accomplishment, very great. And these feelings of love for mother and love for father supported by this ritual of bowing down, this later on develops in devotion to Almighty Great Father.'[27]

As a youngster, Mahesh puzzled over the topic of God, and man's suffering:-
> 'This has been the one question in my mind ever since I was

young: God is omnipresent and God is almighty and God is merciful and in the heart of everyone, why should a man suffer having God within himself? And what is the value of oneself if he keeps suffering'[28]

Perhaps the rumour is correct which suggests that Mahesh left his family home early in life. Certainly, he maintained very close links with Raj R P Varma (said to be Mahesh's uncle), and nephew, Girish Chandra Varma, so it might be speculated that Mahesh spent some of his childhood with them, which might explain the confusion over the family name. The name 'Varma' is a term of address for any member of the prestigious *Kshatriya* caste, whereas the surname 'Srivastava' places a family as belonging to the *varna* (caste) of *Kayastha* (Scribe), which is a sub-caste of the *Kshatriya* (Warrior) caste. Some individuals prefer to dispense with formal surnames altogether, electing instead to use their first and middle names, as seems did Mahesh Prasad.[29]

According to Umesh Shrivastava, the nephew of one of Mahesh's friends, Mahesh's father's job entailed the family moving quite often, so Mahesh attended various schools. It is suggested that at one time Mahesh attended Hitkarini High School in Jabalpur.

Sources in India also suggest Mahesh studied at the K.P. Intermediate College in Allahabad:-

'I was completely dissatisfied with what I studied in college. Because I knew – this can't be the whole knowledge. I was searching for something complete whereby I could understand everything.'[30]

The word 'college', as used in India, is commonly applied to an institution that offers education at Year 12 (American 'Junior College' or English 'Sixth Form'), or where degree courses are available, the colleges being affiliated to a regional university.

At one time an online listing existed of 'Distinguished Alumni' of the Ganganath Jha Hostel of Allahabad University, which included a 'Sri M.C.Srivastava (Universally known as Maharishi Mahesh Yogi)'. Curiously, the listing has been removed.[31]

As a young man Mahesh worked for a time at the 'GCF', the Gun Carriage Factory in Jabalpur. There, one of his colleagues was Jagdish Prasad Shrivastava, and it was apparently through Jagdish's brother, Shri Jugal Kishore Shrivastava, that the seventeen-year-old Mahesh was introduced to Swami Brahmananda Saraswati. Several accounts of this initial meeting exist.

Mahesh's brother, J.P., recalls:-
> 'Visiting innumerable Sadhoos and Sanyasis during his school and college life the Maharishi at last came in contact with Gurudeo in 1939.'[32]

Actually, the date given for the initial meeting between the young Mahesh and the elderly *guru* varies, as do details of the location:-
> 'One day someone in the street whispered to me, "there has come a great saint, but he does not want to be known by the people. If you wish, then we shall go quietly one night." I said, "There could be nothing better than that."'[33]

> 'We were a few men who had gone to visit Guru Dev. We sat outside his door a long time until we were finally admitted. We sat down by the door, which had been left open. Guru Dev sat in darkness. We could only sense his presence – he didn't talk to us. Suddenly a car drove by on the road and the headlights momentarily shone through the open door. For the first time I was able to see Guru Dev's face. Oh, it was a wonderful sight! I have never seen anything so wonderful. Immediately I experienced a deep reverence and devotion to him and I decided to do everything in my power to be in his surroundings.'[34]

> 'I was fond of visiting saints, and when I heard there was a saint - this was in some Summer vacation - "Some saint has come but it's very difficult to approach him and he is far away," and all

that, all that. Then I made more enquiries; "Where is he? And what?", then I found one can only see him about midnight or something, because no one is allowed to go there, and you have to go in all darkness without making noise and all kinds of things. I met some friends here and there and just we went there and, on a small house somewhere far into the, in the forest somewhere.

There was a terrace, small terrace, and there, it was all dark, absolutely dark. About ten or eleven we arrived there. I and someone, or two more.

And there was a *brahmachari* on the ground floor. He said, "How you are here?" and "Who told you?" and, "You are not expected to come!"

And said, "So maybe we forgot our way and we are here then, *darshan* coming. And tell us about the saint, and we want to hear.." I said.

And he said, "Don't talk, don't talk, just sit quietly." And he disappeared and he went up and after about half an hour he came back. He said, "Follow me very quietly." I said, "Alright, alright."

We quietly went up, there was nothing to see, it's all dark and somehow we felt someone was sitting on a sort of chair or something, reclining, comfortable. We sat down quietly, we found two or three other men were also sitting. No one was talking, whispering, it was all dark, everything. It so happened, about maybe fifteen, twenty minutes passed and it happened that far distance a car was coming and it showed the light on the terrace, and that was the first sight of Guru Dev. Just on the flash of the car, maybe a mile away from the car, but it just turned, it just turned for a moment and I was.. It was just enough to have a glimpse of him. And then I thought, "Yes, it seems the time has come." That one glimpse of a flashy light and that was enough to take decisions.

Then I came, and I came, and I came, and I said, "Could I not be at your service?"

He said, "What you are doing?"

"Studying."

"Oh better finish your studies."

"And then, where will you be?"

"Oh you will find me somewhere."

'And I was asked to complete my studies. And then I did not argue with him because once I saw him, I know he knows best and whatever he said was my action.'[35]

JP Shrivastava recalls that his brother was captivated by the *guru's* words:-
> 'On hearing his 'updesh' [teaching] for a few days, Maharishiji decided "This is the Divine light I have been searching for", and he requested Gurudeo for initiation, but was told to wait for some time, "There is no hurry about it" he said.[36]

So, the young Mahesh had no choice but to accept the *guru's* decision, that he was not yet ready to be given personal instruction:-
> 'Then Guru Dev was gone back to the lonely forests. It was hard to locate from where he had come and where he had gone, because those who knew him were strictly prohibited to tell others his whereabouts. There was no way to keep contact with him.'[37]

Raj Varma meets Swami Brahmananda Saraswati

Raj Rajeshwari Prasad Varma is believed to have been Mahesh's uncle. He was also a photographer and artist who lived and worked in Jabalpur in the Central Province of India.

On 24th August 1940 Raj went to visit Swami Brahmananda:-
'It was when Guru Dev had come out from the jungle that I first met him.'

'Guru Dev was the pure and holy man with strict rules of life that he had been reputed to be. He was not interested in acquiring disciples and was therefore extremely restrained on the subject. In the 24 hours the public was allowed to meet him for half an hour.[38]

'… One day a friend came and said "I know you don't care for *gurus*, but now there is a *guru* in Jabalpur (that was the town where they lived) whom you must see, he is completely different from all those I have known. You must accompany me tonight." - "Alright" said Dr. Varma "I'll come with you, but I don't know how to behave with such people." – "Don't worry," said his friend, "you just copy me."

So that evening they went to the house and knocked at the door. A Brahmachari opened and they told him they wanted to see the *guru*. He noted down their names and said he would ask. After a short time he came back. "Yes, you can come in, follow me."

They came to a large room. Along the walls people were sitting in silence. An elderly man was at the end of the room. The Brahmachari gave a sign to Dr. Varma's friend that he could approach the *guru*, so he went forward and bowed down deeply before Guru Dev and stood before him with folded hands and then went to the wall and sat down.

The Brahmachari gave Dr. Varma sign to go forward. So he went towards Guru Dev, bowed down and then with folded hands looked at Guru Dev's face, and he looked—and looked—and looked—completely fascinated by the beauty and majesty of that personality.

Suddenly he realized that he had been staring at Guru Dev for such a long time and was quite bewildered at his own behaviour. Then the thought came: It is His fault, it is His powerful influence! I could not help it! He bowed down deeply again and then sat down near his friend, still bewildered.

There was absolute silence in the room. Then he thought: I wish I could hear his voice, I wish he would speak! – Guru Dev said: "I usually do not speak; I speak only when somebody asks me a question."

Dr. Varma was frightened! "He can read my thoughts!!!" Nevertheless he wanted to hear him and there was a question in his mind, something that had always bothered him, so he asked: "Why are good people, who live a good life suffering and bad people have a comfortable life and are powerful and wealthy?"
Guru Dev smiled and began a story which beautifully answered the question: ~~~
"Once there was a farmer, an honest man, who worked diligently and earned a good living for himself and his family. He had a good wife. His children were well-behaved and he lived in harmony with all his neighbours. He could have had a happy life, but in that area there was a gang of robbers.

In the night they would knock on the door and he had to open it knowing that otherwise they would have broken it down. Ten men would rush into the house threaten everyone, take what they wanted and then shout at them: "Don't dare to inform the police that we were here! If you do we shall kill all of you!"

On what they had left the family could barely survive. They were not the only ones who suffered; almost all the farmers were robbed and threatened by the gang which terrorized the area in the nights. They worked hard and the robbers were well-fed and had a comfortable life, whereas the farmers constantly lived in fear.

One night our good honest farmer heard a knock at his door. "If they take away what is left then we will really starve", he thought. Trembling he opened the door. But there was only one man, one of the robbers.

"You need not be afraid of me, I've run away from them, I was so fed up with that kind of life, always afraid that the police might find out, I want to lead an honest life, I want to work for my living and I want to make up for the bad things I have done. Please help me! Please!"

"Well, you know that I have not much food left, but I have plenty of work, if you want to help me you can stay here and work in the fields tomorrow, come in and lie down rest." So the robber worked with him in the fields all day long and he thanked him because he felt so happy with his work.

After a few days there was a knock at the door in the night. "They have found out that he is here." the farmer thought. "What will they do?!" Trembling he opened the door. There was only one man! Another of the robbers.

"You need not be afraid of me! After my friend had left us we found out that he was working with you. So I said I would watch him closely and I saw that he looked so happy when he worked with you and talked to you. So I thought I am so fed up with this life in constant fear of the police, I want to be happy and I want to make up for the bad things I have done. Can you help me, I don't want to be in prison, I want to help the farmers I robbed. Can you help me, please?"

The farmer said: "your friend has been working well and if you want to help me, there is plenty of work. Come in and rest and tomorrow you start working." so the two men helped him and were happy even though he could offer them only a little food.

A few days later there was a knock at the door in the night and another robber told him he had escaped from the gang where he felt so unhappy and after watching his friends working in the fields and seeing how happy they looked, he had such a desire to work and be happy like them and make up for the bad things he had done and would the farmer please help him and not tell the police! So the third robber worked for the farmer and was most grateful to him for letting him work and be happy.

Two more robbers came in the next nights. And eventually there were five men outside with no intention of attacking. The gang leader said he need not be afraid, they would do no harm; they simply could not go on doing what they had done, their number was too small, and they had seen how happy the men looked who worked for him.

"We, too, want to make up for what up for what we have done to the farmers, we want to work for all the farmers that we have robbed. But please don't tell the police, we don't want to go to prison, we want to work and be happy. Please help us so that we can work!" So the plague of the area had come to an end and robbers and farmers became happy people.

It is a law of nature that a good man, who lives according to the laws of nature, may suffer for some time; he may have to learn how to cope with difficult situations and be an example for others and help others by living and behaving according to the laws of nature. But he will never suffer forever, because that is a law of nature. And he will always get help, because that also is a law of nature.'[39]

'But when I got Maharaj Shri, fortunately I became earnestly desirous to make him my Guru. So on the fifth day of his *darshan*, I requested him reverentially in loneliness, to make me his disciple. He said "To make a Guru, one should test him thoroughly."

I said, "Maharaj Shri, I have no knowledge to test a Guru but this much I know that your revered self is far beyond any test. The very moment I got a message of your arrival in Jabalpur, while I was going to the market on the road, my mind became restless to have your *darshan*, for I have heard that only by the *darshan* of a Yogi Mahatma the beholder is benefitted. Kindly, therefore make me your humble disciple."

Maharaj Shri said, "There shouldn't be hurry in choosing a Guru."

I said, "I am 41 years of age now and think that I am already very late to make a Guru. At what age should a man make a Guru Maharaj Shri?" At this he was silent. Then I asked him, "Should a man make a Guru, in his old age when his senses are weak enough to act to the wishes of Guru Dev?"

Maharaj Shri said, "No, not in old age." Then again I requested him kindly to make me his disciple. Maharaj Shri said, "The Guru also has to see whether a man is worthy of being a disciple."

I said, "When a name is enough to read the character of a man, I am here in person. Maharaj Shri, your revered self needs no time to know about me."

Maharaj Shri then said, "You are getting late to get home, so you may go now."

I said, "Maharaj Shri, kindly excuse me for taking so much of your valuable time." I bowed down and left saying that "My humble request is still at your lotus feet.'"[40]

It took about two weeks of repeatedly visiting the *guru*, before Raj Varma was given permission to come for 'initiation':-

'Maharaj Shri then approved me to be his disciple and very kindly said to me, "Come this time tomorrow, (i.e. on September 14, 1940), with some *puja samagri* for initiation."

I bowed down at his lotus feet with great joy and took leave to go.

Next morning, *puja samagri* (things required for worship) such as camphor, incense sticks, sandal wood paste, rice, sacred thread, flowers, garland, coconut and some fruits etc., were gathered. I took bath and got ready to start. I reached the *ashram* at the fixed time. The *brahmachari* opened the door, allowed me to come in and asked me to sit for a couple of minutes.

I was called in the room where Maharaj Shri was sitting after *samadhi* (deep meditation). Devotedly I performed the *puja* of Maharaj Shri and he gave me a suitable *mantra* to repeat daily in a particular way. I was very grateful to him and bowed down at the lotus feet of Shri Guru Dev. Thus I got Maharaj Shri, the most illustrious *Siddha Yogi*, as my Guru Dev.'[41]

Raj recounted in detail the story of becoming accepted as a pupil of Guru Dev:-

"Guru Dev, I want to be your disciple, would you please initiate me?"

Guru Dev said: "No, you are married, you have children, you are a businessman, you do not have the time."

"But I can spend all the night with you, I am never tired when I am with you." No reply.

So night after night he asked the same question. Eventually Guru Dev said: "ask me again in three days." so Dr. Varma was happy to ask him again on the third day. And Guru Dev answered: "you have shown good perseverance. Tomorrow morning come before sunrise and bring fruit and flowers and I will give you your *mantra*."

Dr. Varma asked: "should I not also bring some good cloth for you to wear?" Guru Dev smiled: "Look at my clothes, they are still alright. But when you see that they are not good any more, then you may bring new cloth."

So before sunrise Dr.Varma came full of joy to his initiation. Guru Dev did the *puja* with his fruit and flowers and then gave him his *mantra* and asked him to sit down. He gave him a rosary. An Indian rosary has mostly 108 beads. Guru Dev told Dr.Varma to close his eyes and repeat the *mantra* and with every *mantra* touch a new bead so that the rosary would go forward in his hand with each *mantra*.

Then he told him to only think the *mantra* easily without speaking it any more while his fingers moving forward touched the beads. The rosary has one extra bead attached to it where you start and where eventually you finish the round of 108.

When Guru Dev saw that Dr. Varma had reached the end of the round at the extra bead, he told him to stop thinking the *mantra*. After some time he told him to open his eyes slowly. He asked him how he felt.

Dr. Varma said he felt very good and happy. "Very good," said Guru Dev, "now you go home and sit in your room and do three rounds. Then come out slowly, have breakfast and then open your shop and do your work. In the evening after closing your shop go to your room and again do three rounds. Come out slowly and have some food and then you can come to me and tomorrow morning before sunrise come again to me and report your experiences. So the next morning Dr. Varma was most happy to report all the beautiful experiences he had had during the day, business was so good, customers were so friendly and

told him he looked so good, he managed to do so many things.
But as to his meditation he was not quite happy. He said: "I felt so happy with my *mantra*, but I kept forgetting it while my fingers were moving automatically. In each round this happened! What can I do about it?!"

A wonderful smile was on Guru Dev's face. "FOUND!" he exclaimed. "You have learnt to transcend the *mantra*! Excellent! You transcended the *mantra*, which wants to go back to the source. The best thing that can happen! When you are aware of having forgotten the *mantra* you quietly pick up the *mantra* again and continue happily. This was very good meditation. Continue meditating like that now and tonight and report to me tomorrow morning." So very happy checkings followed.[42]

Installation of Shankaracharya of Jyotirmath

It appears that for several decades there had been discussions about the restoration of the post of Shankaracharya of Jyotirmath, and, allegedly 'Karpatri' Hariharanand turned down an offer to be Shankaracharya of Jyotir Math, in favour of his *guru*, Swami

Brahmananda. It is also said that it took twenty years to persuade the *swami* to accept the post.

But Swami Brahmananda was not entirely convinced about his assuming the role, so, just prior to the ceremonial investiture being made, he slipped away from his *ashram* in Benares, and made himself scarce. At that time the committee might have directed its efforts at finding another candidate, but instead the members held out hope for the *swami's* return.

Several weeks later, under cover of darkness, Swami Brahmananda slipped back into his *ashram*, and his long awaited return prompted an immediate resumption of the plans to install him as Shankracharya, though this time it was decided to perform the ceremony there and then, at his *ashram*:-

'Swami Gyananand Ji Maharaj, the senior founder of Bharat Dharma Mahamandala, Pujya, had long wished for the restoration of the *peeth,* so he proceeded to Sidhhigiri Baag hoping for the fulfilment of this desire. With a great declaration from Shri Charan ['Shri Charan', meaning 'Blessed Feet' was a favoured epithet for Swami Brahmanand] to restore the northern seat of Dharma, the *shodashopachara puja* (of sixteen offerings) was done and the *abhisheka* was accomplished by about ten o'clock.

In the afternoon there was a magnificent great procession of the Shankaracharya, and at the proper time Maharaj Shri was brought in to the *pandal* (marquee) for a meeting.

Profuse applause of *"Jagadguru* Bhagwan *Shankaracharya"* echoed in all directions. The sounds of *mantras* from Vedic scholars of the four *Vedas* resonated up to the canopy of the sky. The anointing was performed by a special Vedic Karma Kandi (ones who perform religious ceremonies) of Kashi [Benaras], and the king, Maharaaj Dhiraaj Shri Darbhanga, announced the great anointment and the ascension to the *dharmapeeth* of Dharmacharya Shri Jyotishpeethadhishwara Jagadguru Bhagwan Shankaracharya. After having cheered *"Bhagwan Shankaracharya"* again and again they did *abhivadana* (deferential salutation) to Shri Jagadguru Shankaracharya Maharaj.

In this way, on fourth *shukla* day of Chaitra in the Vikram year of 1998, on 1st April 1941, Maharaj Shri was throned as the extremely worthy Dharmaachaarya (religious preceptor) 'Ananta Shri Vibhushit Bhagwan Ji Maharaaj', on the Sinhaasana (lion throne) of *dharma* at Uttaraamnaaya Peeth, Badrinath. The seat had been empty for one hundred and sixty-five years. Accordingly, news of the saviour of Jyotishpeeth spread by newspapers and periodicals everywhere in the country and abroad.

Realising that the *peeth* was being saved, all four organisations of *sanatan dharma* had cause to rejoice and necessarily sent congratulations in praise of *'Acharya Charanon'* (the 'Teachers Feet'), and voiced their obedience to the *acharya*. In north India an unprecedented huge wave of religious awakening occurred, and invitations came from all directions.

* * *

At this time the chief two tasks before Acharya Shri in relation to the restoring the *peeth* were:-
(1) Creation of a new *math* (monastery) and *mandir* (temple) at the place of the *peeth*.
(2) Returning the people of north India to the Vedic path, back to the conduct of *dharma*, and to revive the standing and perfectly glorious ideal of the *peeth*.

These two tasks you were to start simultaneously. Some people of the community of wise men of Kashi suggested to Maharaj Shri that since all the tasks for restoring the *peeth* should be done in a very beautiful form then a lot of wealth would be necessary. Therefore, they suggested that some programmes should be made for the prevalence of *dharma* in well-off cities such as Bombay (Mumbai) and Calcutta, and from that there will be a spiritual awakening and also funds for the restoration of the *peeth*. Now Maharaj Shri answered these learned men like this:- 'You people gave me to sit on the Dharma Sinhaasana (the Lion Throne of *dharma*), and I am sitting on it, and all the tasks relating to that are given to us too. Therefore, you people should now sit free from anxiety. Subsequently, responsibility for the regeneration of Jyotishpeeth is now ours, and that restoration will indeed happen.'

After all that, you travelled southwards. For a few days you stayed in Katni before gracing Jabalpur and making your abode in Baldev Baag. A retinue of faithful devotees was attached to him, and more and more people came and joined his company. An immense crowd rushed for *darshan*, coming constantly for *upadesha* (counsel). *At this time, near the border of Madhya Pradesh at Khandwa in Burhanpur, a Maharudra Yagya was being held, and you were invited there.* This was a traditional religious ceremony and to that end it was magnificently spiritual. It took a lot of arranging, with hundreds of thousands of people gathering together in the same place. *In one place, so many more were getting the wealth of darshan of Maharaj Shri's magnificent authority, whereas it had been difficult for people to get your darshan. For to make darshan easy, three benches made of planks were put one upon the other, and on these was placed your seat. This was done on your advice and accomplished by the folk.*[43]

The Shankaracharya of Jyotir Math Recruits a Secretary

Mahesh Prasad Srivastava wanted to take initiation from Swami Brahmananda, and shortly after the *swami* became Shankaracharya of Jyotir Math, Mahesh had the opportunity of regaining contact with the *guru*:-
'About three years later, I saw him in the market of a big city of north India, being carried in a big procession. And this was when he visited the city as Shankaracharya of north India.'[44]

'That was the time when he came to... mmm, when Shankaracharyas used to come, they take him out on great processions, with great all, big paraphernalia. In one of the processions I happened to see him, and when I saw him, first time, I said now "fine, this is it", that was the flash to me, and then I surrendered myself.'[45]

"He had become the Shankaracharya of Jyotirmath. To become a Shankaracharya is a very, is a democratic thing. All the *pandits* and saints and all that, they join together and they elect the Shankaracharya. The head of.. the custodian of Hindu religion."[44]

Apparently, before accepting Mahesh into his *ashram*, Swami Brahmananda first consulted with Mahesh's father:-
"I think this is common in the parents. It all depends ... that their son should live happily, and happiness is – he should have the comfort of a home and good family and he should live all the joys, and he should not go to the Himalayas where there is nothing and where will he sleep and do what he has to do and all that ... because monks' life is a very hard life. No home, nothing, nothing – you sleep under the trees and meditate in the caves or wherever, whatever. So there is nothing definite in the

life of a monk, particularly in India. Here in the west the monks are more organized and the church is there and they take care of it, but in India when one leaves home – he doesn't take care of himself, because he has no means to take care. He is out of society; no one asks him to do some work and pays him wages or anything – nothing. So now he is all in the faith of God – now that he is left with just his faith. So the life of a monk is a very, very hard life. Therefore the parents don't generally like the children to take such hardships now – out of love."[46]

"By the time I had finished my studies, he had become Shankaracharya in Jyotir Math. I was told that many people were going to that place and I went there and found Guru Dev, and then I stayed."[47]

'Two years after his first request for initiation, Maharishiji got initiation, and within a few months, started life in the ashram of Gurudeo. He found in Gurudeo the deep ocean of learning where all other depths looked shallow; the lofty heights of Yoga and renunciation where all other heights looked low. In him he found the incarnation of Dharma and Tapasya. He saw how easily the doubts and difficulties of aspirants were removed by Gurudeo, an their path made clear for practice of meditation and devotion.'[48]

Raj Varma offered this insight into Mahesh's enthusiasm for his new life with the Shankaracharya:

'He came to the ashram as a youth bubbling over with mirth, full of energy and joy of living. He became so devoted to his master in everything …
At night he lay down outside Guru Dev's door.'[49]

This vision of the new disciple's devotion to his teacher is echoed in Maharishi's own recollections.

'Right from the beginning the whole purpose was just to breathe in his breath. This was my ideal. The whole purpose was just to attune myself with Guru Dev, and that was all I wanted to do.'[50]

When Mahesh joined Shri Brahma Niwas *ashram,* at Varanasi

(Benares), he discovered many learned people there:-

> 'Right in the beginning, I joined the *ashram*, I came, and then I was amongst thirty or forty *brahmacharis,* and *pandits* and all that, all that. And they were very wise people, *pandits* of all the six systems of philosophy, and *pandits* of all the *smrittis*, *shrutis*, and all that. The whole learning round about Shankaracharya was vast retinue of learned people and I was absolutely insignificant. I had some knowledge of Hindi, and some of English, and a little bit of Sanskrit, but in that big huge learned assembly, this was absolutely insignificant, and English, of course, it was not necessary at all.
>
> And then it was about a week and as everyone in the morning would go and do the prostrations and come out and then there was nothing to do. And one week passed and then I thought. "It's ridiculous to waste all this time." Was just once in the morning and once in the evening, go and prostrate and come out. So I made friends with a man who was cleaning his room, something like that, like that. Adjusting his table, this, this, this.
>
> I said, "Oh, could you not take rest? You must be feeling very tired," and something, something.
>
> And I said. "I could..."
>
> But he said, "You can't. You can't come in this room," and this and this.
>
> But I said, "Maybe when Guru Dev is not here, when he is taking his bath, and I could clean or something."
>
> And he said, "Yes, that time you can come but get out quickly, and don't disturb things." Like that. So I started on that, some cleaning of the floor, something, something, adjusting something.'[51]

A *pandit* dealt with the administration of the *ashram*, and during a temporary absence of the *pandit*, Mahesh saw an opportunity for himself. Checking through the incoming mail he then offered to read certain of the letters out loud to Swami Brahmananda:-

'One letter was there. It came for his blessing from some state in India asking that they are going to perform a big *yagya* and they want the blessings of Shankaracharya. And that letter was there and that date was approaching, about a week was left. And that I thought was a letter very responsible for the organisation to answer.

And I asked Guru Dev, "Oh, oh, the answer of this letter?"

And he would just not mind it, because in his eyes just one organisation doesn't mean anything, or something.

But, I thought it's a very great responsibility of the organisation, it's if someone wants Shankaracharya's blessing then it's for the organisation to reply, and reply his blessings and create goodwill and inspire that organisation.'[51]

Over the following days Mahesh again and again attempted to solicit a response from the *guru,* but without result, and then went so far as to suggest that he write something himself:-

'One day I said, "It's only about four, five days left. Shall I make a draft and read to Guru Dev, or anything?"

And He said, "What you will write?" And that was the end he said.'[51]

Mahesh returned to his own room in order to gather his thoughts:-

'I said, "Now come on, I have to write an answer to this. What? What? How to write? What to do? Now supposing if I was a Shankaracharya? What I'll say in that letter?" And I just imposed "Shankaracharyaship" on myself. And I said. "Yes, all the religious organisations look to Shankaracharya, head of the religion. The main thing is, that they should get inspiration from the blessing of Shankaracharya. As an organisation doing this great *yagya*, inspiring the people in the locality for religious life, so they should have the approval of Shankaracharya for this good act of religious value." I somehow wrote. And in the evening - it was just a very short thing, because nothing very long has to go from Shankaracharya, who is a great authority on religion, so very short inspiration. I made some few lines.

In the evening when I opened the door and entered and I read out that thing, in one simple breath quickly. And it sounded so apt, so appropriate.

And then he said, "Will these people get it if you write? Then send it."

I said; "Yes, they can get it, it's yet four days."

That's all he said.

Then I quickly wrote and put on a seal of Shankaracharya and did the whole paraphernalia, and sent it. From that day probably I gave an impression that I could write something useful. That was the first thing. And from there, the letters came to me for replying and I was replying and sometimes reading to him.'[51]

From the time he went to stay at the *ashram*, Mahesh wished to get close to the *guru*, as did so many others:-
'What happened was, naturally people came to the *ashram* from all over India to pay respect to Guru Dev, once or twice a year according to their own convenience. And when they were come, they were narrating all sorts of stories: the child was sick; they had a lawsuit, all sorts of difficulties. And then, thinking of Guru Dev, that thing disappeared.

Hearing all these things for a long time one night I asked Guru Dev: 'What is this? These people don't even write to Guru Dev. Guru Dev doesn't know they are in difficulty on the surface of life. And then, how do they report they had a vision or some thought of Guru Dev and from that time everything started to be smooth? If they wrote a letter and the difficulty came to the notice of Guru Dev and then they got out of their difficulties, I could understand it. But they don't write letters, they just have the devotion to Guru Dev and they have some thought of Guru Dev.'

And Guru Dev's reply was: "It's the department of the Almighty, and he does it."

'It took me about two years to understand - because I quite remember the time - what was meant by 'It is the department of the Almighty.'[52]

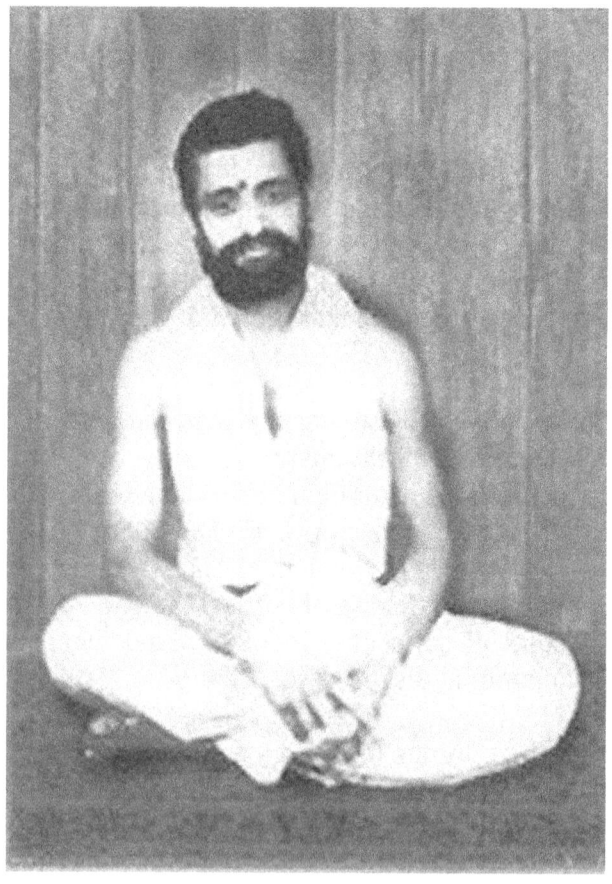

Mahesh's ambition was to try and attune himself to the master's thinking:-

'And it took about two and a half years, and I thought two and a half years were wasted, but it came out to be quite early to adjust myself to his feelings. And the method that I adopted was just to sense what he wants at what time - what he wants. I picked up activity as a means to adjust to his thought, to his feelings.'

'Just about two and a half years for my thoughts to be mainly flowing in tune with his - how much perfectly, there was no way to measure, but I knew I was making very, very rare mistakes, no mistakes almost.'

'And from there on for me the whole thing was very light and beautiful, no obstacles, clear, everything. Then I was living around him without even feeling that I was living. It's a very genuine feeling of complete oneness with Guru Dev, just like that. People who have seen me moving with Guru Dev know that I was not as if in this isolated, single body or something.'[53]

'Even ignorant people like me were blessed, and this was his great, extreme value of adaptability, He could adapt himself to even such sheer ignorance, and raise the value. This adaptability is what I found most useful for me, as far as Guru Dev is concerned. Very great fortune to have found him.'[54]

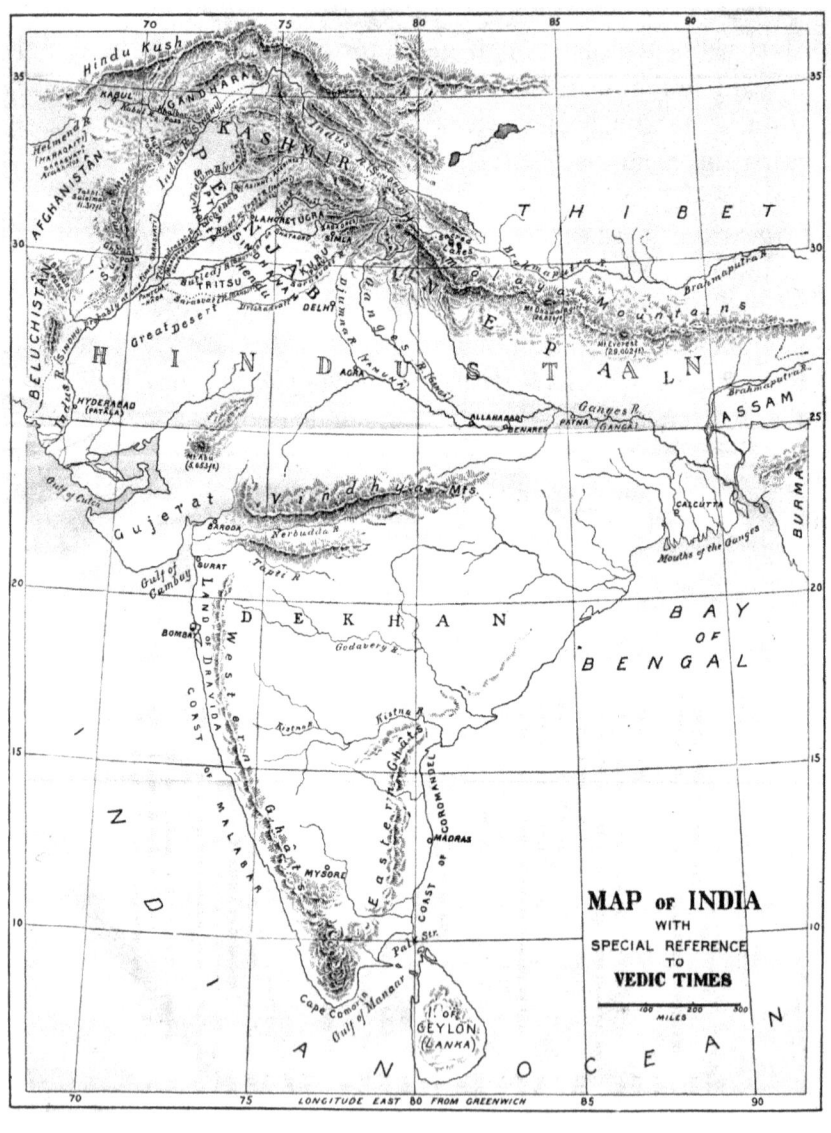

Vedic India

The country we nowadays call India has a long history and rich culture, which stretches back eons into pre-history.

Some consider that the civilisation of India was brought about by an influx of outsiders, known as Aryans, who some believe came from Europe, who are said to have written, and brought with them, the scriptures known as the *Vedas*.

But, according to descriptions contained in the *Vedas*, the geography of *'Sapta Sindhu'*, the land of the 'Seven Rivers', would seem to be a description of the northern area of India, as it was then, rather than somewhere else outside of India.

The *Vedas* are held to be the oldest known record of human thought, and have survived due to being memorised and transmitted from generation to generation. Regarding the origins of *The Vedas*, some believe *The Vedas* are actually *'apaurusheya'* "not of human agency" and are supposed to have been directly revealed. Thus *The Vedas* are called *shruti* ("what is heard").

Indian religion is called Hinduism though the term 'Hindu' is not Indian but a word created by non-Indians to describe the Indian peoples. Actually, both the words 'Hindu' and 'India' relate to the name of a prominent river, the Sindhu. It was the ancient Persians, who called the inhabitants of the area 'Hindus', and the Greeks who called the river the 'Indos' and the geographical area 'India'. The Muslim invaders then called the country 'Hindustan'. Those who live in India refer to their country as 'Bharat', it being named after a former king, Bharat or Bharata, a brother of Lord Rama.

The plains of Northern India are very fertile, watered as they are by the five rivers of the Punjab, *'panjab'* meaning 'Five Rivers', But in early times there were two other rivers, thus the area was known as Sapta Sindhu, the 'Seven Rivers'. On account of its resources, North India has attracted the attention of marauders, and has suffered wave upon wave of attacks, with a series of invasions, and foreign rule, dating back at least to 715AD. For two and a half centuries, during the period known as Mughal India (1526-1765), the country was ruled over by a series of largely Muslim emperors.

The year 1776 saw America become independent from Britain, but in India British interests gained sway, with the East India Company taking greater control there. Coincidentally, 1776 was the year that the post of Shankaracharya of Jyotirmath, the defender of the religious values of *'Sanatana Dharma'*, fell empty. After a long, long lapse, of 165 years, the seat was again set to be filled, and on April 1st 1941, Swami Brahmananda Saraswati was installed as the official Shankaracharya of Jyotir Math.

For Swami Brahmananda, a lifelong recluse, this was a major step, for not only had he to deal the routines of meeting and greeting visitors, and with public speaking, but he had also to raise funds and restore the buildings and the dignity of the teachings.

The Teachings of Swami Brahmananda Saraswati

── ★ ──

The *ashram* issued a regular newsletter in the format of a broadsheet newspaper, under the title of *'Shri Shankaracharya Upadesha'* – 'The Teachings of Shri Shankaracharya', in which transcripts of discourses were published alongside news and inspirational Scriptural quotations. Some of Swami Brahmananda's discourses were also published in the occasional book produced by his *ashram*. Recordings survive of sound reels, wire-recordings, which contain examples of his voice, with him giving discourses and singing *bhajans* of Shankara.

As Shankaracharya, Swami Brahmananda took it upon himself to spread the philosophies and teachings associated with Adi Shankara. These include the *'Smarta'* teaching, which harmonises the devotional worship of various deities, viz Shiva, Vishnu, Shakti, Ganesh and Surya, and the *'Advaita'* teaching, of 'non-dualism', of there being no real distinction between the *'Atman'*, individual spirit and *'Brahman'* (Unchanging entity).

Swami Brahmananda had also to convey and interpret the various *Shastras* (Scriptures), including the *Vedas*, *Upanishads*, *Puranas* (ancient folk stories) and the *Bhagavad Gita*.

In order to impart information on a wide array of topics and systems, Swami Brahmananda could be surprisingly direct:-

'Take a look and consider one time; "Who are you?"

However much you experience in *samsara*, you are separate from all that - body, mind, intelligence, breath etc. - all that you regard to be your own. It is said; "Our body." "Our mind." "Our intelligence." It is clear that to some extent you think that you are the owner, but your existence is separate from this, in the manner of your house, your temple. The *mandir* (temple) is yours; but you are not the temple. In this manner, the body, the mind, the intelligence, the breath etc. are yours, but you are not them - you are a separate thing from that. You are a part of the Paramatma *sachchidananda* form, but because of *aviveka* (absence of discrimination) and because of *agyaan* (ignorance), you have made such a close association with the body, mind, intelligence, breath etc. that you have become attached to understanding this form as yourself.

If a hand, foot etc. or an organ of the senses is destroyed then you will stay living. If an organ of perception such as the eyes or the ears etc., is destroyed then you become deaf or blind. Your existence is not destroyed with the destruction of the sense of perception. On some occasion when you are sick with a very dire illness then you say this, that really; 'If the breath will stop then we are happy', that is to say that you understand that the whole of *samsara's* agonies will be terminated with the stopping of the breath. In this manner the *prana* (breath) is also a thing separate from you. You are also not breath. However much is visible and can be experienced, you are separate from that. Understand, whatever things you can relinquish; you are separate from these things. Your real form is that which you can never relinquish. The experiencer of all, the witness of all, you are a part of the perfectly awake liberated human form of *sachchidananda* (Truth, Consciousness, Bliss) Eternal Paramatma.

Experience one's own form as separate from body, senses, breath etc. and the entire world; then again you will be released from pain and distress etc. of living in *samsara*. In order to experience one's own true self, trust on the *Veda Shastra* and with support provided according to the instructions of *sadgurus* (genuine *gurus*) proceed with *upasana* (worship, service).[55]

Swami Brahmananda was concerned that people were suffering:-
Nowadays, in all the four directions people appear to be disturbed and unhappy. The real cause of this is lack of knowledge. By reasoning together with discernment it becomes clear that outer surroundings cannot influence us, if we make the effort to strengthen our natural tendency to be unaffected. When the mind allows external environments to give happiness or to give trouble, then they make us happy and sad, if we are continuously experiencing the existence of our *sthula* (gross), *sukshma* (subtle) and *karana* (causal) bodies. We are beyond these three bodies. You are the soul, you are *sachchidanandamaya*, pure Truth, Consciousness and Bliss, then in whatever the surroundings you are, you cannot be experiencing suffering.[56]

Swami Brahmananda often extolled the path that leads to closer identification and eventual merging of the individual with the Absolute. Here the *guru* expounds on '*Aham Brahmasmi*'; a teaching that translates as 'I am Brahman (the Ultimate Reality)':-
As much as *samsari* (worldly) people desire to obtain wealth, children and respect, that much effort is not made in worshipping Bhagavat (the Lord) and in becoming knowledgeable. That *sadhana* (means) of [obtaining] uttermost happiness is disregarded. *Sadhanas* of collecting and amassing suffering are done. From any worldly thing there can never be any happiness. From worldly things the pleasure gained is like the wish of a childless woman preparing for the son's marriage. If there is not a son who is fit to be reverenced then how will there be a marriage? At whatever time happiness is not really in worldly things such as wealth, woman, son etc., then how will

happiness be got from these? But by absence of discrimination, the mind has gone in pursuit of *anishta* (mishchief, evil).

The purpose of life is to desire doing something for the future; 'If the bucket is to be filled, and is to be emptied, this is all there really is'. Then human being existence is going to be really useless. So consider; 'Fill the bucket of the stomach at dawn and empty it by the evening.' If this is really how life has been then to live is really useless. You desire life because just now you have not had *darshan* (vision) of Bhagwan. For this *darshan* one is alive, for doing *sadhana*.

When a seed is roasted then no sprouting appears. This is like the mind of a man when, from the heat of knowledge and devotion, it is roasted. Then afterwards birth and death does not sprout. Therefore, make an effort to become devout and knowledgeable. But similarly don't become a *gyaani* (a learned one) of wealth, woman, sons, in love with worldliness and at the same time chanting:-

"शिवोहं । शिवोहं"

"Shivoham, Shivoham"
'I am Shiva, I am Shiva'
[ref: *"chidananda rupah shivoham shivoham."*
'The Bliss Consciousness Form, I am Shiva, I am Shiva.'
(*Atma Shatakam* or *Nirvana Shatakam,* of Shankaracharya)]

"ॐ । ॐ"

"OM, OM"
and

"अहं ब्रह्मास्मि"

"aham brahmasmi"
Brihadaranyaka Upanishad 1:4:10
'I am Brahman'

When people call themselves Brahman then afterwards go far from *dharma* and *karma* too, in this way, that condition [of oneness with *Brahman*] is not nourished but is destroyed.

Therefore, until you shrink from love of worldly things, then for as long as you are not returning to Brahman, you should do worship of Bhagwan. Keep doing *bhakti* and when you will very much desire Bhagwan, then afterwards you will be freed from *"janma-marana ke chakkara"* - the 'wheel of birth and death'.[57]

Which people go to hell?

In those days [when] I was living alone in the jungles, one time there was a temple on the bank of a river in a jungle near Rewa, right there we stayed. A little way off was a village.

A man came there and did *puja* and asked of us; 'Maharaj, the *gyaani* person gets *moksha* on the strength of his own *gyaan* (knowledge) then, for the *bhakta* person the *bhakti* (devotion) is the cause that they will cross over (attain salvation), and the one who is fallen obtains the support of Bhagwan. Then again, which people go to hell?'

We said that; 'The answer to this I will give tomorrow.'

At dawn the very same man came in the temple praying before Bhagwan saying:

"पापोऽहं पापकर्माऽहं पापात्मा पापसम्भवः ।"

"paapo aham paapakarmaaham paapatma paapasambhavah."
[*Pradakshina*]

This kind of sentence he said for a very long time, that 'I am a sinner, I am a wicked soul, I am the doer of evil *karma*.'

When he had said all this he comes to me, then I said to a *brahmachari*; 'Remove this evil one. Where has he come from this morning to be before us? His face is not fit to be seen. Quickly drive away this evildoer, far away.'

Getting out of my way he told to the *brahmachari* that 'I am not such a sinner as Maharaja is understanding.'

Hearing this I called to him and said that; 'We are not calling you a sinner, we are giving an answer to your question of yesterday. We called you a sinner, then you felt bad. From this it is obvious that inside yourself you don't consider yourself to be evil. However, you come every morning in front of Bhagwan saying this *"paapo aham, paapakarma aham"* - 'I am evil, I am an evil doer.' So you are saying this then in front of Bhagwan, but in your own mind you don't consider yourself to be evil. Thus it is really;

"मनसि अन्यत् वचसि अन्यत्"

"manasi anyat vachasi anyat"
'Thinking one thing but saying another'

Such people go to hell that have something in their mind and yet outwardly say something else. This is the answer to your question. You should be identical on the inside as the outside. According to that which is in the mind, you speak that and like that indeed do, then you will not deceive any other, and you will also experience happiness and peace.'[58]

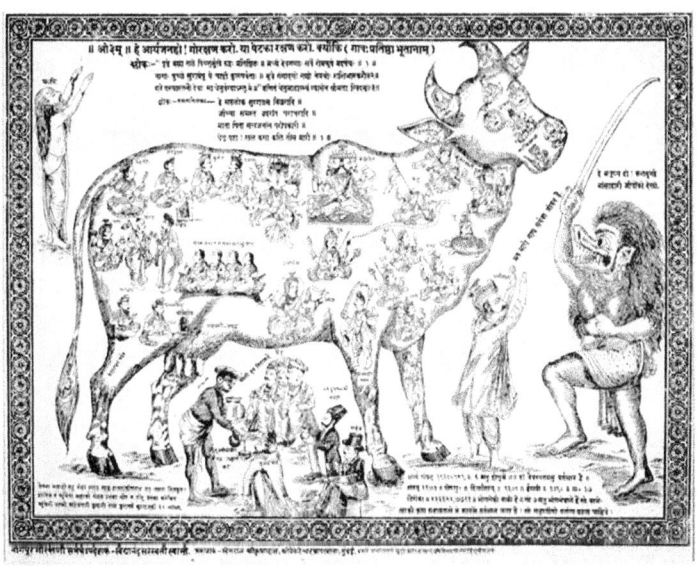

Cow Protection League

यद्गृहे दुःखिता गावः स याति नरके नरः ।

"yadhgrihe duhkhitaa gaavah sa yaati narake narah."
'The man who gives suffering to the cow goes to hell.'

'But our civilisation and culture have been become intermixed with the culture of Westerners, from that time, the extensive disappearance of the Indian method of teaching has caused ignorance of the *Shastra*, *Purana* etc - that the cow, the Brahmana etc are the same, this devout scriptural knowledge is disappearing.'

'Schemes to slaughter and kill are the downfall of the cow and its progeny, and injure the holy and financial delights of both *raja* and *praja* (subject). So for this reason everyone should make an effort to put a stop to these gristly practices. Several states have done laudable work in this connection, but unless central government will be compelled, it is impossible to satisfactorily inform of the effects. For the sake of this, effort should be made countrywide.'

'Together everyone should make an effort to promote the old custom of houses of cow protection, all householders, landlords, land owners, merchants, money-lenders etc should progress cow houses, from where can be gained ideal able-bodied cows and bulls. Nowadays the [lack of] establishment of grazing ground is lamentable. In this connection Manu wrote:- "On the four sides of every village and city there should be sufficient ground for pasture of cows." All capable farmers, landlords, merchants and money-lenders should make arrangement for centres to provide proper pasture for cattle. Also you should always consider advancing the cows. In this is the honour of India and Indian civilisation kept true.'[59]

As a child Swami Brahmananda was named Raja Ram, 'King Rama' and through the death of his grandfather heard the message that *'Ram naam satya hai'* 'Ram's name is truth', in later life he remained true, extolling the virtue of studying the *Ramayana*, the epic poem tale of the god King.

Umesh Srivastava, the son of one of the *swami's* most notable devotees, Jugal Kishore Shrivastava, recalls the *guru's* advice:-

'Shri Gurudev asked me – a child of six years of age – "Who is your chosen God?" – I replied– abruptly – "Lord Ram ". Shri Gurudev said follow the instructions of your parents. After the age of 8, I started reading the epic "Shri Ram Charit Manas" as per the instructions of my father.'[60]

Umesh's elder sister, Shrimati Vidyawati Shrivastava, also recalls receiving such advice from the *guru*:-

"After initiation in the year 1942. One day I went to Shankaracharyajee for his darshan. I asked Shri Gurudev "What more I should do for my spiritual development?" Shri Gurudev said "Read Ramayan" i.e. Ramcharitmanas of Goswami Tulsidas.

I requested him for further instructions for my spiritual development – again and again. But Shri Gurudev didn't reply. Previously my father, a close disciple of Shri Gurudev, instructed me to complete Ramayan *paath* [reading] whenever possible daily."[61]

Another devotee, Bhai Gurudasjee, declared:-

"It was my good fortune that I was initiated by Shri Gurudev Jagatguru Shankaracharya Maharaj in the year 1941. "As a piece of paper, when waxed, stands the test of time, a trimmed lamp will shed its light for longer hours. As a person flying a kite in a wind-swept sky controls it by a string, an appropriate antidote can cure a snake bite. As a king travelling incognito best observes the state of his subjects, it is by such relative supports that the *guru* guards his disciples"[61]

Swami Brahmananda knew all-too-well that some people might become drawn to spiritual teachings for the wrong reasons, and in particular he knew of the peculiar lure that supernatural powers have for some. To those people he gave a solemn warning:-

'Nowadays most people seek the *siddhis*, desiring to meet with any kind of *siddhi*. Few people have a *siddhi*, but by their greediness for *siddhi* a good many people become cheated. Our wish then is [for them] to be wary. We are like the village guard who calls *"Jagtay raho!"* ('Be awake!'), in this way we people are remaining attentive. Be cautious folks, beware of cheats. The watchman's raises his voice; his *"deputy"* work is done. Later, how could he be blamed if anyone is senseless asleep! It is the one who is sleeping that gets looted. Our wish is to perform the everyday affairs of the watchman. We are awake and awakening others.

There are five kinds of *siddhis*:-

"जन्मौषधिमन्त्रतपः समाधिजाः सिद्धयः"

"janmaushadhimantratapah samaadhijaah siddhayah."
Yogadarshanam 4:1
'Siddhis are attained by birth, drug, *mantra*, *tapa* & *samadhi*.'

The significance of this is that if miracles are seen in any person this is not the true measure of a *yogi*. Seriously, there are *yogis* in whom miracles occur and they do not perform miracles for their wealth or reputation. They only want for happiness in the world, tenderness and compassion. Understand that folk should be saved from misunderstandings about these *siddhas*.

Do *bhajans* (hymns) to Bhagwan (God). You should become a ruler to the *siddhis* then *siddhis* will wander behind you.

How to be made a ruler? Not to belong to the world of the imagination. Until such time as your world is of a different kind, not longing for a son, for wealth, for a wife, for prestige and reputation, until then you will really be bereft of strength. The proverb is that 'God is scared of the beggar'.

Withdrawing from the fancies of the world, grow in desire of Paramatma (the Supreme Self, God) then a multitude of *siddhis* will wander behind you, but no *siddhi* will occur when you seek them. The way that one should possess is where one's own honour is not sacrificed. When you can be in the steady presence of the Almighty Paramatma, then it would be a calamity if you were to go stumbling behind, here and there, following trifling *siddhis*. Be sure of this, the *siddhis* behind you will run away when they see you. If you do not wish for *siddhis*, if you obstinately make a boundary with the *siddhis* that obstruct your spiritual progress, then *siddhis* will stay surrounding you.'[62]

Swami Brahmananda would constantly press his listeners to live in the present, reminding them again and again of the transience of life, encouraging them always to be ready for death.

'Every day be ready, bedding packed. Nobody knows what time the *"warrant"* comes. Death *"warrant"* is the arrest *"warrant"* - for you there is no scope for *"appeal"*, all at once it occurs you are to leave. Wherever one is, at that very place you will be falling down. If you are ready in the first place, then there will be no suffering at the time of death.

He who remains ready to go, from him there will never be sin. Really it is by overlooking the other world that one becomes wicked and lives sinfully. If all this is remembered every day that one day one is going to let go, then henceforth a man will never lie or behave badly.

Consider this; that when father, grandfather, great grandfather is not living then it cannot be that we will remain. When it is settled that we will go, then really if we are ready beforehand, then the travelling will be a pleasure; but if one is not ready then afterwards you will be suffering. Be careful of doing any work that you regret afterwards, at the time of going.

If you are not careful then you cannot escape falling down. The stream of worldly existence takes a downward direction. The inclination of the senses is opposed to a man and in opposition one again falls into the wheel of desires, not considering the suitability. Therefore it is always necessary to be careful.

At the time of death that which was good and bad in a man's own lifetime all come to be remembered. That sin that has been done remains, the fearful effects are remembered at the time of death - much repenting and much sadness occurs. Therefore you should be careful that no sin occurs to be regretted at the time of death.'[63]

Swami Brahmananda would liken life in this world to making a short visit to a *'dharmashala'* (a guest house for the temporary accommodation of pilgrims):-

'This world is a *dharmashala*. In this place it is not proper to involve the mind very much. The general way is to do the work and put your vision on the *yatra* (journey, pilgrimage). It is really a folly to ensnare oneself in the arrangement of this *dharmashala*. So, behave according to what a thing is. In four days of existence putting on a show of emotion is not good. For as long as you are breathing, pass the time praying to Bhagwan. In everyday affairs proceed with proper behaviour. In case everyday affairs have intruded into the mind, then again and again there is a return to the eighty-four hundred thousand births, fallen and rolling in the wheel. For this reason very carefully perform everyday affairs; by the body and wealth are everyday affairs done, and with the mind thinking of Paramatma. Apportioning in this way, on this account people can well experience happiness and peace.'[64]

This teaching, about the world being but a *dharmashala,* was one that the *swami* often returned to:-

'The world then is a *dharmashala* (a stopping house for pilgrims). Four days you remain here, then you proceed further. Don't get very involved in any of the difficulties in your abode at the *dharmashala*, accomplish the work needed in order to go. If there is anything lacking then people are not much troubled; considering that they are to stay in the *dharmashala* only two days then they will be permitted to leave. If arrangements at the *dharmashala* are to be in accord with one's own wishes then all the time passes in making arrangements, and the work for which he came from his town or village, that he will not obtain.

You should accept that the world is really a *dharmashala* too. Life is a few days; we are not to remain here permanently. For this reason, don't put a lot of interest in arrangements of the world, do only that much to get that portion for one's maintenance. Always remember this, that however many plans you will make, they cannot all be fulfilled. For this reason, in making *"schemes"* one's hopes hang by a thread, restlessly thinking about them day and night, ruining this time and to no advantage.

However much you make arrangements in the world, afterwards there will still remain some lack. Therefore if there is an item you cannot own, there is really no purpose in trying to reach out for it. Exert yourself in the normal way passing your life according to the *Shastra* and importantly do *purushartha* from which you gain permanent happiness and peace. By performing *purushartha* principally for gaining Bhagwan, for gaining earthly things put your trust strictly in:-

"यदस्मदीयं न हि तत्परेषाम्"
" yadasmadiyam na hi tatparesham"
'That which is ours cannot be another's.'

That which is in one's destiny, that will certainly come into one's own possession, none can hinder it. So be resolute in the world. Don't become too busy on account of earthly tasks; perform everyday affairs as a matter of routine. Set the primary relationship in Paramatma. By so doing you will experience peace in life and the way ahead will also be made clear.'[65]

At the cessation of hostilities after World War II, Swami Brahmananda was asked for his opinion about victory over enemies. The *swami* took this opportunity to stress the work we all must undertake in order to obtain peace and freedom from suffering. Instead of talking about national or international conflicts he spoke of conflicts closer to home, and the means to bring about 'True Victory':-

> 'In truth then victory is really this; for the one who has no risk of inner defeat. In truth, by the suppression only of outer (usual) enemies no one can become permanently victorious; because from those enemies there is no lasting suppression. True knowledge of victory occurs then from obtaining control over internal enemies. Really, only by the permanent subjugation of internal enemies is the subjugation of the external enemy achieved; because the inner enemy gives rise to the creation of the external enemies.
>
> The internal enemies are *kaama* (lust), *krodha* (anger), *lobha* (greed), *moha* (delusion), *mada* (intoxification) and *matsarya* (jealousy). This is really the *shadari varg*, the group of six inner enemies which create any external enemies of the world; therefore if you wish to experience happiness and peace one must gain victory over all one's gross enemies, then you should cut off the place of birth of the six subtle enemies, *kaama* (lust), *krodha* (anger), *lobha* (greed), *moha* (delusion), *mada* (intoxification) and *matsarya* (jealousy). Without gaining victory over the *shadari varg* (group of six enemies) then you cannot completely eradicate the external enemies. This is fixed.
>
> This is the proven experience of those who have gained victory over these internal subtle enemies, that if the birthplace of the external enemies becomes destroyed and all enemies have become eradicated then afterwards no enemies remain and in truth this is considered to be a real victory. For him the true and lasting storehouse of happiness and peace is opened.
>
> To be completely free from enemies, that country should be wholly settled in happiness and peace, and for that it is required that the creator of that region or the leader has gained victory over the *"antarika shadari varg"* (the group of six inner

enemies), otherwise this is what really occurs that; 'of one's own accord one's life is destroyed' and 'of one's own accord one is choked'. The past history of many hundreds of years is a witness to this statement, which the chief leaders of the new countries did, by their own inner *kaama* (lust), *krodha* (anger), *lobha* (greed), *moha* (delusion), etc, instigate the colouring of the earth blood red, many times. This is brutish. On whom the burden of running a kingdom befalls, he should acquire the special characteristic of powerful insight. To have trust in a gust of agitation of the emotions, of *kaama* (lust), *krodha* (anger), *lobha* (greed), *moha* (delusion), etc, is not a great wish or humane to the whole world.

Up to what extent can we suppress our outer enemies? We subdue one but are intimidated by another, this then is the suppression of an enemy but there is no sign of triumph. Whilst victory over the internal enemies is not obtained then this will remain the condition. Therefore, this much is necessary, that the leader of a country obtains triumph over his own inner *antarika shadari varg* (group of six inner enemies). Thus if the leader of society is really victorious, then they can successfully demonstrate the path of lasting happiness and peace for the country and the whole world.

It is not very difficult to obtain triumph over *kaama* (lust), *krodha* (anger) etc. But without understanding, people are habituated to presuming it is out of their reach. Mostly people have become resolved that only a *mahatma* (a great soul) on the *nivritti margi* (the path of renunciation) can attain triumph over the *shadari varg* (six enemies); but this determination is really based in ignorance. The basis of the *nivritti margi* (path of renunciation) then is giving up and severing all connections with the root cause of *kaama* (lust), *krodha* (anger) etc. So for him there is no question arising of victory or defeating anybody. It is assumed that a victor over the *shadari varg* then is he who can engage continually in *vyavahara* (daily business, employment etc.); but that on him desire and anger cannot accumulate and gain monopoly. So the enemy can constantly have the opportunity to make an attack; but that power to attack will not be strong enough; for this reason then he (the enemy) will surrender, as he is flawed and defeated. The continuous flow of daily business is no trouble in getting victory over *shadari varg* (the six enemies).

The birthplace of all enemies of *samsara* (mundane existence) is the collection of subtle enemies. The willingness for obtaining a victory by awakening physical preparation for battle and making the period of disquiet of life and death is not necessary. For this only it is only necessary to become dispassionate and act with strong discernment.

One who is a *samadarshi* (one who is impartial, dispassionate) is one who is said to see very well - he who sees a thing for what it really is said to be *samadarshi*. In the real form of a thing and in seeing it he makes no distinction, he is in a complete inner state of harmony and remains fit. In his vision the perception of a thing is correct, that is to say there is no confusion. If *samsara* (mundane existence) is delusory then there is no change in the truth of that; and if the absolute is truth then he really accepts the truth. The falsehood of *samsara* (transitory existence) and the permanence of the *atma* (soul) - when a man becomes strong then he becomes *samadarshi* (impartial, dispassionate). And, then he sees all things in their real form.

The meaning of the falsehood of *samsara* is this, that the nature is to change, become reversed, and to perish in an instant. No more learning is necessary for anybody to understand this - all are experiencing this, that everything in *samsara* is transient, has a tragic end - subtlest of the subtlest and grossest of the gross things are changed. This is apparent to every individual life that in front of us. How many individuals are born? How many are being destroyed? All this speech is not original and one day I also will no longer remain. If *samsara* is broken in an instant then it is not necessary to make a great effort to understand this. Man is experiencing this day and night; but then again he is not considering it.

He who has once given careful thought to the perishability of *samsara*, in his own heart, he gains victory of the *antarika shadari varg* (the group of six internal enemies); because to that man, all the material world is instantly destructible, so that he cannot have *lobha* (greed) or *moha* (delusion) for anything; because he knows that what he has *lobha* (greed) and *moha* (delusion) for today, tomorrow is automatically changed; therefore *lobha* (greed) and *moha* (delusion) are to no purpose, in effect they are really connected to remorse and anxiety; therefore *lobha* (greed) and *moha* (delusion) are not to be grown in the inner self. The very seeds of these become destroyed and if there are no seeds of *lobha* (greed) and *moha* (delusion) then *matsarya* (jealousy) also becomes destroyed. He is also without *matsara* (wrath). No jealousy of worldly glory and wealth remain, no arrogance or jealousy, then in him anger becomes perfectly destroyed. Thus man's narrow wishes become attached to those of God's, and with dutiful mind all business is accomplished. His behaviour is very naturally disciplined and in his worldly life he is like a lotus leaf, detached and pure. Thus by such dispassionate natural activity man is really triumphant over the *shadari varg* (the six enemies) - In this way there are no outer enemies of man - he governs over all of nature alike - moreover, none becomes capable of destroying the reign of peace. So really the *samadarsi* (the impartial, dispassionate one) is the great conqueror, he can remain exhibiting the fruit of happiness and peace.

Let that be! Triumph over the *antarika shadari varg* (group of six internal enemies), that is the best and true victory, and for this great victory man should incline his efforts.'[66]

In keeping with the views and beliefs of Adi Shankara, Swami Brahmananda conveyed the *'Smarta'* teaching, the understanding that all deities are equal, and that all deities are but aspects of one Deity. This position challenges any individual who convinces himself or herself of the supremacy of any god or goddess to see the same divinity in any aspect of creation, even in another god or goddess:-

'In *samsara* (worldly life) there are two sorts of people - *astika* (religious) and *nastika* (unbeliever) - in the world of the atheist there isn't any *guru*. Of the world of the *astika* (religious) that *guru* should really be called *"jagadguru"*. Amongst the religious there are two kinds of believers. Some folk are setting their belief in a *sakara* (form) of Brahma and some in the *nirakara* (formless). The one who holds the ability to be *guru* to both, those who are speakers of the *sakara* (form) and those who are speakers of the *nirakara* (formless), the very same can be called a *jagadguru*.

The meaning of this is that; of the *sakara* deities there are five Vedic deities, that is to say; Bhagwan Vishnu, Shiva, Shakti, Surya and Ganesha. There are different instructions for worship of all of these and for those who do not believe in the five deities he can also give instruction, the same is really a *jagadguru*. The person who instructs in the method of worship for *devata* (deities) is similar to the lowly paid *vaidya* (physician) who sets phials of medicine for all diseases, without also having the status of a *"compounder"* but calls himself a *"civil surgeon"*.

Anybody can name their own son Rama. Who can stop them then? But merely from a name he does not become Rama. Then who stops anybody writing *jagadguru* in front of his own name? But when you ask the mark of the *jagadguru* then the proper indication really is this that nobody with faith in any deity goes away from the door disappointed. Recently *sampradaya* (sects) have allotted a relationship of worshipping Shiva, Shakti, Vishnu etc., this is improper. In the five deities there is not any inferiority or superiority. Every deity is similarly capable of dealing with the welfare of their own devotees, however much a worshipper they are, all are *Vaishnava*, since all deities are parts of Bhagwan. Bhagwan states that:-

ज्ञानं गणेशो मम चक्षुरर्कंअः

शिवो ममात्मा ममशक्तिराध्य ।

विभेद बुद्धया मयि ये भजन्ति

ममाङ्गहीनं कलयन्ति मन्दाः ॥

gyaanam ganesho mama chakshurarkamah
shivo mamatma mamashaktiradhya.
vibheda buddhaya mayi ye bhajanti
mamangahinam kalayanti mandah.

'That is, Ganesh ji is the head of Bhagwan,
Surya are the eyes of Bhagwan,
Shiva is the *atma* of Bhagwan,
Adya Bhagavati is the *Shakti* of Bhagwan.'

Therefore these five gods are several equal parts, which cannot be measured and split from one another, and they are to be worshipped as equals. [If not] then worship is not being done but [instead] the cutting off of parts is being done.'[67]

Swami Brahmananda supported worship of a variety of divine forms, as Bhagavan (God), but also that the One Reality exists in a formless state, as Paramatma - the Transcendental Self.

'In the manner that in milk the formless form of butter exists, pervading the drops of milk, in that manner Bhagwan (God) is in this world, present everywhere in the world of the moveable and the lifeless; and that method of churning the milk produces the butter, that very method in the form of *upaasanaa* (worship, devotion), having stirred with the stirring spatula, you stir the formless form and obtain the concrete form of Bhagwan (God).

That manner, that in milk the creamy substance is butter, in that manner, in this world the creamy material is Bhagwan (God); and that method, on extracting the butter from the milk, but all the strength and nourishment and the fullness is in the butter, and the milk is devoid of fullness. Really, that kind is the quintessence of the world of the sentient and the lifeless, who by gaining God, at once acquires complete health, wealth and greatest peace, and the experience of unlimited *aananda* (bliss), and then this world is altogether unsatisfactory.

In this manner, prepare the means for gaining this understanding, of Bhagwan (God) being both formless and having a form. Come, be engaged in *upaasanaa* (spiritual exercise) and having digested this knowledge of these words, automatically gain that highest pleasure.'[68]

Swami Brahmananda, though teaching the highest spiritual truths, never lost sight of his devotees' very human-ness.

'One day a man who was considered to be very wealthy came to Guru Dev. He said to him:

"I have been so happy whenever I have come to you. Would you allow me to donate something for your *ashram*?"

"No," said Guru Dev, "I do not want money but I want from you what is dearest to you."

"I have precious jewels."

"No, I want what is dearest to you!"

"Do you want my estates?"

"No, your estates do not belong to you, you have so many debts."

Now the man was deeply frightened!

Guru Dev continued quietly: "you have a little box in your pocket, what is in it, that is what I want, for that is dearest to you! For that cocaine you have been spending all your money and have made your family unhappy."

Trembling the man took out of his pocket a little box and handed it to Guru Dev. He prostrated before the master for a long time and then thanked him from the deepest depth of his heart for having been cured of his addiction.

Guru Dev said: "Now go and work and make your family happy!"[69]

Swami Brahmananda would suggest to his followers that they surrender their flaws to him, and he forbade them from making financial donations – a board was displayed to this effect. It is not known how he was able to pay the costs of running the *ashram*, the rebuilding Jyotirmath monastery, and all the costs related to travel expenses, and food for of himself and his entourage. He was conferred the Sanskrit title 'Ananta Shri Vibhushit', meaning 'Bestowed with Infinite Wealth'. It has since been stated that:-

'This is an expression in Sanskrit Language which was used for the first time in the history of India, to synthesise his Greatness.'[70]

Since Swami Brahmananda was himself a monk it might be assumed that he advocated and encouraged others to become monks too. Nothing could be further from the truth. In fact, Swami Brahmananda was very concerned that only those who might really benefit from becoming a *swami* did so. He even reassured his devotees that they did **not** need to become monks in order to be at peace with themselves:-

'Be a *mahatma* living at home wherever that is, he can become a *mahatma* wherever he is living. One does not become a *mahatma* from clothes dyed in ochre or the mark of a *tilak* (a mark on the forehead as an emblem of a sect). Benediction does not come from costume, the welfare comes from faith. In the *vritti* (fluctuations, activity) of the mind the state of *mahatma* exists. Therefore be here, staying there alter the flow of the mind a little from thinking inside of *samsara,* and think more of Paramatma.'[71]

With respect to the tradition whereby only certain *varna* or *jati* (castes) are qualified to become a *sannyasi* or become a *guru*, Swami Brahmananda was very clear about his position:-

> 'There is no talk that one must be a *brahmana* in order to get *mukta* (liberation). If *bhakti* (service) of Bhagwan is done then [all] is well, [but if] not then *brahmanas* also come to the ruler of hell, and the devout *shudra* can gain Bhagwan. Wherever happiness is to be, there nobody is *brahmana*, is not *kshatriya*, is not *vaishya*, is not *shudra*. In Paramatma there is no difference in anyone, the difference then is in everyday affairs.'[72]

> 'Having been doing *puja*, worship and chanting, accomplishing the *sadhana*, then all can gain knowledge, all have the right of devotion in Bhagwan, but not everyone can be a *guru*. Actually, only *brahmanas* are in the position to be a *guru*. In addition to *brahmanas*, - *kshatriyas, vaishya* and *shudras* can become *shishya* (disciples), but not a *guru*. Women also have no right to be made a *guru*.'[73]

> 'Nowadays *kayastha, vaishya, teli* (oilman), and also *kalavara* (seller of spirits) are taking to wearing the colours of the *sadhu* (holy man) and are eagerly wishing to make *shishya* (disciples) of their own. Actually both these kind of *guru* and *shishya* (disciple) are to get their downfall. Actually this speech we are saying coincides with the *Shastras*, it is not something of our own that we have made up.'[74]

Swami Brahmanad was also a firm supporter of the wider tradition of *'varnashram dharma'*, the division of humankind by different occupations, and adherence to the sequence of *'ashramas'*, the four stages of human life:-

1. *Brahmacharya*, student life
2. *Grihasta*, house-holder life
3. *Vanaprastha*, forest-dweller life
4. *Sannyasa*, ascetic life

Yoga Teachings of Swami Brahmananda

The principal teaching of Swami Brahmananda Saraswati was that one should routinely practice a system of meditation, in order to bring about change in one's consciousness and realise the purpose of one's life. This teaching of meditation was most often referred to as *'japa dhyana'* – *'japa'*, being the mental repetition of a *mantra,* and *'dhyana'* being the practice of meditation. Swami Brahmananda explained his position, that as a *guru* he was there to assist, by virtue of his ability to choose a *mantra* that would be suitable for a particular individual:-

'The *guru* is really a boat to get across the ocean of life. In *samsara* (earthly life) everything is easily obtained, but it is very difficult to obtain a *sadguru* (perfect teacher). The *Veda Shastra* (traditional Indian Scriptures) are full of *mantra*, there is no shortage of them. But books of *mantras* are similar to a pile of cartridges: There are piles of cartridges of different kinds by the fifties and the gun is also there, but until someone will tell which "number" cartridge is fit to kill the beast, the pile of cartridges will really be next to useless. In the manner that an expert hunter desires several "numbers" of cartridges for hunting tiger, elephant, deer etc., that kind of experienced *guru*, observing the *shakti-pravritti* (energy and inclination) of those people devoted to spiritual achievement, in accordance to their qualification, deduces the beneficial *mantra* which would be of benefit to the spiritual seekers.'[75]

Swami Brahmananda counseled that the choice of *mantra* relates to the form of God that one prefers;

'Understand from any experienced *sadguru* (good tutor) the *mantra* and meditation method of your *"ishta"* (favoured god); you will surely soon become attached to regular *"ishta mantra japa"* (mental repetition of the *mantra* of one's favoured aspect of God).'[76]

*

'Using a good method to find a *satguru* then of his words it is necessary to appreciate the *"mula mantra"* ('mula mantra' means 'root *mantra*' but it can also mean 'essence of advice'). Afterwards your welfare will be improved.'[77]

Swami Brahmananda repeatedly extolled the value of *mantra japa* and meditation:-

'There is no doubt that *siddhi* (realisation) comes from doing *japa*.'

जपात् सिद्धिर्जपात् सिद्धिर्जपपात् सिद्धिर्नसंसंशांशयः ।

'japaat siddhirjapaat siddhirnasamshayah'
"*japa, siddhi japa, siddhi* from *japa* there is no doubt."[76]

*

'To the best of your ability obtain a *japa mantra* and by practicing, sin is destroyed.'[78]

*

'From the act of *japa* [the effects of] sins are destroyed.'

जपतो नास्ति पातकम् ।

'japato naasti paatakam'
'Sins are eliminated by reciting the name of God'.[76]

*

'The method to join the mind to Paramatma is; *japa* of Bhagavan's *mantra*, and *dhyana* (contemplation / meditation) of *swaroop* (true nature) of Bhagavan).'[79]

*

'Shiva, Vishnu, Shakti, Surya, Ganesha are actually all forms of Bhagavan, do *japa* of the names of any of these too and do *dhyana* (contemplation / meditation) of the *swaroop* (true nature) of that fit *mantra* - right here is the method of Bhagavan's *bhajana* (worship).'[79]

*

'The *Veda* and *Shastra* are similar to a list for gaining Paramatma; and according to the command of *Veda Shastra*, *japa, dhyana* etc are the ways to dig for the treasure of Paramatma.'[80]

*

'Have endless devotion in one's own *ishtadeva* (one's chosen deity), without *darshan* of the *ishta* there is endless difficulty.'[81]
'For climbing aloft it is necessary to acquire the aid of stairs. Forsaking steps nobody can go. The staircase for meeting the *ishta* is by way of the *guru's* instruction.'[82]

*

'If you devote yourself contemplating, worshipping and singing in praise of your Adored One you ought to feel something or other and your desire ought to be more steady. If it is not so, be sure your devotion is not of right kind.'[83]

*

'There is a tenet of Ayurveda that sins of previous life appear in the shape of different afflictions, i.e. physical diseases. They are cured by medicine, chanting of some particular *mantra*, *havana* and worshipping Him. Hence when a disease is not cured by medicine other remedies, too, should be tried.'[83]

'Devotional song is sung in four voices; namely *vaikhari*, *madyama*, *pashyanti* and *para*. These days, devotional songs are sung in *vaikhari* voice with the help of playing *kartal* (small cymbals or wooden clappers) and *sistrum* (resonant percussive device).

Singers of such songs should not spend their whole life in singing in *vaikhari* voice. They should try to produce the other three kinds of voices with the help of veteran *gurus*. The same applies to chanting of *mantras* too. Chanting of *mantras* has several stages. Contemplation too is of many kinds such as internal-external, concrete, subtle and ultra subtle. Hence devotee should keep searching great veteran *gurus*.'[83]

Swami Brahmananda warned his devotees of the dangers of using an incorrect *mantra* for *japa* meditation:-
'Many people have not done the work of consulting the *Shastras* in order to determine what is authorised and what is

not, they look here and there and from this they understand what they should do to engage in worship. Some people set great measure by the magnificence of the *japa* of ` ॐ (*OM*).

In *Bhagavad Gita*, Bhagavan certainly said that "I am the *pranava*" [ॐ *OM*]. But if the purpose is to attain Bhagavan's special form, then why not use the method of grasping the lion as well, since he is also that too? Bhagavan Shri Krishna Chandra said that:-

मृग्गानां मृग्गेन्द्रोऽऽऽह

"mrigaanaam mrigendroaham"
[Gita ch10 v30]
"Amongst beasts I am the lion"

What actually happens to those who proclaim the greatness of using only *OMkara ka japa*, our experience up until recently we are informing, listen; 2, 4, 10, 20 times constantly repeating (*OM*) then no particular effect there will be. But if 2, 4 thousand unceasing repetitions then in a short time [the connection with] the worldly surrounding will become weak. Arsenic is a destroyer, but taking a little, then the effects will not be very rapid. If some excessive dose is taken then it actually kills. Those who use the method alone of *OMkara ka japa* taking it to be the special form find that their worldly discipline certainly weakens; working and regular meals go into decline; wife and son etc become unhealthy and also die.

Five, six years ago, we had gone to Lucknow for the occasion of *Laksha Chandi Yagya*. On that occasion one old woman came to us, and 2, 4 people came along also. These people did say that Mataji was a great devotee, all day long she would remain in prayer and worship, but only very recently her two sons who were in the prime of life had died.

To this we asked; "Were you practicing *OMkara ka japa*?"

She answered to Maharaj! "The very same is our portion, all

day long I did do *japa*."

We said that; "well done that for your *samsara* (worldly life) you have dropped [ॐ OM] *japa*, at this moment do not renounce [the world]".

However, by adherence to the practise something very excellent she will destroy, right here is the effect of *oMkara ke japa*.

This then is done somewhere without love and if love's work is being done then the meaning and the object of love will be be annihilated by the influence of *oMkara ka japa*.

For this [reason] "*grihasthom*" (householders) are not authorised to do *oMkara ke japa* alone. *Shastra* with a view to grant good fortune do not give authority. If there were any benefit to be derived by "*grihasthom*" (householders), by using *oMkara japa*, there would be no reason for the *Shastra* to prohibit.

Mantras [sometimes] contain a mixture [of sounds including] ॐ *oM* that are given for auspicious purposes. Another thing is this that women are prohibited from practicing *japa* with an *oMkara-yukta mantra* (a *mantra* conjoined with ॐ *oM*). Wherever at the beginning there is the *purusha* (male) *mantra* (ॐ *oM*) then instead women should apply the sound 'श्री *SHREE*'.

Bhagavan Shankar (Lord Shiva) giving instruction to Parvati on *japa* explained that for women "*oMkara-sahita mantra ka japa*" (connected *mantra*) can be like poison and for happiness they should only do *japa* without "*oMkara*". Due consideration should be given that Shankarji gave this information to his own wife. If *oMkara* is beneficial for a woman to do, why would he instruct his own wife against the practice?'[84]

*

'[If you] will do only *japa* (repetition of a *mantra*) then the mind will flit here and there. By doing *dhyaana* (contemplation, meditation) the mind is restrained, therefore you should set in motion both *japa* and *dhyaana* together.'[85]

'At daybreak and in the day do that *puja* (ritual worship), *japa* and *dhyaana* (meditation) etc which is appropriate, but at night you should certainly do 10-15 minutes of *japa* (repetition) of the *'ishta mantra'* and *dhyaana* of the *'ishta murti'* (desired form) before sleeping. Rapid advancement occurs by this *upaasanaa* ('sitting near' / devout meditation).

In darkness (nightime) you should sit with eye closed and do *japa* of the *mantra*, and in the same way with eye closed you should do *dhyaana* of the *ishta* with the mind. Not on their whole body, you should look on the foot or on the mouth area of the head, seeing our favourite *ishtadeva* full of compassion, appearing infused with tenderness. The vision of the *ishta* is really for one's own use. You should not envisage the eye of the *ishta* to be closed. This manner of having seen the vision of the infusion of tenderness, doing *dhyaana* of the *ishta* in the heart, you should remain doing *japa* of the *ishta mantra*. From this, the image of the *ishta* will grow and provided that the mind gets strengthened and held with the *ishta* then in the end it will stay in this condition. On the strength of this you will be going across the ocean of *samsaara* (worldliness).'[86]

Swami Brahmananda also advocated daily sessions of this type of meditation for householders, to be practised morning and evening, using the *mantra* of the deity to whom the meditator was devoted (the "Ishta"): -

'At daybreak and in the day do that *puja*, *japa* and meditation etc which is appropriate, but at night you should certainly do 10-15 minutes of *japa* of the *'ishta mantra'* and *dhyaana* of the *'ishta murti'* (desired form) before sleeping. Rapid advancement occurs by this *upaasanaa* ('sitting near' / devout meditation).

In darkness (nightime) you should sit with eye closed and do *japa* of the *mantra*, and in the same way with eye closed you should do *dhyaana* of the *ishta* with the mind.'[86]

'Those people who are always attached to worldly works, in truth they are generous, since the work they do will come for all others, none will go to them. Besides, those people who are giving, doing the *dharma* (duty), practising *japa* (repetition of *mantra*), doing *tapa* (penance) etc., are collecting *punya* (meritous action). In truth they can really be called stingy because all fruits of anything they are doing here are made into a *"parcel"* in their own name, in the future only they will obtain it - nobody else. In this manner those people who are said to be *punyatma* (pious) in truth can be said to be stingy. Thus become a skinflint, then you will be celebrated in this world and will get the Supreme state in the other world, this is really the principle of *Veda Shastra*.'[87]

'You must get to know the Mantra of your 'ISHTA', and the method of 'DHYAN' thereof, through an experienced 'SADGURU' and somehow or other devote some time every day in Japa of the 'Ishta mantra' and Dhyan.'

'Through Japa, "SIDDHI" (Realisation) shall result. There is no doubt about this. "JAPAT SIDDHIR JAPAT SIDDHIR JAPAT SIDDHIR NASAMSAYAM."[88]

Contemporary Meditation Teachings

Swami Brahmananda was teaching a traditional meditation practice that also seems to have been taught by other *gurus* of his day.

Sri Ramana Maharshi

Ramana Maharshi (1879-1950), a famous holy man from South India, taught a very similar meditation system for householders as that advocated by Swami Brahmananda.

In this quote from Ramana Maharshi, he explains the value of silent intoning of a *mantra* in *japa* meditation, explaining that it 'vanishes into its source', reminding us of the words used by Swami Brahmananda when teaching Raj Varma; "You transcended the *mantra*, which wants to go back to the source".

In January 1937 Ramana Maharshi was asked a question about *japa*:-

'D.: Is not mental japa better than oral japa?

M.: Oral japa consists of sounds. The sounds arise from thoughts. For one must think before one expresses the thoughts in words. The thoughts form the mind. Therefore mental japa is better than oral japa.

D.: Should we not contemplate the japa and repeat it orally also?

M.: When the japa becomes mental where is the need for the sounds thereof? Japa, becoming mental, becomes contemplation. Dhyana, contemplation and mental japa are the same. When thoughts cease to be promiscuous and one thought persists to the exclusion of all others it is said to be contemplation. The object of japa or dhyana is the exclusion of several thoughts and confining oneself to one single thought. Then that thought too vanishes into its source - absolute consciousness, i.e., the Self. The mind engages in japa and then sinks into its own source.'[89]

Swami Sivananda Saraswati

Another contemporary teacher of *yoga* meditation was Swami Sivananda Saraswati, an eminent *guru* living on the banks of the river Ganga in Rishikesh. In 1939 Sivananda published his description of the process of *mantra* meditation leading to loss of the *mantra*, and juxtaposed this to a process of concentrating on the *mantra*:

'In the beginning you should combine Dhyana with Japa. As you advance the Japa drops by itself; meditation only remains. It is an advanced stage. You can then practice concentration separately. You can do whatever you like best in this respect.'[90]

Interestingly, both Ramana Maharshi and Swami Sivananda point out that the state where the thought drops off is an 'advanced stage' of meditation, but neither indicate that this stage would necessarily take a long time to attain.

* * *

यौगिक सफलता की कुंजी

[पूर्वोपदेश का शेषांश]

वेद के कर्म-काण्ड का यही चरम लक्ष्य है कि कर्म-योग द्वारा ही जीव के अन्तःकरण की शुद्धि कर उसे सच्चिदानन्द परमात्मा से मिला दे ।

वेद के उपासना-काण्ड के अनुसार चित्त-वृत्ति के निरोध को योग कहते हैं । इसका अन्तिम लक्ष्य अन्तःकरण की वृत्तियों को साधन द्वारा निरुद्धकर परमात्मा के स्वरूप का अनुभव कराना है । निश्चल तरंग-रहित जलाशय में जिस प्रकार मनुष्य अपना मुख देख सकता है उसी प्रकार चित्त-वृत्तियाँ निरुद्ध होते ही कूटस्थ आत्मा का प्रतिबिम्ब अन्तःकरण में स्पष्ट दिखलाई देने लगता है । यही आत्म-दर्शन है ।

In 1947 a book of Swami Brahmananda's Hindi discourses was published, entitled *'Shri Shankaracharya Vaksudha'*, compiled by his secretary, Mahesh Prasad Ji.

In this volume Swami Brahmananda refers to the 2nd sutra of the famous Indian Scripture *'Yogadarshanam'*, Patanjali's collection of *yoga sutras*. The short Sanskrit verse is transliterated as; *'yogashchittavrittinirodhah'* and is of great importance as it defines the word *'yoga'*. Here Swami Brahmananda explains the meaning of this verse and in so doing offers a very clear description of the goal of *yoga* meditation. Here is a translation of his inspirational words:-

'According to *Upasana Khand* of the *Vedas* we are told:- *"yoga"* is stopping the fluctuations of consciousness.'

'The ultimate aim is this, that by the practice of having stopped the fluctuations of the inner self, to experience the Supreme form of the Self, calm without a ripple in any part of the pool of water, that manner a person can see his own face.'

'That really is the method; stopping the fluctuations of the consciousness is really giving a clear reflection of the imperishable self in the instrument of inner vision. This indeed is "*darshan*" (sight) of the "*atma*" (self or soul).' [91]

Swami Brahmananda & the First Presidents of India

A wide mix of people gathered to hear Swami Brahmananda's teachings, mainly those from the Hindu community, but many others were attracted too. He was admired by people from all classes of society, and those of differing creeds and denominations, thus justifying the title given to him, of *'Jagadguru'*; meaning 'Universal Guru'.

Swami Brahmananda was even visited by politicians, amongst them two future Presidents of India, Dr. Rajendra Prasad and Dr Sarvepalli Radhakrishnan.

Shankaracharya Swami Brahmananda addressed a gathering of eminent philosophers at Calcutta in 1950, at which 'Justice' Professor Paul stressed the importance of Swami Brahmananda's guidance:-

'To-day we are here to do homage to his Holiness, Shri Jagatguru Shankaracharya Ananta Sri Vibhusita Swami Brahmananda Saraswati of Jyotirmath, Badarikasram - the Superman, the seer, the sage, who is one of the few rare individuals amongst the billions of the citizens of the world, whom we would unhesitatingly choose if and when we would be called upon to describe the spiritual and cultural capital of our nation, if and when the world would feel the need of evoking the part our nation can play in it, who is beyond any controversy, one of the rare few who have contributed and can still contribute something to universal peaceful progress, who have risen by their talent and genius above their fellow countrymen, above their fellowmen of the world and have thus gained a place for themselves at the head of humanity, at the extreme spearhead of civilization.

Standing here at a time when everywhere in the world

everybody feels not a little bewildered at an immense increase in the sense of human power, we can hardly exaggerate the necessity of teachers like his Holiness the Jagatguru.

You will pardon me if I venture; at this assemblage of eminent philosophers, to refer to an aspect of our Hindu Philosophy which seems for the time being, to be too much belittled by the power-intoxicated world.

Our Vedic philosophers.... ....
The civilized world today is indeed in an age of spiritual chaos, intellectual doubt and political decadence. Civilized man today no doubt has acquired immense scientific and mechanical resources, but seems hopelessly to lack the wisdom to apply them to the best advantage. This is why we witness a growing sense of frustration seizing every mind almost everywhere. The whole world seems to be suffering from an epidemic of hysteria.................

We do not know which way the truth lies. Perhaps even here it will be true to say that every truth, however true in itself, yet taken apart from others, becomes only a snare. In reality, perhaps, each is one thread of a complex weft, and no thread can be taken apart from the weft. But this much seems to be certain that there is this paralysing fear and alarm almost everywhere in the world-everywhere even the most powerful minds have not succeeded in escaping it altogether. Everywhere humanity is beginning to feel that we are being betrayed by what is false within, - we are almost giving way to find ourselves spiritually paralysed.

This indeed is a deadly malady. The patient here must first of all be brought to see that he is sick and to want to get well and to do of himself what is needed to get well. Perhaps something is away both with the heart and the brain.

The world needs philosopher-teachers like His Holiness Shri Jagatguru Shankaracharya who can reveal the world of values and can make us realize that, that is the real world. The world badly needs guidance to a creed of values and ideals. The world needs a teacher who can dispel our fears and can remove all sense of frustration or least in so far as it is only an internal malady.

We need a teacher who has succeeded in gaining for himself freedom to be alone, who does not require any power, who can cure both heart and Brain. We are in an age in which the meeting of the traditionally alien cultures of the Orient and the Occident has become inevitable. We need a teacher with sufficient gift of intellectual imagination and divine inspiration who can help the smooth working of this meeting, the working out of this meeting in such a way that the values of each civilization complement and re-inforce rather than combat and destroy those of the other. We cannot avoid the sight of conflicting economic, political, religious, artistic and other ideological doctrines and the consequent fear and feeling of helplessness, We need a teacher who can teach us how to get out of the crisis in valuation in this realm of conflict, who can teach us how to avert the danger of spiritual paralysis facing us.
His Holiness Sri Jagatguru Shankaracharya, having gained the freedom to be alone, did also fully realize the means of escaping from loneliness. In these days of doubts and difficulties if we can at all safely turn our eyes for guidance to any one it should be to this superman the overpowering influence of whose genius appears indeed in the light of divine inspiration, the superman who has succeeded in ridding himself of any ambition for power.

Saintly guidance from a seer like Sri Jagatguru alone can ensure an abiding peace.'[92]

Dr Radhakrishnan addressed Swami Brahmananda as 'Vedanta Incarnate'. Shortly after the gathering of philosophers Dr Radhakrishnan made a visit to the *guru*, taking along with him two scholars from the USA who wished to meet the *guru* in person. When they arrived the *guru* was sitting in quiet contemplation on the flat roof of the building, whereupon the doorkeeper presented himself and announced the arrival of visitors. Brahmachari Mahesh was in attendance and wrote an account of the meeting, in Hindi, in which he tells of Swami Brahmananda's response to the news of the visitation:-

> 'The gate-keeper came and informed – "Dr. Radhakrishnan ji accompanied by two scholars from England and America has arrived to seek His Excellency's *dar*s*han*."'

> 'I thought – "It's for the good. These people are world-renowned scholars. Due to their visit, Maharaj Shri will hold a marvellous intellectual discourse.'[93]

But it seems that the *guru* had no mind to receive guests at such a late hour, for he commented:-

> '"What's this for a time to meet? No appointment had been given."

> Listening this much I became cautious; it felt as though Maharaj would now say – "Tell them I cannot meet". Because generally it happens that after saying words like "This is not a time to meet" and "No appointment had been given", people often say, "Tell them I cannot meet".

> Before Maharaj Shri could say so, I carefully requested – "If His Excellency finds it suitable, kindly give them a few minutes. Maybe other people surround these visitors during the day. They might have come at nighttime with the aim of meeting with you in private."

> Maharaj Śhri said – "If this is the case, please bring them in." As the visitors reached upstairs, one light in the hall was switched on by which the terrace also got lighted up a little.'[93]

Swami Brahmananda answered the questions posed to him and before the visitors left, Dr Radhakrishnan told the *guru* how he would like to visit him again:-

"These days I am very busy with political affairs here, otherwise I would definitely prefer to spend some time in your company. However, it is my sincere wish to spend two months with you whenever you are in Jyotirmath."[93]

* * *

Swami Brahmananda at Lucknow, March 1952

Brahmachari Mahesh, Lucknow, March 1952

On Wednesday 15th October 1952 a press release was issued:-

The Great Saint of the Himalayas is Coming to Shower His Blessings on the Metropolis.
The Statement issued by: BAL BRAHMACHARI SHRI MAHESH JI.

Press conference convened by Shri Shankaracharya Reception Committee, Delhi on the 15th Oct., 1952 at 5 p.m. in the Young Man's Tennis Club Queen's Gardens, in connection with the visit of HIS HOLINESS SHRI JAGATGURU SHANKARACHARYA MAHARAJ OF JYOTIRMATH.

******

My own self in different forms.

It gives me a great pleasure to welcome you all and have your company here this afternoon. It gives me enough encouragement and support to acquaint you with the details of the mission for whose fulfilment His Holiness Shri Jagatguru Shankaracharya Swami BRAHMANAND SARASWATI MAHARAJ will be visiting your city about the 12th of November 1952 and stay here for about a month for Dharmopdesh.

Swami Brahmand Saraswati Maharaj, the present Shankaracharya of Jyotirmath Badarikashram (in the Himalayas) is a magnetic personality with a sweet amalgam of High Wisdom and Love of humanity. He combines in himself the Knowledge of the self with the mysterious powers -- the siddhis arising out of yogic perfection and hard penances, which he has undergone throughout his life. He is a great living yogi and scholar and is revered by millions of Hindus as their Supreme Religious head.

This great Saint of the modern age was born in U.P. in a well to do and renowned Brahman family in 1871 and was enthroned to the seat of His Holiness Jagatguru Shankaracharya in 1941 at Benares, during the ninth session of the All India Sanatan Dharma Maha Sammelan convened by the Bharat Dharma Mahamandal in conjunction with a countrywide support of almost all the ruling princes and different socio-religious institutions all over the country. It may be recalled that it was a long persuasion of about twenty years which could convince Param Virakt Swami Brahmanand Saraswati to accept the great responsibility of the Shankaracharya at the age of seventy.

From the tender age of nine when he came out of his home in Search of God, till this time, his life was mostly spent in the lonely hidden regions of the Himalayas, Vindya Giris and the Amarkantakas which are rarely frequented by men and are chiefly inhabited by wild animals. For years together he has lived in hidden caves and thick forests where even the midday sun frets and fumes in vain to dispel the darkness that may be said to have made a permanent abode there in those solitary and distant regions.

But today he is easily accessible as he is now the presiding head of Shri Jyotirmath which is the greatest religious institution of the Hindus of Northern India, covering all different creeds and sampradayas and branches lying under the fold of Hindu Religions.

One unique principle of the great Sage that distinguishes him completely from other living saints of today is that he does not accept money as gift from his visitors or disciples.

This brief description attempts to mirror a few hurried and short glimpses of the life journey of this great living sage who has actually transformed into a living fact the inner latent potentiality of the soul. He has known the great universal Truth, whose realisation is the aim of the entire scheme of life. For him the mists of ignorance have completely disappeared and having known the Divine Reality he has verily become an embodiment of the great Divinity.

His aim of life, if the life of a realised soul can be said to possess any such aim, is to broadcast the message of the Great Divine light that he has himself realised, the Light that is the Soul of all human beings. Having himself attained the pinnacle of Self development, he aims at transforming the worldly minded people into the Godly minded, and through his inner Divine touch to change the materialistic hearts of iron into spiritual hearts of gold.

His entire personality emanates the sweet perfume of spirituality. His face radiates that rare light which comprises love, authority, serenity and self assuredness that comes only by righteous living and Divine Realisation -- one feels as if some ancient Maharishi mentioned in the pages of the Upanishads has assumed human form and feels that it is worth while leading a pious life and to strive for the realisation of the Divine.

His Spiritual teachings are simple and clear and go straight home to heart. He strictly adheres to the course of inner development laid down by the Systems of Indian Philosophy and ethics and he raises his voice never in opposition but always in firm support of the Truths and principles contained in the Hindu Scriptures.

According to the tradition from the worldly point of view, the dignity of the Shankaracharyas throne has got to be maintained by the rich paraphernalia around his Holiness, but those who have come in his contact know the fact that the private life of the Sage is quite simple and renunciation.

I believe that he is a living embodiment of titanic spiritual force. If I were asked on the basis of my personal experience, about the living saints of today, as to who is the greatest amongst them, I would unhesitatingly name Shri Jagatguru Shankaracharya Swami Brahmanand Saraswati Maharaj of Jyotirmath the Beacon Light of the holy sanctuaries of the Himalayas.

Shri Shankaracharya Maharaj has clear insight into the mind and the thoughts of the modern age. His teaching and commandments are based on sound reasonings which are quite agreeable to any reasonable thinker. He is a great critic of prejudices and narrowmindedness arising out of irrational love of caste, creed, nationality or any "ism". His life is a living proof of the Truth of the Vedas and Shastras. He has opened a new era of renaissance of True Religion. He extends his recognition to anything that is good in any religion. He is accessible to all. Everyone can enjoy and derive benefit from his holy Darshan and elevating discourses.

He is coming shortly to shower his blessings on the busy and restless souls of the metropolis. I beseech you, my friends, to extend your hearty co-operation for the great cause in the interest of each individual of our society, in the interest of our nation and in the interest of the world at large. The great Saint of the Himalayas is coming in your midst and in the fitness of the great occasion, I appeal to your good sense to extend your valuable support so that his elevating discourses may reach the masses in every nook and corner of our country and abroad.

Thanking you for giving me a pertinent hearing, I would like to say something, in short, about the shrine of Jyotirmath, the prime spiritual centre of Northern India and the headquarter of Shri Shankaracharya Maharaj. Jyotirmath is one of four seats established by Adi Shankaracharya in this continent -- two thousand and five hundred years ago. It is situated in the heart of the Himalayas 173 miles up from Hardwar and only 18 miles south of Shri Badrinath and may be said to be the queen of the Himalayas for natural beauty and spiritual values. Jyotirmath it was that the first Shankaracharya selected for his stay in Himalayas where he taught the highest philosophy of existence -- the Vedanta - to his disciples, wrote his immortal commentaries on the eleven principle Upanishads, the Bhagavad Gita and Brahma Sutras and established a seat of Spiritual light to function as sansorium [sic], a supreme centre of the Eternal Religion of India to keep the Light of Pure civilisation and culture burning for all the millennium to come. It is an ancient culture centre of yoga, the Light House which has preserved and disseminated the Light of the Sanatan Dharma all the way down the ages.

Swami Brahmananda in Delhi, December 1952

Whilst Swami Brahmananda was in New Delhi, the President of India, Dr Rajendra Prasad, and his mother, went to see him at various times:-

'On 4th December at twelve o'clock in the day, President Dr Rajendra Prasad came in the *shivira* (camp) for *darshan* of Maharaj Shri. He did *darshan*, *shraddhanjali* (offering of faith) of surrender and for *"charanodaka"* (the holy water that washed the feet).

Shri Bhagwan Shankaracharya conversed with the Rashtrapati (President) saying, 'Before, the kings would have discussions with *tapasviyon* (ascetics) and *maharshiyon* (great saints) for their advice on the tasks of government. Because of *yoga* and *tapasya* (austerity) their minds had become clear. There existed neither greed nor worldly desires, and they did not fear the king becoming displeased with what they said. Those who were given advice, that advice was beneficial for both *raja* (king) and *praja* (subject). But now things have gone to hell on account of *rajas* neglecting to keep the company of *maharishis*.'

**Shankaracharya Swami Brahmananda Saraswati
and President of India Dr Rajendra Prasad, Delhi, 4th December 1952**

Having related this he said afterwards, 'What advice can your servant give you? Only that which your eyes will see. Therefore, first you should wish to accept advice from *maharshiyon* who can also imagine the future. You people should not remain confused about this, opposing religious guidance and statecraft. Us folk make mankind righteous by giving *upadesha* (instruction). However righteous mankind will be, then, that much the government also proceeds with a very beautiful appearance.'

His Eminence the President listened to the words of Shri Shankaracharya Maharaj with utmost seriousness. In a summary on the profundity connected with *upasana* (intercession) Maharaj Shri cast light saying; 'The student cannot make the syllabus for himself. For this an academician is indispensable. By this manner, to understand the way of real happiness and peace, the experienced *guru* becomes indispensable.' In this connection, in an extract of his own lifestory, listen as Shri Charan also throws light of some experience of his own Gurudeva. He told that when he met Guru Ji in Uttarkashi; 'At that time, before anything else we said, "Firstly, you ought to give me such knowledge that I do not have to outstretch the hand outwards. Afterwards we will understand *paramartha* (the greatest treasure, salvation)". This is the effect of Their kindness that from the beginning until the present we have never extended the hand in front of anyone!'

In one-and-a-half hours of conversation, Shankaracharya Maharaj explained to the President the chief elements of how to better the individual and the society, so that ultimately the ruler and the ruled would benefit. Rajendra Babu was charmed and enamoured with all that he heard, of the simple and succinct theories. According to the programme of Rashtrapati Ji's fixed period of conversation with Maharaj Shri there was an additional twenty-five minutes more. But when Maharaj Shri spontaneously gave him leave, only for this reason did he go.'[94]

President of India and Brahmachari Mahesh

Many came to Swami Brahmananda's meetings, from all over India, including his own disciples. Back in October 1951, Swami Brahmananda had initiated 38-year-old Ramji Tripathi, as a *sannyasi*, naming him Swami Shantanand Saraswati:-

> 'At that point of time, Swami ji (Swami Shantanand) was in severe penance on the banks of the Ganges. The popularity of the teachings of His Holiness had spread word of his whereabouts, which Swamiji got to know of.
>
> Keen to get blessings from the *guru*, Swamiji went to Delhi. Staying with Swami Vishnudevananda in a tent, Swamiji participated in the spiritual retreats for a few days.
>
> His Holiness Swami Brahmananda Saraswati was on the last stage of his life. He wanted an eligible disciple of high spiritual orientation to shoulder the responsibilities of the *math*. For centuries the *math* had been instrumental in directing spiritual seekers, so the successor of His Holiness had to shoulder the big responsibility of guiding the aspirants in the path of spirituality.'[95]

It is said that at this time, in December 1952, Swami Brahmananda's health was deteriorating, and that he set about writing a *vasiyat*, or Will, naming his successor:-

> 'In 1948 His Holiness had once selected his successor, one of his favourite disciples, Swami Hariharananda Saraswati. He was also known as Swami Karpatri. The responsibilities of the *math* were transferred and registered in the name of Swami Hariharananda Saraswati in the Allahabad High Court. But his (Karpatri's) political motivations were greater than his spiritual aspirations. His Holiness had tried to convince him to take up the spiritual path to uplift mankind, but in vain. Karapatri said that he had decided to serve the nation through politics. Hence he refused to take up the task given by the Guru. Once again he (Swami Brahmananda) had to search for an eligible spiritual aspirant to lead the followers of the math.'[95]

'This historical incident was to be accomplished in 7 Canning

Lane, New Delhi. Maharaj Shri sent for his two close servants, Rameshwar Prasad Tiwari and Shyam Narayan Gupta from Prayag, and Chowdary Krishnagopal, an advocate from Etawa, to accomplish the task mentioned above, for making the Will. Maharaj Shri chose his new *"uttaradhikari"* (successor) and wrote his name and whereabouts.'

'Maharaj Ji had Willed the entire peeth in the name of Swamiji, and named three other successors, with his signature, and witness signatures in front of advocate Chowdary.

He had completed all the formalities, registered with the Registrar here in Allahabad and taken back the previous documents.'[95]

After returning to his *ashram* in Varanasi, Swami Brahmananda then made a trip to Calcutta where his health deteriorated. He lived only a short time longer.:-

'At about one o'clock on 20th May 1953, the doctor saw him and said, ' *"Sab thik hai"* (All is well)! The state of the heart is *"thik"* (fit). The pulse is moving, "*bahut achchi*" 'very good'.

After the doctor went, Maharaj Shri relaxed and about ten minutes later he suddenly opened his eyes and said, ' *"Uthao"* - 'You must lift (me)!'

Having arisen, he quickly drew both his feet to sit in the posture of *sukhasana* ('easy seat' - cross-legged) and closed the eyes. In this way he was sitting.

At one-fifteen, having abandoned his own body of the five-elements he became absorbed in his own Self. The Self arose from the form of the gross body, from the surface of the world.'[96]

* * *

News of Swami Brahmananda's death soon reached those in the

guru's ashram at Banaras. One of his devotees, Brahmachari Satyanand, recalls:-

'When in 1953 Guru Dev left this mortal frame and attained *nirvana* I was at Benares, another place of pilgrimage for Hindus, and at that moment I was staying in the *ashram* of Guru Dev. Everybody knew that I am very attached to Guru Dev and devoted to Guru Dev, and then news came to Benares that Guru Dev has attained *nirvana*. I was sitting somewhere with a group of my friends and the news was relayed there. When my friends heard that Guru Dev was no more they were very anxious about me and when they conveyed that news, they were rather alert to appraise whatever reaction is and what happened, I simply, when I heard that news I became very sad, very sorry and I just kept my head on the table before me. And all of them were very anxious what will become of me. But soon after, while I was very morose, sorrow, sad, entire world was empty for me and I did not understand what to do without Guru Dev, just a half a minute or two seconds after, a flash came and it appeared to me that Guru Dev was scolding me;

"What a fool you are! You have been with me for all these many months and years, and you heard my discourses too. Is it a moment of feeling sorry? Why should you be sorry today? And you think that I am gone, where am I gone? Till now whenever you wanted to meet me, you had, you had to come to the place where I was, and today when I have attained *nirvana*, I am everywhere, I am omnipresent. Where have I gone? Very foolish for you to mourn on this occasion. I am with you, here, there, everywhere. Why should you be sorry?"

And the moment this flash came, my face became very brilliant, I became very cheerful. And when I raised my head, my friends who were standing there, very anxious and held in suspense, they were upset to see my brilliant and cheerful face. And then they said, "What has happened to you?" I said, "No you can't understand, nothing has happened to me, I am alright, now let me go back to the *ashram* and make the necessary arrangements".'[97]

A New Shankaracharya of Jyotirmath

Three weeks after the passing of Swami Brahmananda Saraswati, a Will was produced which named one of his disciples as his successor, and on 12th June 1953 the scene was set for the induction of Swami Shantanand Saraswati as the 'Abhinava Shankaracharya', the new Shankaracharya of Jyotir Math:-

'In charge of the ceremony was Swami Govindanand ji Maharaj, who had left the place without informing anybody. He was in possession of the essential things for the ceremony. But the general secretary Pt Balakrishna Mishra with the help of other members such as Pandit Kashipathi Tripathy, Lohiya Pandey, Brahmachari Mahesh, Shankar Brahmachari, and Brahmachari Ramprasad tried hard to make all arrangements and invited all the dignitaries from across the nation. Representatives of all the religious centres, sannyasis, scholars, and spiritual leaders arrived at the predetermined time and the ceremony began. With the blessings of saints and sages of the entire world, the ceremony was successfully completed.'[95]

But less than two weeks later, on 25th June 1953, Swami Karpatri challenged the *guru's* Will and established Swami Krishnabodashram as Shankaracharya of Jyotir Math. Apparently, Swami Krishnabodashram laid a condition that he would not involve himself in any legal disputes, and this condition was accepted.

So now there were two claimants to the title of Shankaracharya of Jyotir Math, Swami Shantanand Saraswati and Swami Krishnabodhashram.

An account of Swami Brahmananda's funeral rites, and the *guru's* last instructions were soon published, in a latter issue of *'Shri Shankaracharya Upadesha',* the newsletter of the Shankaracharya of Jyotishpeeth's *ashram*, published on the 20th July 1953.

श्री शंकराचार्य उपदेश

अनन्त श्री विभूषित ज्योतिष्पीठाधीश्वर जगद्गुरु शंकाराचार्य ब्रह्मीभूत
स्वामी ब्रह्मानन्द सरस्वती का अन्तिम आदेश

अनन्तश्री विभूषित ज्योतिष्पीठाधीश्वर जगद्गुरु शंकराचार्य ब्रह्मीभूत स्वामी ब्रह्मानंद जी सरस्वती के समाधिस्थ होने के पश्चात् जो घटनाएँ घट रही हैं पत्रों में उनके सम्बंध में भिन्न भिन्न प्रकार के समाचार पढ़कर अनेक शिष्यों को चिंता होना स्वाभाविक ही है । वास्तविकता जानने को उत्सुक शिष्य-मंडल की चिंता एवं भ्रम निवारणार्थ यह लेख प्रकाशित करना आवश्यक प्रतीत हो रहा है ।

ब्रह्मीभूत शंकराचार्य स्वामी ब्रह्मानंद जी सरस्वती ने अपनी दैहिक लीला कलकत्ता में २० मई, ५३ के मध्यान्ह को प्राणायाम साधकर समाप्त की । तदुपरांत उनका पार्थिव शरीर रेल द्वारा काशी लाया गया । महाराज श्री के ब्रह्मीभूत होने का समाचार टेलीफोन, तथा तार द्वारा भिन्न भिन्न नगरों में प्रमुख शिष्यों को दे दिया गया था । फलत: सैकड़ों शिष्य स्त्री और पुरुष अपनी अपनी सुविधानुसार रेल, मोटर तथा आकाश मार्ग द्वारा शीघ्रातिशीघ्र काशी पहुँच गये । आचार्य चरण के विग्रह को मुगलसराय स्टेशन पर रेल से उतार कर मोटर द्वारा काशी स्थित ब्रह्मनिवास आश्रम में लाया गया । प्रातःकाल से ही अंतिम दर्शनार्थ उपस्थित जन-समुदाय में महाराज श्री के पार्थिव शरीर-दर्शन से शोक की लहर व्याप्त हो गई । अनेकों स्त्री पुरुष बालकों की भाँति फूट फूट कर रोने लगे । आचार्य चरण के नित्य-निवास के कमरे में उनके शरीर को विधिवत स्नानादि कराने के पश्चात चंदनादि तथा नवीन वस्त्रों से सुसज्जित कर एक सुन्दर विमान में पधराया गया । समस्त जन-समुदाय ने पुष्पमालादि से भगवान को अंतिम प्रणाम किया । यद्यपि ब्रह्मीभूत हुये ३० घंटे से अधिक हो चुके थे फिर भी भगवान के मुख का तेजोमय भाव दर्शनीय था । पुलिस बैंड तथा अन्य गाजे बाजे, एवं संकीर्तन मंडलियों के पीछे एक सुरक्षित मोटर ट्रक पर आचार्य महाराज का विमान सुरक्षित था ।

ब्रह्मनिवास से प्रस्थान होने के पश्चात भीड़ उत्तरोत्तर बढ़ती ही गई । दशाश्वमेध घाट पर तो ऐसा लगता था कि जगद्गुरु के अंतिम दर्शन के लिये काशी के सभी आबाल वृद्ध उमड़ पड़े हैं । घाट मकान मार्ग सब जनपूर्ण थे । अनेकों बजरे तथा डोंगियें गंगाजी में दर्शकों से परिपूर्ण जलमार्ग को ही अवरुद्ध कर रही थीं । दशाश्वमेध घाट पर पहुँच कर भगवान को स्नान करवाया गया और विमान विशाल बजरे पर स्थित किया गया जिस पर चारों ओर यतिमंडली तथा प्रमुख शिष्य गण बैठे थे और कीर्तन चल रहा था । बजरे के श्री केदार घाट की ओर चलते ही छन्नेकों बजरों और डोंगियों ने उसे घेर कर चलना प्रारम्भ किया । गंगा तट पर एकत्रित जन-समुदाय भी गंगा जी के तीर तीर उसी ओर बढ़ने लगा । केदारघाट पर एक पाषाण मंजूषा में दंड कमंडल सहित जगत्गुरु के पार्थिव विग्रह को पधराकर बीच धार में जगत्पावनी गंगा की अगाध जलराशि में समाधिस्थ करते देखकर सहस्रों भक्त जनों ने अपने को निराधार एवं असहाय होने का अनुभव किया । इस भांति १६० वर्ष तक लुप्त रही ज्योतिष्पीठ का उद्धार तथा उत्तर भारत में आस्तिकता, धार्मिकता को जागृत कर एक अनुपम ज्योति पुंज को जाह्नवी की धारा में विलीन होते देखा और उसी के साथ आस्तिक वर्णाश्रम धर्मावलम्बी जनता का सौभाग्य भी ।

स्वामी श्री करपात्री जी की अध्यक्षता में एक 'अंतरिम ज्योतिष्पीठ प्रबंधक समिति' का निर्वाचन किया गया । स्वामी स्वरूपानंद सरस्वती इस समिति के प्रधान एवं पं॰ बालकृष्ण मिश्र एम॰ ए॰ एल॰एल॰ बी॰ प्रधान मंत्री तथा अन्य १० सदस्य, जिनमें विशिष्ट शिष्य, आश्रम निवासी, ब्रह्मचारी तथा सन्यासी थे, निर्वाचित किये गये । निश्चित कार्यक्रम के अनुसार जगत्गुरु के और्ध्व दैहिक संस्कार, भंडारा,

The Last Instructions
of
Ananta Shri Vibhushit Jyotishpith Adhishwara
Jagadguru Shankaracharya Brahmibhut
Swami Brahmananda Saraswati

After the *samadhistha* (state of absorption in *samadhi*) of Ananta Shri Vibhushit Jyotishpithadhishwar Jagadguru Shankaracharya Brahmibhut, Swami Brahmananda Ji Saraswati, disciples have been reading many things in the papers in connection with occurrences taking place, so it is very natural for them to become anxious. For the circle of anxious disciples to understand the reality and to prevent suspicion, it is necessary for this article to be published.

Brahmibhut Shankaracharya Swami Brahmananda Ji Saraswati's own physical *leela*, devoted to spiritual accomplishment, performed *pranayama* at midday on 20th May 1953 in Calcutta, and afterwards Their worldly body was brought to Kashi (Varanasi) by rail. News that Maharaj Shri had become *brahmibhut* (merged with *brahma*) was relayed to principal disciples in various towns by telephone and telegram. Consequently, numerous disciples - female and male – quickly arrived at Kashi by rail, motorcar and airway. The body of Acharya Charan arrived at Mugalsaray Station, was placed in a motorcar, and taken to Brahmanivas Ashram. From daybreak, really, the community was on hand, seeking *darshan*. At the sight of the material body of Maharaj Shri a large wave of mourning pervaded. Discordantly, many women, men and children cried. In the room of Acharya Shri's regular residence, Their body was duly washed etc, decorated with sandalwood and fresh raiment, and afterwards seated on a beautiful *vimaan* (bier). The entire community did a last *pranaam* to Bhagwan with flower garlands etc. Despite it having become merged with *Brahman* for more than 30 hours, the face of Bhagwan was still seen to be of a brilliant appearance. The police band and another band of instruments played, and a gathering sung *kirtan*, behind which was the decorated *vimaan* of Acharya Maharaj on a motor truck. After their departure from Brahmanivas the crowd really grew. At Dashashwamedha Ghat it was as if everyone of Kashi, young and old, surged for a last *darshan* of Jagadguru. On the road to the Ghat there were all mankind. Many *bajara* (large roofed or covered boats) and *dongee* (small boats) afloat in Gangaji filled to the brim with *darshan* seekers continuously coming to the waterway. Having arrived at Dashashwamedha bathing *ghat* the ablution of Bhagwan was caused to done, and the *vimaan* was placed upon a huge *bajara*. On four sides were seated a circle of ascetics and a group of disciples doing *kirtan* (musical recitation). Whilst the *bajara* proceeded in the direction of Shri Kedar Ghat, many *bajara* and *dongee* began to encircle. On the shore of Ganga people collected at one place, and also swelled to the shores of Ganga Ji. Opposite Kedar Ghat, the earthly body of Jagadguru was seated in a stone casket, together with *danda* (wooden staff) and *kamandalu* (water pot), and placed in the current at the middle waters, *samadhistha* (absorbed in *samadhi*) in the very deep ocean of Ganga. Having observed this, thousands of followers had the experience of being forlorn and helpless. In this way it was for as long as 160 years, [until] the revival of Jyotishpeeth and the *astikata* (belief in the existence of God) in Northern Bharat (India), the awakening to righteousness. The one incomparable mass of light [now] was seen to have become hidden in the stream of Jahnavi (Ganga), together with the happiness of those religious folk supporting *varnashram*, and righteousness.

Under the supervision of Swami Shri Karpatri Ji, an Interim Committee for the Arrangement of Jyotishpith was elected. Swami Swaroopanand Saraswati, the President of the Committee and Pandit Balakrishna Mishra MA. LLB. Principal *mantri* (chairman), and another 10 members were elected, of which were prominent disciples, *ashram* inmates, *brahmachari* and *sanyasi*. According to the settled custom, until 6th June were *bhandara* (feast given to *sadhus*), giving *dakshina* (donation) and food for Brahmans, the celebration of the festival of Basant (Spring *puja*), and the Pandit Sabha (Assembly of Pandits) etc.

Actually, this then was known, that in Delhi, because a spectacular amount of effort, that Maharaja adjourned further *upadesha* (instructional) meetings in New Delhi. His tent was erected at the dwelling of number 7 Canning Road. He conversed with the Honorable President Dr Rajendra Prasad for about 80 minutes, and within a week he placed his *antim vasiyat* (Last Will and Testament) in a sealed envelope and it was placed securely with the Master Registrar of Prayag (Allahabad). Pandit Dwarika Prasad Ji, of endless service and disciple of Maharaj, was sent to Prayag to make the deposit, and Maharaja caused his First Will to be removed by him. This [new] Will was written in December 1952 and was deposited at that time. The Interim Committee obtained a copy of the Will from the Registrar's Office, in which was written a perfect elaboration and explanation of the management of the Peeth (the seat of Shankaracharya), and in the Will was also the *kram* (series) of *uttaradhikar* (those who the inheritance would revert to).

The two principal ideas of the *vasiyat* (Will) are like this:- First of all, it is a description of founding and restoration of Jyotishpeeth, by the whole great righteous society of Bharat (India). After that it is about finding someone to install on the Peeth (seat) of Acharya, by way of the great sphere of righteousness of Bharat, and a description of entrusting of the land of Jyotish Peeth. After this, Jagadguru describes in detail about maintaining Jyotish Peeth, the school, the kitchen, the Shri Purnagiri Devi Ji temple and the installation of a statue, and the creation of a *gopur* (gate) and garden. The purchase of the *kothi* (mansion) from the Rajah of Dalipur, Brahma Nivas, located at Prayag (Allahabad) and a detailed description of the *ashram* at Jabalpur with the temples on the shore and *ghats* etc. of Narmada. Afterwards is a description of the organisation of those buildings in Kashi (Varanasi) constructed in holy memory of his own *gurudeva* - the description of the organisation of the *ashrams*, the school and the temple of Brahmaneshwar Mahadev Mandir.

Movable and immovable properties were both described. Due arrangement of the names of the successors are given:-
- (1) Swami Shantanand Saraswati
- (2) Pandit Dwarika Prasad Tripati
   (if he comes to accept *danda*)
- (3) Swami Vishnudevanand Saraswati
- (4) Swami Paramanand Saraswati MA.

Consecutively, one after the other to be Jyotishpeethadhish Shankaracharya. To the last, fourth *acharya,* is given the right to choose the future successor. Afterwards, all acharyas will have the right to choose their successors. In this connection is detail given that in the election of Jyotish Peeth *parampara* (succession), that he must be a *dandi sanyasi*, born a Panch Gauda Brahman in Bharat (India). This instruction was also given, that whilst a suitable *dandi sanyasi* of the Saraswati *sampradaya* is known of then they should be acquired, otherwise for successors of Jyotish Peeth, *sanyasis* of another *ashram* (hermitage) of a *tirth* (sacred place) etc. should not be made Shankaracharya [i.e. *sanyasis* of other *ashrams* should be chosen only in the absence of suitable candidates from the Saraswati line].

In the circumstance that the possibility of the series of Shankaracharya succession becomes severed, first of all one that is born in Bharat, in the disciple *parampara* of Saraswati, accepts *varnashrama*, virtuously follows *dharma*. And if a suitable disciple cannot be obtained of the Saraswati *sampradaya* (tradition), then this day pick an *acharya* of another *ashram,* of another *tirth*. In time, make all moveable and immovable property the *acharya's* own, [but] to them is not given the right to take a loan or to take to their hand any other property by any means.

Actually, to the Shankaracharyas of Jyotish Peeth are also consigned the management of several *ashrams* situated in Kashi (Varanasi).

In connection with the *vasiyat* (Will), there have been erroneous false words printed in the newspapers. The correct news is this, that in the *vasiyat* are many pages of type, and and Maharaj Shri signed on each and every page, and at the end is the signature of eye-witnesses. The *vasiyat* had been inserted in a heavy envelope and enveloped in cloth, was stitched and all were enclosed in another envelope, and on that were attached seals. The hypotheses that the signatures of Maharaj Shri were obtained without his knowledge, or in a condition when he did not have the strength to notice, are completely baseless. The process of producing the *vasiyat* is dependent on the rule of the Registrar, according to which it had been produced.

According to the determination of the aforesaid Interim Committee, on 12th June 1953, in Brahmanivas Ashram, completed as prescribed by the Scriptures, was the *abhishek* (installation) of Shri Swami Shantanand Saraswati Ji. Wise *dandi sanyasis*, town leaders, and a collection of disciples were in attendance. And according to the *vasiyat*, he is the Jagatguru Shankaracharya of Jyotish Peeth. Also, by Them is the management of the Peeth functioning.

Some people making erroneous publicity in connection with the *vasiyat*, they are writing untrue words in the newspapers, whose proper response is right here in the *vasiyat* in *anka* (issue number) 50, *varsh* (year) 3, of '*Shri Shankaracharya Upadesha*' (the *ashram*'s news sheet). After the great shock of reading this, if he has any doubts those good selves can look to redress from the *mantri* (chairman) of the Prayag circle of disciples. Here, for the circle of disciples, in the *vasiyat* is given all instructions, from which all disciples fulfil the desires of Brahmibhut Jagadguru, and they understand what is proper for them to do. In his own *vasiyat*, Maharaj did write:-

"Before today I wrote a closed *vasiyat* on 23-10-43 (23rd October 1943) and placed it securely with the Registrar gentleman in Prayag. Now, by way of this present *vasiyat* I refute and cancel the above-mentioned *vasiyat*. This new *vasiyat*, if I shall not get cancelled or exchanged in my own life, this then will signify my last *vasiyat*, and accordingly, afterwards according to this *vasiyat* will the management be done of Shri Jyotish Peeth and Shri Swami Krishnanand Saraswati *ashram* and the connected *pathshala* (school), Brahma Vidya Niketan and the *mandir* (temple) of Brahmanadeshwar Mahadeva.

Therefore, together with earnest good consideration, without being influenced by opportune wilfulness or anything else, by way of writing my own *vasiyat* in this form, the *parampara* (succession) of Shri Jyotish Peeth *acharya* with stay uninterrupted, *sanatana dharma* (eternal *dharma* – i.e. Hinduism) and supporter of *varna,* the standing rule of Jyotish Peeth and clear aim of detailed instructions of the institution pertaining to Jyotish Peeth, the appointment of their own successor as Shankaracharya, and their duties, I am writing a detailed description of the suitable authority, also that settled to my own holy remembered *gurudeva*, the Shri 108 Swami Krishnanand Saraswati Trust, and the settlement and burden of arrangements of all the connected property, and by this *vasiyat* is consigned my own successor the *parampara* of Jyotish Peeth Adhishwar, by means of this above-mentioned *vasiyat*, management and adjustment, the first *vasiyats* having been terminated, this *vasiyat* is proved by my own signature, this is my very last *vasiyat* and it is really the chief obligation that I will protect my disciples.

> Paush Shukla 2 Guruvar *san*. 2006,
> accordingly, 18th December 52
> (signed) Brahmanand".

Studying the aforementioned sentences written in the *vasiyat* of Brahmibhut Acharya Charan, how could there still be doubting, in his own decisiveness, in the heart of any devotee? The *mantra moola* (principal advice) is really, the words of the *guru* demonstrate the path of us disciples and will remain. In Shri Ramacharit Manas (the story of Rama), Goswami Tulsidas Ji wrote:-

गुरु कें बचन प्रतीति न जेही ।
सपनेहुँ सुगम न सुख सिधि तेही ॥

'guru ke bachana prateeti na jehi.
sapnehun sugama na sukha sidhi tehi..'

"He who has no faith in the words of his *guru*,
he cannot hope to win either happiness or success,
even in a dream."
[v79, *Baal Kand, Sri Ramacharitamanasa*]

Therefore, by us all, *guru* devotee disciple brothers, to annihilate mountainous obstruction, Brahmibhut Acharya Charan did, after earnest thought, made a decree, the very same we all should respect, together with faith and trust. Those people who today, for any reason or wish, are attaching any shortcomings to the conduct, reasoning in the mind of Acharya Shri, and them by means of useless gossip in relationship to the *vasiyat*, we should remain careful of them, whoever else they are, why not? When the time comes their own remorse will be. Understand that envy, malice, self-interest, political gambles, deceit and craftiness, move in the form of Narayana (God), *sanyasi*, in the field of *mahatmas* (great souls) are those showing increasingly to be trapped in worldly illusion. To us householder people having seen that, they are viewed with boundless amazement. Bhagwan give to us the gift of keen intelligence, protect the *dharma*, Bhagwan give to us the gift of keen intelligence, protect the *dharma*, erase *adharma*. Produce goodwill amongst living beings and universal happiness. This is really the request at the lotus feet of Shri Gurudeva.

mantri, Shri Shankaracharya Sevak Mandal, Prayag[98]

**Brahmachari Mahesh and Swami
near Gyaan Mandir, Gyansu, Uttarkashi**

Brahmachari Mahesh Ji

After service as the *guru's* clerk and secretary, Mahesh had then acquired the status of *brahmachari*.

> 'Brahmacharya or spotless chastity is the best of all penances; a celibate of such spotless chastity is not a human being, but a god indeed. To the celibate who conserves the semen with great efforts, what is there unattainable in this world? By the power of the composure of the semen, one will become just like myself.' - Lord Sankara'[99]

Though still involved in the administration of the *ashram*, Brahmachari Mahesh received spiritual instruction from Swami Brahmananda, however, this period was lamentably short - about two or three years - cut short due to the *guru's* sudden death.

On account of his Kayastha *varna* (caste), Brahmachari Mahesh could never have hoped to succeed his master nor could he ever become a *guru* himself.

Swami Shantanand was now the Shankaracharya of Jyotirmath, but his position was looking increasingly precarious.

Brahmachari Mahesh, the *ashram* secretary for over a decade, left the *ashram* in Varanasi and headed off for the foothills of the Himalayas to a valley called Uttar Kashi, in the far north of India. Brahmachari Mahesh's destination in Uttarkashi was an *ashram* called 'Gyan Mandir', which means 'the Temple of Knowledge Ashram'; that likely once belonged to Swami Krishnanand Saraswati, Swami Brahmananda's *guru*, whom he had met at Uttar Kashi when he was but a child.

Far from the commotion caused by the succession dispute, this little *ashram* in a tranquil valley offered a place for peaceful *'sadhana'* or 'spiritual practice':

> 'Where I stay in a small Ashram in Uttar Kashi, the cave is like a small basement under a room. The entrance is through an opening only big enough for one person to enter.'

> 'Food is not always needed, but when I am eating, a man comes from the village and cooks vegetables. I do not break silence by seeing or talking to anyone.'[100]

* * *

But things were far less tranquil for Shankaracharya Swami Shantanand, because in January 1954, at the Munsiff Court in Lucknow, followers of Swami Krishnabodhaashram applied for an injunction against Swami Shantanand, restraining him from interfering with any of the Jyotir Math properties. It is also recorded that another suit was filed with the Court of District Judge, this one in Varanasi, brought by Swami Paramanand Saraswati and three others, versus someone referred to as Ram Ji Tripathi - Swami Shantanand Saraswati's name before he became a *sannyasi*.

* * *

But instead of returning north to Varanasi to help his *gurubhai*, his fellow devotee, Brahmachari Mahesh, after several months spent in self-imposed seclusion, traveled south.

> 'After about one year of ascetic seclusion at Uttarkashi, in a place called "valley of the saints," Maharishi Mahesh Yogi accompanied his ailing aunt from Calcutta to a medical facility at Madanapalle in the southern state of Andhra Pradesh. By his own admission, he was responding not only to the request of his relative but more directly to an irrepressible impulse to "go south" and visit the temples of pilgrimage at Kanchi, Rameshwaram, and Kanya Kumari.'[101]

> 'Among the ardent devotees of Poojya Gurudev Brahmananda Saraswati, there was one elderly lady in Kolkatta, West Bengal,

belonging to a well known family of zamindars. Mahesh affectionately called her "Mathaji" ['Mother']. She too was most impressed by Mahesh's devotion to the great Guru, and she was fondly calling him "Beta" ['Son']. This lady was deeply hurt and felt desolate after Gurudev passed away, and became very sad and depressed. Her health failed. For necessary treatment she was advised to go to Madanapalli, in Andhra Pradesh (South India). She called "Beta" Mahesh to accompany her. Taking it as an opportunity to serve Mother as well as Gurudev, Mahesh accompanied her to Madanapalli.'

'Mathaji was admitted into the sanatorium and Mahesh had to find a place to stay in the small town of Madanapalli.

One Krishna Iyer and his brother Narayana Iyer were running a small coffee hotel in Madanapalli Town. But there was no provision for travellers to stay overnight in that hotel. After having his meal in that hotel, Mahesh asked the Iyers for a place to stay. Since there was no provision for lodging, they suggested that he may sleep on the steps, in the nearby temple. In the rain and cold of that place it was not possible to stay outdoors. So the problem was serious. Mahesh saw a very small room next to the kitchen of the hotel and asked for permission to stay there. But it was stacked with firewood and was quite uninhabitable. Somehow Mahesh prevailed upon the owners, neatly stacked the fuel in one corner and made enough space to stretch himself. He was quite pleased with the arrangement, and the others sympathized with him too. During the day he would be spending time at the hospital to look after Mathaji and later, in the evening, he would come back to his corner at the Town Hotel.

In Madanapalli, there is a branch of The State Bank Of Mysore, and one Mr. T. Rama Rao was its manager then. He was a well educated person with deep interest in philosophy and was living a virtuous life. It was his routine, at the end of the day's work in the Bank, to have coffee in the local hotel of Rama Iyer and spend the evening on the steps of the temple near by, with a few of his office colleagues, talking about various matters of general interest and also covering religious and philosophical topics. During that time, one evening, they saw Mahesh sitting all alone, with a gentle smile of deep contentment. His bright eyes, the charming smile on his lips and total composure attracted Rama Rao and his friends. They enquired about Mahesh's identity. They were most impressed by his smiling response, pleasing voice, gentle laughter as well as easy handling of subjects of religious and philosophical import. Clad in unstitched pure white silk, having long black curly hair and beard, innocent, ever twinkling eyes, soft but very clear voice, easy rendering of religious and philosophical subjects, at once impressed the group. Day after day, they engaged themselves in covering topics of righteous living based on religion and Indian philosophy. They were eagerly looking forward to the meeting every evening. The hotel owner brothers too joined the group.'[102]

It has also been suggested that Brahmachari Mahesh drew attention to himself by putting up a sign saying 'WHO WANTS INSTANT ENLIGHTENMENT?', allegedly, the means by which this was achieved was by a blow on the forehead!

'Sometime in June or July of 1954, he acquired his first students at Madanapalle and initiated them into "transcendental meditation". According to T. Rama Rao, perhaps the very first initiate, the technique of meditation and its instruction was exactly the same as it is taught today by TM teachers throughout the world. Mr. Rama Rao was at that time the manager of the local branch of the Bank of Mysore, a position requiring a command of English (enabling him to translate for Maharishi, who could not speak the vernaculars - Tamil and Telugu) and affording contacts with businessmen throughout South India. Sree Narayana Iyer was another businessman who contributed to the construction of the first "permanent meditation hall" at Madanapalle. That both men were English speaking businessmen and Tamil brahmins suggests the social base of the movement at this earliest stage in Andhra Pradesh and, through their contacts in other South Indian states, the social base in centers where Maharishi travelled subsequently.'[101]

'Meanwhile, at the sanatorium, Mataji's health began to fail. In spite of the best treatment she received there, within a few days she breathed her last. Mahesh felt totally lost and bereaved as if he lost his own mother. He now felt like an orphan. After fulfilling necessary obligations to the Mother, Mahesh felt desolate not knowing where to go and what to do next. Suddenly the old message - "Go South" flashed across his mind. He enquired of Sri Rama Rao where and what was there in the "South" and how far. He learnt that 200-300 miles down south of India from Madanapalli on the east coast, there was the town by name Rameshwaram, where there was a very large and ancient temple dedicated to Lord Shiva established by Lord Sri Rama himself. It has become famous over these centuries. Mahesh was thrilled to hear this and remarked - " Surely that is my destination. I must go there! I now see how and why I have been brought here by Mataji. Thank God."

Thereafter Sri Rama Rao made arrangements for Mahesh's travel to Rameshwaram.'[102]

After touring around the temples and holy shrines of Rameshvaram, Brahmachari Mahesh moved down to the southernmost peninsula of Cape Comorin to spend time at Kannyakumari and then to the Guruvayur Krishna Mandir in Trivandrum.
'I went to Kanyakumari - I had a divine revelation. I left and went to Trivandrum, to the biggest temple. I was followed by a man and he asked me to speak about the Himalayas - he arranged a 7 day lecture program and he supplied the topics.'[103]

This request resulted in Brahmachari Mahesh giving a week of talks, followed by others too. Clearly he began teaching spiritual practices, as is evident from a note he hand wrote, giving his contact address as being in Uttar Kashi, Himalayas.

Prostrations to The Holy Feet of Shri Guru Deva Swami Brahmanand Saraswati Maharaj the Jagat Guru late Shankaracharya of Jyotirmath, Badarikashram Himalayas

~~~~~~

Stick to my instructions and you will progress

Bal Brahmachari Mahesh
Uttar-Kashi
U.P. (Himalayas)

8.00 A.M.   14th April 1955.

Perhaps he took a shine to public speaking, for he continued touring around Kerala; from Trivandrum he visited Quilon, and in June 1955 moved on to Ernakulam, Allepey and Kottayam. The *brahmachari* also felt inspired to show people how to meditate, but though he lacked the status of being a *swami*, or the credentials of being a *guru*, he decided to teach meditation in the name of his illustrious master, Swami Brahmananda Saraswati, the former Shankaracharya of Jyotirmath:-

'And now I remember when I begin to look into the past, what I, what happened, the first such thing happened somewhere in Kerala, where I went from Uttar Kashi to Kerala, *dakshina* [Hindi for 'south'].. South India, and people wanted to learn this practice of meditation.

I thought: "What to do, what to do, what to do?" then I thought, "I should teach them all in the name of Guru Dev. I should design a system, a system of *puja* to Guru Dev."

And in that *puja* the reality came out, the reality of Guru Dev, the totality of Guru Dev and what it was:
"Gurur Brahma", the Creator, *"Gurur Vishnur"*, the Maintainer, *"Gurur Brahma"*, the Creator, *"Gurur Vishnur"*, the Maintainer, the Administrator, *"Guruh Sakshat Param Brahma"*, totality of knowledge, totality of enlightenment. *"Gurur Brahma, Gurur Vishnur, Gurur Devo Maheshvarah"*, silence, *"Shiva, Gurur Brahma, Gurur Vishnur, Gurur Devo Maheshvarah, Shiva"*, silence, eternal Purusha. *"Guruh Sakshat, Param Brahma"*, transcendental *"Brahma"*

Totality of all, infinite diversity, that is the *guru* – *"na guror adhikam"*[104], *"na guror adhikam"* – "there is no one greater than *guru*", *guru* is everything, Creator, Maintainer, Sustainer, everything is the *guru*, the *guru*, the *guru*.

I formulated the *puja* to Guru Dev; I started through that instrumentality to transfer Guru Dev's reality to the one who wanted to teach meditation [the *brahmachari* himself]. So what flowed was, totality of Guru Dev, flowed through the *puja*.'[105]

Apparently, as an act of devotion, Brahmachari Mahesh would colourise monochrome photographs of his master, Swami Brahmananda, and it seems that one such hand coloured photograph was passed to a graphic artist, M.T.V. Acharya (1920-c1992), for a portrait painting of the *guru* to be created by him, to be revered by those who the *brahmachari* lectured and taught meditation. As an artist, M.T.V. was then best known for his illustrations in *'Chandamama'*, the popular children's monthly magazine.

The finished painting, signed by M.T.V. Acharya, is quite similar in fact to the work-in-progress photomontage, but it differs greatly from the original photograph in many ways, such as:-

1. The addition of the *swastika*, (ancient sun sign, fylfot cross, and symbol of auspiciousness),

2. Moving the carved image of the open lotus flower.

3. The addition of the Sanskrit symbols; ॐ *'OM'* and श्री *'SHREE'*, superimposed one upon the other.

4. The addition of the *danda* staff, perhaps to reinforce in people's minds that Maharishi's master was a proper *bona fide* holy man. Or perhaps this is because of the custom that the *swami* and the *danda* stick should not become separated.

the late Shankaracharya of Jyotirmath
Swami Brahmananda Saraswati

1955 artwork utilising photo of Swami Brahmananda Saraswati

**Portrait of Swami Brahmananda Saraswati
created by M.T.V. Acharya, from photograph**

During his time in the south he spent several months in Kerala moving from town to town advocating a method of meditation. The technique he taught necessitated repetition of a *mantra*, a practice he claimed was easy and very effective at bestowing happiness. Responding to an advertisement in a local paper, Mr and Mrs Menon attended a three and a half-hour talk at Ernakulam and afterwards met with the speaker.

Mr A.N. Menon said to him:-

'"It is very easy for your Holiness to talk about mind control. But for us to put it in practice is very difficult – when we sit for meditation our minds fly nine thousand miles away – that is our experience". Our Revered Maharshi laughingly replied, "That is my responsibility and not yours – I will see that you get it within a few days. It is easier for you to practise and experience it than for me to lecture and convince you".'[106]

Mrs Thankamma N Menon explains how she learned meditation:-
'Maharshi asked us about our Ishta-Devata and advised us to go to him the next morning for Pada Pooja of Guru Deva, Maha Yogi Raj Ananta Sri Vibhushith Sree Sankaracharya Brahmananda Saraswathi Maharaj of Jyothir Math who was going to be our Guru. The next day morning we met Maharishi and both my husband and myself were initiated. Instructions were given to us to meditate for an hour both in the morning as well as in the evening. We strictly followed Maharshi's directions in Sadhana thereafter. Maharishi's discourses at the T.D.M. Hall continued for fourteen day; we attended the lectures regularly and we were highly enlightened and all our doubts were removed.'

'This great spiritual secret hitherto kept concealed in the valleys of the Himalayas are now being revealed through the universal benevolence and generosity of our Revered Maharishi – the beacon Light of the Himalayas, and who in Kerala, functioning, we find as a torch bearer of divine effulgence.'
'Jai Sree Guru Deva'[107]

Apparently, both Mr and Mrs Menon were happy with their lesson in 'mind control':-

'I went to Maharshi in the morning with my wife, received initiation and to our greatest surprise in life, we were able to have full cent-percent concentration in the second sitting of our practice and we found it was followed by feeling of great joy, indescribable great Anandam during our further Sadhana. When we reported this experience of joy to Maharshi he explained it to be Samadhi Sukha'[108]

It is clear that the erstwhile *brahmachari* was by now being referred to as 'Maharshi'. Later, he explained:-
'In South India this word is more prevalent for good saints, and when I travelled South India the newspapers wrote, and then it came from one newspaper to the other, like that, just, a spontaneous thing, and this is not a title conferred as a degree in a college or somewhere. It's the, I think, just like a "sage", or a "seer", or a "saint", they're not the degrees, it's the symptom of a man, a symptom, a feature, and then people start calling him, but there is no confirmation of the title or anything. That is it.'

"Rishi" and "Maharishi" – "*rishi*" is a Sanskrit word and that means "the seer of the *mantras*", "the seer of truth" - the *mantras* and are the Vedic hymns. So "*rishi*" is equivalent to "a seer", a seer sees the truth, "*maha rishi*" means "great seer", "*maha*" is "great".'

'Generally, people don't remember the name. A North Indian name [viz. Brahmachari Mahesh] is not so easily remembered by the South Indians, like that, like that.'

'I didn't object to it. (audience laughter) Otherwise I have to explain why they should **not** call me "Maharishi", but just call me something else.'[109]

'Maharshi' is certainly a name with which most people are familiar with in South India, for it is the name of a very popular local saint, Sri Ramana Maharshi (1879-1950).

Many were interested in learning this easy method of meditation, taught by Brahmachari Mahesh, amongst them Sri C R Vaidyanathan.

> 'Somebody said that Swamiji was giving initiations and if one followed his directions he would get Bliss quickly. I was really sceptic about this "Ananda" business.' I asked, not alone whether any useful purpose would be served by the initiation and mantras given by him. I felt the fittest person to whom these questions ought to be addressed was none other than Swamiji himself and so on that Wednesday evening I along with Sri Bua interviewed Swamiji. Swamiji's reply was that we ought to take initiation even though we have been chanting Gayatri and other Mantras. He wanted none to change his Ishtadevata or Ishtadevatha mantra, but to learn the effective method of meditation, at the feet of Gurudeva. Such as were interested were advised to go there the next day at 10 A.M. to take the initiation and Sri Bua and myself parted with a decision to do so. I casually enquired of somebody there whether any fee was charged for this initiation when I was told that I need not spend any money and it would suffice if I took a few flowers from the same garden!
>
> The very next morning when I met Sri Buva he told me that he had already taken initiation, the previous night itself. I thought him a more fortunate person. I presented myself with the necessary puja materials on Thursday. Swamiji made me offer puja to Guru Deva and under closed doors gave me Mantra of the Ishta Devata I chose and asked me to repeat the same and also gave the necessary instructions in the new method for meditation.
>
> A word in this connection about the choosing of my Ishtadevata. Being Smarthas we have been taught to consider all the Panchayatana Devats equally, nonce superior or inferior. Really

I could not conceive of any difference between Siva, Vishnu, or the Mothers. But a few suggestions from Swamiji made me decide about my Ishtadevata. After that Swamiji gave me some instructions about meditation and asked me to practice daily both in the morning and in the evening for at least an hour. I did accordingly but with no success, except that when I was repeating the mantra m during my first sitting after the upadesa, a clear vision of Murali Manohar presented itself and passed out after sometime. After a time came a similar vision of Guru Deva. After that, there was a vision of the Samadhi of Sankaracharya's mother at Kaladi and inside that Sankara Bhagavadpada doing meditation sitting cross-legged. These were not the result of my thoughts wandering to these subjects at all but I considered them of no consequence and I reported this to Swamiji and he said that they were very good omens for the beginning. "Your Ishtadevatha and Guru Deva both have come and blessed you. Now you will find quick progress, in your Sadhana but be regular in your practice. The next day also I sat for one hour scrupulously, doing strictly what I had been asked to do. I got, not any Ananda but only some ache in my legs. Fortunately my Yogasana practices minimised the ache, and it passed away soon. I went to Vignanaramaneeyam. Swamiji was asking everybody whether they experienced Anandam during their Sadhana and were saying they had. Some said they were feeling very very happy. Some others said that there was such an on-rush of Ananda and they were at a loss to know how to check it. Others felt Ananda throughout the day. To some, Ananda was coming in jerks. To others it came at intervals. I was really ashamed to note that I alone amongst them should have been deprived of this Ananda in spite of my pretensions to Adhyatmic learning and good conduct, when all others were getting it so easily. I even took consolation in the thought that these persons who were really suffering from the on-rush of Ananda were nerve-strung people, but I dared not express it out. I did not want to utter a falsehood, and that too before Swamiji. At this moment Swamiju turned to me and asked the now familiar question. I made bold to say that I had nothing of that thing. Swamiji encouraged me and advised me to continue my practice and added that I was certain to get it ere long. On that day in the course of his talk, Swamiji narrated the experience of an initiate whose onrush of Ananda with such force that he did not know what to do at that time and how to manage it. This sadak could not refrain from suddenly crying out in great joy. Of course this reminded me of Vivekananda crying out in the ecstasy which he got through the blessings of Sree Rama Krishna Paramahansa. This created an upheaval in my mind coupled with the feeling of hope because swamiji had spoken to me in a very encouraging manner that I was going to get if very soon; with this background of Maharshi's blessings I went home.

Sri. V.D. Nair had asked us all, the initiates to assemble to hear swamiji's special instructions and address to them. I decided, "took a vow," will be too strong a term – not to go but sit through the whole night if necessary in meditation to see whether bliss would come to me after all. I determined "to dig deep to strike water" and steeling my mind sat on that Saturday evening in meditation. The mantra was playing hide and seek and finally in about two hours time completely faded out like a gramophone song when the winding exhausted. After this there was a vast, full stillness like the sight of a vast tank full of silent water. I would have sat on for hours together, but the mantra returned in about forty-five minutes again. I rose up and left to hear Swamiji's lecture feeling really joyful, not that I had my experience of Bliss but I was able to consciously still my mind for sometime at least. I was just in time for the lecture where Swamiji was explaining the four stages of perception of sound viz, Vaikhari, Madhyama, Pasyanti and para and how the concentration of the mind on the mantra, brings about Samadhi. I was a splendid classroom lecture with diagrams and all. Later on I investigated these matters in the shastraic Books and I have been able to find passages for every word that Swamiji had spoken and unimpeachable authority for every direction from meditation given by swamiji.

I told Swamiji at the end of the lecture of my experience of that day's meditation and as usual he asked me whether I experienced any positive ecstasy or Ananda in that state of stillness of mind. I told him that I did not experience any positive bliss. He said "your experience of the state of vacancy for about 35 minutes is very good progress for two days of Sadhana. You will experience Anandam shortly, within 2, 3 sittings." This came out to be literally true. It is not an exaggeration when I say that I am able to experience positive bliss in the shortest time. There is **spiritual as well as material prosperity** all around, which can attribute only to swamiji's blessings.'[110]

Professor P S Atchuthan Pillai observed:-

'His talk, behaviour and everything about him are as though he is in constant contact with his Gurudev. That is a feature which has surprised many of us closely moving with him. Maharshi Bala Brahmachari always acts as the messiah between his "Gurudev" and his own disciples. He modestly claims to be only the conduit pipe conveying the Gurudeva's blessing on to his devotees in Kerala, or to use his own expression, he is only the "bulb through which the spiritual electrical current from Gurudev shines in radiating light on all".'[111]

After several months in south India, the 'Maharshi' seemed set to stay longer, so, clearly, he had no immediate plans to return to his cave at Uttar Kashi. A. N. Menon recalls:-

'In every place where Maharshi happened to stay for ten or fifteen days, people were inspired to take initiation. The feeling of peace and joy that the initiated began to enjoy made them naturally meet one another with feelings of joy and thus everybody felt the need of a common meeting place and in every place 'gurubhais' began to meet once a week according to their convenience. This is how very naturally as if by a divine call, Adhyatnic Vikas Mandals sprang up in each place. When Maharshi was requested to give a name and organise all the Mandals in a manner so that 'gurubhais' of different places may contact each other and be profited by mutual give and take of the spiritual experiences. I have known it from the gurubais of Quilon, that Maharshi very much discouraged them for the formation of a regular institution like that. He said, "I am not at all for forming an institution or society nor, would I advise you to spend your energy in this line. It is enough that you meet amongst yourselves, and be benefitted by mutual give and take of the experiences of your sadhana, and if at all you want to make an institution of 'gurubhais' you may make it after I leave Kerala, so that I may not be taken to be the promoter of any institution. My approach to the people is individual and not institutional, and let it be like that.'[112]

It was announced that Maharshi would be leaving Kerala, and Mr Menon responded by suggesting a farewell meeting:-

'Having read Maharshi's programme of leaving Kerala, devotees began to write enquiring where they could meet him before he leaves for the Himalayas. Thus I found the best time for my scheme. I put up to Maharshi, that the devotees wanted to meet His Holiness once before he leaves Kerala, then why not a time of three days be fixed for all to come and meet and the same opportunity be utilised for a big congregation, which will inspire not only Kerala, but the whole country. Maharshi gave a minute's thought over it, and consented.'[113]

In fact arrangements and preparations were put in place for a series of *yagyas* (religious rituals) to be performed in the major city of Cochin in late October 1955. The occasion was organised by barrister A.N. Menon who had first heard the *brahmachari* some three months before, in Ernakulam. The conference was to be an opportunity to celebrate the life and teachings of Swami Brahmananda Saraswati, with invitations sent far and wide to his devotees, including the Vice-President of India, Dr. S. Radhakrishnan, and others in high office.

ADYATMIC VIKAS MANDAL AT ERNAKULAM.

It seems that supporters in the various towns that 'Maharshi' had visited, organised themselves into groups called the Shri Shankaracharya Saraswati Adhyatmic Vikas Mandal - 'Adhyatmic Vikas Mandal' means 'Spiritual Development Circle'.

On 30th September 1955 the Madanapalle group wrote in support of the proposed celebrations:-

'WE the members of Shri Shankaracharya Saraswathi Adhyatmic Vikas Mandal, Madanapalle are happy to express our fraternity and heartily associate ourselves with your efforts to bring about a spiritual regeneration of our Society. There is now a general awakening in humanity towards spirituality. All through the times several Rishis and Saints who had direct and positive experience in the field have been giving their call to the rest of mankind. But so far the majority had not responded, due to their egocentred life and in illusion of an empty materialism. Having realised the utter futility of gross materialism, they now appear to be ready to respond to the call of the Rishis and Saints. It looks as though mankind is taking a turn. Life of Sadhana which was possible only for a few is now becoming possible for all.

It is at this juncture great Rishis like our revered Guru Maharshi Bal Brahmachari Maheshji are springing up to hold the beacon light and lead us all in the path of "Atma Gnana". We have to enlighten and elevate ourselves under the loving care of our revered Guru Maharshi Shree Bal Brahmachari Maheshji and simultaneously strive to kindle the spirit in our brothers around us. We had the unique privilege of sitting at the feet of Maharshi Maheshji and having him amidst us for months. We all drank profusely the nectar of his sweet talks and experienced an inexpressible joy in his company. Our spirits were kindled and nursed by the intimate care of this messenger of the "Call Divine". The tender care and love of our Guru Dev, Ananta Shree Vibhushit Shree Shankaracharya Brahmananda Saraswathi Maharaj are always with us and his spirit will always guide us in our noble mission.

On this memorable occasion where you have all congregated under the banner of our most Revered Gurudev to bring about a collective spiritual regeneration, we cannot but express our extreme joy and wish you Godspeed in your work. We prey God to bless this noble task of yours with crowning success.

With fraternal regards,
At the feet of GURUDEV,
The Members of the
Shree Shankaracharya Brahmananda Saraswathi,
Adhyatmic Vikas Mandal, Madanapalle. (Andhra)[114]

Maharishi Mahesh Yogi

The *'Beacon Light of the Himalayas'* is a 168-page booklet published following a four-day event held from 23rd to 26th October 1955 at the auditorium of T.D. High School, Cochin, in south India. A souvenir booklet, published later, contains a wide array of materials, including a biography of Swami Brahmananda Saraswati, over a dozen messages in support of the event including one in Sanskrit by Swami Shantanand Saraswati and one written on his behalf in English, from his *ashram,* at Brahma

Niwas, Alopibag, Allahabad U.P., which conveyed the following message from the Shankaracharya:-

"Spirituality is the backbone of India. India can restore her ancient glory only through Religion and Spirituality. All religion is simply an attempt to unveil the essential nature of ourselves. This ultimate Truth can be realised through self-purification. I hope your efforts will promote the development of spirituality, nobility, calmness and bliss. Remember the teaching and the ideal of Shrimad Bhagawat Gita:-

यत्करोषि यदश्नासि यज्जुहोषि ददासि यत् ।

यत्तपस्यसि कौन्तेय तत्कुरुष्व मदर्पणम् ॥

This Sanskrit verse is from the *Bhagavad Gita*, Chapter 9 verse 27, and translated says; 'Whatever you do, whatever you eat, whatever you offer or give away, and whatever austerities you perform—do that, O son of Kunti, as an offering to Me.'.

Shankaracharya Swami Shantanand's message continues:-

"I am extremely pleased to know that Bal Brahmachari Mahesh Yogi, the beloved disciple of Guru Deva, Brahmaleen Mahaygiraj Jagadguru Bhagwan Shri Shankaracharya Anant Shri Vibhushit Swami Brahmananda Saraswathi Ji Maharaj of Jyothirmath Badarikashram is helping the cause of spirituality there. May his presence in Kerala inspire you all with **Real Peace and Happiness.**

"I wish your Maha Sammelan every success"

With love and blessings of
His Holiness Jagatguru Bhagwan
Shri Shankaracharya Anant Sri
Vibhushit Swami Shantanand
Saraswathi Ji Maharaj, Jyothirmath
Badarikashram.

A message came from the office of the Vice-President's Secretariat for the Government of India, New Delhi:-

Dear Sir,
  Thank you for your letter of the 7th instant.
  I send my best wishes for the success of the conference.
    Yours faithfully
    S. Radhakrishnan

A note also came from Brahmachari Mahesh's Uncle Raj Varma:-

'It gave us, the Shankaracharya Shishya Mandal, Jabalpur, great pleasure to learn that the devoted disciples of Maharshi are going to have **Maha Yagna** and **Mahasammelanam of the**

Adhyatmic Vikas Mandal with befitting enthusiasm. Their determination to spread the message of spiritual development and unfold the true nature of self and God realisation is really laudable. Although the circumstances did not allow us to be physically present in your midst on this solemn occasion, yet we assure you that we are present with all of you in spirit. May the blessings of Guru Deva, Anantashri Vibhushit Jagadguru Shankaracharya Jyotishpithadhishwar of Badarikashram, Bhagwan Gurudeva Swami Brahmanand Saraswathi Maharaj fill the hearts of all of you there with a spirit of full confidence and enthusiasm to further the cause initiated and enunciated by the Maharshi, for the emancipation of the entire human race.'

Also featured in the publication are selections of Sanskrit verse in praise of the *guru*, and testimonies from meditators, and transcripts of lectures given by a selection of speakers, and photographs. There are also a large number of photographs of the event.

The publication is printed in blue ink throughout – and on the cover the *brahmachari's* message is boldly proclaimed.

FLAG HOISTING

THE DAWN OF A HAPPY NEW ERA
IN THE FIELD OF SPIRITUAL PRACTICES
MIND CONTROL, PEACE
&
ATMANANDA
Through simple & easy methods of Spiritual Sadhana
propounded
by
Maharshi Bala Brahmachari Mahesh Yogi Maharaj
OF
UTTAR KASI, HIMALAYAS.

SOUVENIR OF THE GREAT SPIRITUAL DEVELOPMENT CONFERENCE OF KERALA., OCTOBER, 1955.

BEACON LIGHT OF THE HIMALAYAS

THE DAWN OF A HAPPY NEW ERA
IN THE FIELD OF SPIRITUAL PRACTICES
MIND CONTROL, PEACE
&
ATMANANDA
Through simple & easy methods of Spiritual Sadhana propounded
by
Maharshi Bala Brahmachari Mahesh Yogi Maharaj
OF
UTTAR KASI, HIMALAYAS
SOUVENIR OF THE GREAT SPIRITUAL DEVELOPMENT

CONFERENCE OF KERALA., OCTOBER, 1955

Oh ye of the peaceless and suffering humanity!

My happiness desires to root out your suffering. Will you extend your arm and allow me to lift you up from the mire of misery and peacelessness?

Come on, here is the call of peace and joy for you. Here is an invitation, a cordial invitation for you all to come and enjoy the Blissful Grace and All Powerful Blessings of my Lord the Great Swami Brahmanand Saraswati, the Great among the greats of the Himalayas. I have found a treasure in the Dust of His Lotus Feet and now I invite you to share it with me and make yourself happy.

Come on; I invite you to get into the Blissful Realm of His Universal Benevolence. See, the path is straight and entry is free. Come on with faith and you will find that the very cause of your peacelessness and misery will be eradicated and you will be adorned with lasting peace and real happiness in your day to day life.

Feel not disappointment in life and shrink not from your responsibilities in despair. Whatever are your circumstances, rich or poor, if you are not in peace and if you want peace and happiness, come on with faith and you will have it. Here is the message of hope for you. Here is the Divine call of rescue for you. Peace and joy of living await you. Do not reject it. Come on and have it.

The sun of Guru Deva's Blessings is now up on the horizon. Wake up from the deep slumber of apathy and agony and enjoy all glories of life material and divine.

Bal Brahmachari Mahsh.
29.11.55.

Quite why Brahmachari Mahesh signed himself as '***Mahsh***' in his hand-written message prefacing the *'Beacon Light of the Himalayas'* booklet, is a mystery, but it must surely have done nothing to lessen confusion over the correct spelling of his name?

A Close up of the procession which gives a better view of the MAHARSHI in front of Guru Deva's Chariot.

Maharishi's First Published Discourses

The *'Beacon Light of the Himalayas'* booklet contains transcripts of three lectures given by Maharishi, which together give a clear insight into the shape of his teachings, and the method of the meditation he was teaching. The lectures are reproduced here in full.

On Day 1, Maharishi's discourse was entitled, 'Time is at hand';

JAI GURU DEVA

"It gives me great pleasure this afternoon to be in the company of you all here assembled in the close vicinity of the Maha Yagna Mandapam. From the early morning the atmosphere here is being surcharged with the Divine Vibrations of Rig Veda and Yajur Veda Parayanam and the chanting of the Maha Yagna Mantras. From the morning till noon today when the Shiva - Laksha - Archana was being performed by the learned Vedic Pandits, everybody must have felt the thrilling and Divine presence of the Vedic Gods here. In such a pure, Serene and Godly atmosphere, your Kerala Maha Sammelan has commenced.

It is a matter of good fortune and pride for every one of us that we have assembled here to discuss and decide, as far as it is possible intellectually, about the easy and practical ideologies of mind-control and spiritual development. This auspicious occasion, I find is graciously sanctified by the presence of the great Lord Shiva and his retinue, and the divine radiance of Shri Guru Dev who is famous for his benevolence and generosity in showering His blessings on all.

In this atmosphere of all-embracing Divinity the inauguration of this Maha Sammelan by the speech from a saintly and princely personality has added grandeur to the occasion. His Highness's inaugural address is the most appropriate speech for the occasion. When I came to Kerala I heard that His Highness the Maharajah of Cochin is a very learned and religiously cultured soul. Now after listening to his inaugural address I am convinced that he is fully worthy of the great name and fame he has earned. In his speech he has successfully laid down the essentials of Adhyatmic Vikas of Spiritual Development. He has very clearly explained the distinction between the theoretical and the practical aspects of Adhyatma Vidya. All this shows his clear understanding and unflickering approach to the subject.

The clarification of "Pravrithi Marga" and "Nivrithi Marga" by His Highness is the most remarkable feature of his speech. It leads me to conclude that His Highness is in full possession of the golden treasures of the rich and old traditions of learning. That is why he could clearly claim Jeevan Mukti for the "Pravrithi Margi" also. This is a very important lesson because in the present Atmosphere of too much talk about Vedanta, it is often argued that Peace in day to day life, experience of Atmananda, and realisation of God are not possible without Vairagya or Renunciation. This ideology is basically wrong and I am glad His Highness has spoken what is right.

For such a noble, intelligent and befitting inaugural address I can only congratulate His Highness and pray to Guru Deva to shower his choicest blessings upon him for a healthy, prosperous and long life.

Another thing which encourages me to speak at this stage is the Asirvatham sent by Shri Shankaracharya Maharaj of Sringeri Math. You have heard his Asirvatham. Therein you would have noted the sentence that this Kerala Maha Sammelan of the Adhyatmic Vikas Mandal is the need of the Nation. In this one sentence His Holiness has spoken volumes. If time would permit, hours could be spent in elucidating the glorious principles compressed in this one small sentence. Obviously enough His Holiness means that after the advent of the political freedom of the country, a Spiritual Renaissance throughout the vast continent of India is the need, and now is the time to accelerate the spiritual development, because spiritual development alone will ensure abiding peace and lasting happiness in the country. This spiritual development of India can alone erect a permanent light house of peace and joy, to guide the destiny of the storm-tossed ship of the suffering humanity of the whole world and save it from wreck. Shankaracharya Maharaj has also meant and wished in that one sentence that the Mandal should rise up on a national basis. It is a clarion call of peace and happiness for the people and therefore His Holiness has called it the need of the Nation.

Adhyatmic Vikas or spiritual development is the process which brings to light and to our direct experience, the hitherto unknown and unexperienced glories of the subtler aspects of our being. Adhyatmic Vikas or spiritual development is the process of unfolding the essential nature of the soul and bringing it out to light from the hidden chambers of ignorance - ignorance that stands as a covering and hides the subtle and glorified aspect of our inner personality. Adhyatmic vikas or spiritual development is the process of revelation of the ultimate truth of our life, the Sat-Chit-Anandam, which is the greatest heritage of one and all.

The most treasured heritage is really the fountain head of all joy in life, material and divine. Adhyatmic vikas is the process to unfold the glories of the soul and to enjoy all aspects of life, material and divine. Adhyatmic vikas is the process of bringing out the great fountain-head of peace and joy hidden with us. Adhyatmic Vikas or spiritual development is the process of sharpening the mind to enable it to enter into the kingdom of the soul which is the subtlest aspect of our life, the "Anoraniyan" and directly experience its essential nature which is Sat-Chit-Anandam.

Everybody can have, should have and must have, the great privilege of enjoying the glories of the soul, the glories of the glorified aspect of everybody's life. Caste, creed or nationality is no hurdle in the realm of the soul or on the royal road to it. Soul is the individual property of everybody. It is the natural and inseparable possession, nay, the very existence of every man. Everybody has a right to enjoy his own possession. Everybody has a right to enjoy the Sat-Chit-Anandam nature of his own soul. In the most natural manner everybody has every right to enjoy permanent peace, Bliss Eternal, which is the nature of his own soul. Everybody has a birth-right to enjoy abiding peace and unbounded joy which is the essential nature of his own soul. And I hold **Everybody already possesses the capacity** of enjoying it, because it is already there in the innermost recess of everybody's heart. Nothing from outside can stop a man from experiencing the nature of his own soul. Nothing from outside can stop a man from enjoying lasting peace and permanent joy in life, for, it is the essential nature of his own soul.

The doors of Sat-Chit-Anandam are wide open alike for one and all. The path is straight and entry is free. Then why waste time in helplessness and suffer any agony in life? Why suffer when you can enjoy? Why be miserable when you can be happy? Now, let the days of misery and peacelessness be over and let their operation become tales of the past. Allow not the past history of agony to be continued in the present. Be happy and gay. Come on straight and enjoy the enjoyable. Come on and enjoy the fountain-head of all joys in life, enjoy the overbright chambers of your own inner personality. All suffering will cease, all agony will go, and all peacelessness and misery of life will simply disappear. Today you are under the divine radiance of Shri Guru Deva. Time is at hand. Under the universal benevolence of Guru Deva enjoy all glories of life, material and divine. Let not the caravan of life be tossed about and wander aimlessly in the darkness of ignorance; under the dark clouds of agony and peacelessness. Let it enjoy the royal entry into the gates of protection, peace and happiness; let it enter into the Kingdom of bliss and be blissful for ever.

Under the high flying banner of spiritual development alone can the suffering humanity find solace and peace. Spiritual development of the members of the family of nations, alone can ensure abiding peace in the world. Let the standard of everybody's mind be raised to the heights of his own inner glory and then man will feel for himself the greatness of the higher values of life and would be tempted to bring them down into practical life, and live them. Unless the steps of spiritual development are ascended and the pinnacle is reached, the hope of peace and happiness in life will ever remain unrealised. It was on the basis of this spiritual development that India was once so great and it is the glory of the same spiritual development that can make India great once again, to shine as a rising sun of peace and happiness on the horizon of the world.

I believe in something practical. Mere talks of peace and fussing over it have no practical value in any field of life. If one peaceless and miserable man of the world could be made peaceful and happy, it would mean something of value, positive and concrete for the suffering humanity. If a formula could be brought out to light a formula for transforming peacelessness and miseries of life into peace and joy of a permanent nature, that would be a boon to society and for the whole of mankind. Here we find that great boon, in the dust of the Lotus feet of Shri Guru Deva. Any number, millions and crores of the suffering souls can come and take refuge in the universal benevolence of Guru Deva and can, within a few days of Sadhana, transform their peacelessness and sufferings into real peace and permanent joy. You have already heard the experiences of many on this platform.

What else can be a greater boon in life? What else can be a better sift in lose of humanity? Guru Deva is now out to shower His Grace on one and all. Like a flood has come His Grace here in Kerala. Thousands are enjoying peace and joy in their daily life. Anybody who came, was blessed, and allowed to take the path of peace and happiness. Time is favourable, opportunity is yours. Enjoy, enjoy to the maximum the overflowing grace of Shri Guru Deva.

Mysterious are the ways of destiny. I cannot say, for how long in the atmosphere of the present age, we will succeed in holding on to this great and overflowing generosity of Shri Guru Deva. I can only speak in terms of the present. I can only offer to you the dishes ready in hand today; for tomorrow I cannot promise, for, I have nothing of my own. The bulb is shining here, but the current is coming from the power house. Any time the main switch may be put off and then the bulb will cease to spread the light. Therefore under the light of the shining bulb at hand, lay out your own lines to the powerhouse and be independent and free from the fear of darkness when the light that is, chooses to switch off.

Here is the Divine call for you. Adhyatmic Vikas Mandal of Kerala is the clarion call to awaken the world from deep slumber of ignorance, suffering and peacelessness. Here is the invitation from the universal benevolence of Shri Guru Deva; the invitation, the universal invitation for everyone suffering the agony of peacelessness and miseries, to come out of the dark night of life into the brilliant light of Divine Grace and enjoy all glories of life, material and divine.

Remember, it is nothing new that the Adhyatmic Vikas Mandal of Kerala is saying today. It is not any new message of life that the Kerala Maha Sammelan is broadcasting today. It is the same age-old voice of eternal peace and happiness for which India stands out from times immemorial. It is the same age-old voice of eternal peace and happiness which the child of Kerala, the pride of India, Shri Shankara gave out to the world more than two thousand years ago. Kerala Maha Sammelan is giving out today, on the basis of personal experience, the same age-old lesson of Shri Shankara which declared the unimpeachable universality of Anandam as the Ultimate and Absolute Reality of existence; it is the same principle of Anandam that the Eternal Vedas and Upanishads have been singing down the ages-

आनन्दाद्ध्येव खल्विमानि भूतानि जायन्ते ।
आनन्देन जातानि जीवन्ति ।
आनन्दं प्रयन्त्याभिसंविशन्तीति ।

aanandaaddhayeva khalvimaani bhuutaani jaayante.
aanandena jaataani jivanti.
aanandam prayantyaabhisamvishantiti.
(Taittariya Upanishad)[115]

"From Anandam is the whole creation born. In Anandam do the creatures live and in Anandam shall all this ultimately merge! Anandam is the one reality of the universe, ultimate and absolute. Anandam is the one reality of life eternal and absolute. Anandam is the life of every body. Anandam is the very existence of every being". This is the Anandam which the Adhyatmic Vikas Mandal of Kerala is enjoying and this is the natural and universal Anandam for whose enjoyment Kerala Maha Sammelan is raising a voice and inviting the people. This is the Anandam, which was considered to be so difficult of experience, and which now has become so easily attainable under the grace of Shri Guru Deva. It is this great miracle of Guru Deva that is tempting the Kerala Maha Sammelan to feel for the suffering humanity. Although nothing is new in the realm of the soul, the experience of it which was thought to be very difficult has now become very easy under the grace of Guru Deva. It is the joy of this easy way of approach which is encouraging Kerala Maha Sammelan to raise a voice unique and unheard of elsewhere in contemporary times. Kerala Maha Sammelan is raising a voice, that under the universal benevolence of Shri Guru Deva, MIND CONTROL IS EASY, PEACE IN DAILY LIFE IS EASY AND EXPERIENCE OF ATMANANDAM IS EASY.

The voice of Kerala Maha Sammelan is not a voice of

catch-words and charming sentiments, it is a voice coming out of the acid test of personal experience.

Kerala Maha Sammelan stands only to flash out the age old light of Eternal Peace and happiness, the light Celestial blazoned by the Maharshis of yore and kept alive in the heart of the holy tradition of the Maharshis of the country; the Light serene whose one ray is sufficient to enlighten the dark nights of ignorance misery and peacelessness of the whole world. And you have seen it for yourself, how under the amazing influence of that light, hundreds of miserable and peaceless souls of Kerala have put an end to their suffering and peacelessness and have begun to enjoy peace and happiness in life. Whatever the material circumstances and surroundings of the man, his life has been raised to a high pitch of real peace and joy. Under the flash of this unfailing light of Guru Deva's Blessing, Kerala Maha Sammelan stands to proclaim sure cure for all the miseries and peacelessness of everybody everywhere in the world. This is the one treasure of Adhyatmic Vikas Mandal, on the basis of which it stands "to bring peace and happiness everywhere in everybody's every-day life".

"Today we have considered the nature of Adhyatmic Vikas, the Omnipresence of Anandam, and the aim of the Adhyatmic Vikas Mandal. Tomorrow we shall deal with the theory of Adhyatmic Vikas, the principle of attaining peace and happiness in life.

Jai Shri Guru De...va.

On Day 2, Maharishi's discourse was entitled 'Theory of Spiritual Development':-

"JAI SHRI GURU DEVA"

'What a happy time we have this evening. Yesterday's Shiva - Laksha - Archana Maha Yagna, it seems, has really pleased Lord Shiva much. It was the pleasure of Lord Shiva, that doubled this morning, the programme of Vishnu - Laksha - Archana. Instead of one, two Vishnu - Laksha - Archanas were performed today. This shows the delight of the Almighty Gods, Lord Shiva and Lord Vishnu, in the celebration of this Kerala Maha Sammelan of Shri Shankaracharya Brahmanand Saraswati Adhyatmic Vikas Mandal. In the midst of this great delight of Gods and under the divine radiance of Shri Guru Deva, in this holiest of the holy atmosphere of all embracing divinity, what encourages me most is the Ashirvadam of the great successor of Shri Guru Deva, Swami Shantanand Saraswati Maharaj, the present Shankaracharya Swamigal of Jyotirmath, Badarikashram. I take it to be the Ashirvadam of Lord Shiva appearing on the Lap of Lord Vishnu. Yesterday we performed Shiva - Laksha - Archana and today we received the Ashirvadam and the best of it was that today it was received in the midst of the two Vishnu - Laksha - Archanas. This is not an ordinary coincidence. I find very great meaning in it. 'SHANKARAM SHANKARACHARYAM' Shankaracharya is said to be the Avatara of Lord Shiva. And Lord Vishnu has himself said - 'ACHARYAM MAM VIJANEEYAT', i.e. know the 'Acharya' to be 'My-self'. And therefore according to Lord Vishnu, the Dharmacharya Shankaracharya is Lord Vishnu Himself. So this Ashirvadam of Bhagawan Shankaracharya is the Ashirvadam of Lord Shiva and Lord Vishnu, both. Happy I feel to say that your Kerala Maha Sammelan has really been blessed by the All Powerful Divine influence of both Lords Shiva and Vishnu.

You have heard and received the great Ashirvadam. In

that Divine Message you have heard that "Spiritualism is the backbone of India". In this one sentence His Holiness has spoken volumes and has expressed great truths of Indian Philosophy and culture. Spirituality deals with the realm of the soul, and this is the subtlest field of our existence. It is also the very basis of all the gross aspects of life.

The spirit or soul is the basic motive force of our existence and spirituality is the science of that motive force. The material science of today speaks highly of atomic power. Today the political power of a nation depends upon its resources of atomic energy. But we know in India know that the atomic energy is not the basic motive power of existence. It can only be called the basic motive force of material existence, because it is found to be very gross when compared with the powers of our mental and spiritual existence. That is the reason why India laid more importance on the field of the soul which is the ultimate motive power behind our life in all its aspects; spiritual, mental and physical. That is the reason why India always regarded the science of the soul as the best and most useful of all sciences. This is the reason why His Holiness has called spirituality as the backbone of India. Under the high-flown banner of spiritualism alone can India regain its past glory, and cultured in the spirit alone, can the children of India be great masters of Nature and Universe. This is what His Holiness has meant, when he said "Spiritualism is the back-bone of India". It is the keystone of the arch of all developments. Spirituality trains the mind to rise from the experience of the subtlest field of objectivity and enables it to transcend the field of objectivity for entering the realm of the soul, the field of Eternal Bliss. Spirituality trains the mind to enter into the realm of the soul and becomes all powerful for enjoyment of all the glories of life, mental and material.

By a perfect system of spiritual development, the great sages of yore have given to us the keys to lay open the treasures of great energy and power hidden within us. The Mundaka Upanishad declares that anybody who establishes himself on the highest attitude of spiritualism becomes capable of developing his will-power and mental force to such a great extent that he can attain any object or get into any strata of the universe by a mere "SANKALPA" or a thought. This is the glory of spirituality which can make a man worthy of attainment of everything by the agency of thought alone. This all powerful spirituality is valued and cherished most in India. That is why His Holiness has said it to be the backbone of our country. But this spirituality tends to be ignored today in the heat of the modern currents and Western ideologies. If India is to become strong and great let her not sleep over spirituality, the science of the very motive force of existence.

If Society is to become great, every man has to become great spiritually. Be he a beggar or a millionaire, if only he turns spiritual can he have peace and happiness, and enjoy all the glories of life spiritual, mental and material. This is the great strength of our ancient wisdom, the great efficacy of spiritual development for bringing peace and happiness to every body irrespective of his material standard of life or status in society. This is the reason why His Holiness has said that "Spiritualism is the backbone of India".

We feel the flash of the spirituality of our Guru Deva in the Ashirvadam of His great successor. We in Kerala today are immensely blessed by this great Ashirvadam and in reverence we offer our devotional pranams to the Lotus feet of His Holiness.

Yesterday, we considered the Omnipresence of Anandam. Anandam, which is present everywhere and pervading. As a matter of fact everything is but Anandam in its essential nature. Just as a mountain of snow is nothing but water, so also the whole Universe is nothing but Anandam. Just as the different shapes and forms of pots are made of the same clay, so also the different objects in the Universe are made of the same formless Anandam. Anandam is the ultimate reality of the Universe.

The world of concrete forms and objects is made from the formless. This truth of Indian Philosophy has been supported by the findings of the modern science also. According to the electronic theory of modern science, electrons and protons are the ultimate reality of matter. All these different forms of matter are nothing but involved energy. This solid concrete wall is nothing but abstract formless energy. This concrete mike, all its components and the whole mechanism of it, is nothing but abstract formless energy. All these multifarious material objects in phenomenon are nothing but formless abstract energy. No sensible man can refuse to accept this finding of the modern material science. Now if we are able to conceive that the whole material universe is nothing but formless energy, then it is easy to conceive, on similar lines, that all this concrete universe is nothing but Abstract Formless Brahman "Sarava Khalu Idam Brahma". All this is Brahman and 'Anandam Brahmano Vijnan' i.e. Brahman is Anandam. All this is Anandam. Sat-Chit-Anandam.

To be more clear - Electrons and protons of the modern science, seen through the Indian system of analysis of the universe are manifestations of Agni-Tatwa and Vayu-Tatwa combined. The energy of the electrons and protons is due to the Agni-Tatwa and motion in them is due to Vayu-Tatwa. Thus we find, the present day science has reached up to Vayu-Tatwa in the field of analysis of the universe. But our Indian analysis of the universe has found out much more of the subtler phases of existence. According to our system of analysis - finer than the Agni-Tatwa and the very cause of it is the Vayu-Tatwa; finer than the Vayu-Tatwa and the very cause of it is the Akash-Tatwa; finer than the Akash-Tatwa and the very cause of it is the Aham-Tatwa; finer than the Aham-Tatwa and the very cause of it is the Mahat-Tatwa; finer than the Mahat-Tatwa and the very cause of it is the Prakriti-Tatwa; and finer than the Prakriti-Tatwa and the very cause of it is the Brahma-Tatwa which is the Ultimate Reality, the subtlest "Anoraniyan", Sat-Chit-Anandam. This is the analysis of the universe according to our Indian thought which speaks of universality of Anandam and establishes that Anandam is the ultimate and absolute Reality of existence. This universality of Anandam we have already considered yesterday.

Today we shall try to find out why this Omnipresent Anandam evades common experience. And having found out the cause, we shall try to find out the means to eradicate it. A thing which is present everywhere has gone out of our experience! Obviously it seems to be a great paradox. But this is experience in life which cannot be denied. Omnipresence of Anandam we accept intellectually, but Omnipresence of 'Dukham' is our day to day experience in life. Which of the two is correct? What is the truth of life? Is it to remain a paradox or an unsolved problem of existence? If Anandam is the reality of life then all our experience of the world which are, in one way or the other, allied with 'Dukham' are the experiences of a non-reality. The Reality of life which is Anandam of unbounded nature is not at all being experienced. A real life of all Anandam, the most cherishable aspect of our being is out of our consciousness. What is the reason? Something seems to have gone wrong with our machinery of experience. Our machinery of experience is able to experience only one aspect, the gross aspect of the ultimate reality and fails to experience the subtler aspect of its essential nature.

There are two states of the ultimate Reality Brahman - the unmanifested state, and the manifested state. In the unmanifested state the Brahman is 'Anoraniyan' the atom of the atoms, the minute of the minutae; and in this unmanifested minute state, its essential nature is Anandam Sat-Chit-Anandam; but in its manifested state the Anandam becomes latent to give rise to other properties which come on the scene of the manifested objects, just as the fluid property of water becomes latent i.e. when water becomes ice. Water in its essential nature is Fluid and transparent, but when it becomes ice it is translucent or opaque, and solid. The solidity and opacity of ice are quite contrary to the fluidity and transparency of water. When water becomes ice the transparency of water becomes latent giving rise to its opposite characteristic of solidity. Thus we see, when a thing transforms its original and essential characteristics it becomes latent and gives rise to different characteristics which may even be contrary to the original. These changed characteristics deviate from the original characteristics according to intensity of the change Vapour, cloud, mist, snow and ice are the various manifestations of water; Water itself is liquid, but of its manifestations some are gaseous and others are solids.

This analogy helps explanation of the experience of misery (or Dukham) in the midst of the Omnipresence of Anandam. When the unmanifested Brahman becomes manifested, the Sat-Chit-Anandam characteristics of it become latent to give rise to other characteristics which may even be Asat, Achit and Anandam. The never changing (Sat), absolute existence (Chit) and absolute bliss (Anandam) which are the characteristics of the Unmanifested 'Anoraniyan' become latent giving rise to their opposite characteristics, viz. the ever changing, relative existence, and relative joy characteristics of the manifested objects and universe.

I think it is clear now, why the quality of Omnipresent Anandam is not exhibited on the forms and objects of the Universe. Although Anandam is the essential nature of the ultimate reality of the material objects, it has become latent in them and only the qualities of the gross objectivity are being experienced at the outset.

Hail to the perfect system of Indian philosophy which offers the theory and practice of directly experiencing the Sat-Chit-Anandam; and hail to the Maharshis of India who have opened the gates of spiritual glory in material life and who have laid out practical paths for experiencing the nature of the 'Anoraniyan' in the midst of all this manifested gross universe, and have floated the ideology of Jeevan-Mukti, the most exalted state of human existence, the state of constant experience of Sat-Chit-Anandam.

Today we have to look into this ideology of Jeevan-Mukti, and consider the theory and practice for experiencing Sat-Chit-Anandam.

Our instrument for experience viz. the mind, is constantly engaged in apprehending objects through the senses which can only perceive the gross objectivity. Our physical eyes can see only the gross form. When the form is minute or subtle our eyes fail to perceive it and we need a microscope to see it. Similarly ears can hear only gross sounds. When the sound becomes subtle, our ears fail to catch it. Similar is the case with the other senses of perception. Because these senses can experience only gross objects, the mind, which is always experiencing things through the senses, is able to experience only the gross field of manifested objectivity. Due to the long-standing experience of gross objectivity, the mind itself has become gross and blunt. In its gross condition the mind naturally fails to enter into the realm of the subtlest "Anoraniyan", and that is how it misses the Anandam which is Omnipresent.

If the mind could be trained to apprehend the experience in the subtler fields in objectivity itself, it will definitely become sharp and in its increasing sharpness can definitely enter into the realm of "Anoraniyan", the Sat-Chit-Anandam, and have the direct experience of it. The path of spiritual Sadhana lies therefore in training the mind to march through the field of subtler objectivity, in spiritual development.

For practice we can select the field of objectivity pertaining to any of the senses of perception - sense of sight, hearing, smell or touch. In any of the fields we are required to reduce the objectivity to its increasingly subtler stages and help the mind to go on experiencing them till it reaches the subtlest stage of objectivity, and its experiences.

At this stage when the mind is able to experience the subtlest in objectivity, it becomes sharp enough to enter into the realm of "Anoraniyan" which transcends the field of subtlest objectivity, it becomes sharp enough to enter into the realm of "Anoraniyan" which transcends the field of subtlest objectivity and in this state it tastes the essential nature of that realm, which is Sat-Chit-Anandam.

If the mind is proceeding through sound, the field of Anoraniyan is the field which transcends the field of subtlest sound, which is the field of "no sound", i.e. "Ni Shabdam"; and the Upanishads call it "Paramam Padam", "Ni-Shabdam Paramam Padam". This Paramam Padam is Sat-Chit-Anandam in its essential nature. The man experiencing it, rises to Eternal life of Eternal life - a life of Eternal life - a life of Eternal Bliss and Absolute Consciousness.

For training the mind through sound we can take any word. Even the word "mike" can be taken. By reducing the sound of the word "mike" to its subtler and still subtler stages and allowing the mind to go on experiencing all the stages one by one, the mind can be trained to be so sharp as to enter into the subtlest stage of the sound 'mike', transcending which it will automatically get into the realm of Sat-Chit-Anandam and experience it. Thus we find that any sound can serve our purpose of training the mind to become sharp. But we do not select any sound like 'mike', flower, table, pen, wall etc. because such ordinary sounds can do nothing more than merely sharpening the mind; whereas there are some special sounds which have the additional efficacy of producing vibrations whose effects are found to be congenial to our way of life. This is the scientific reason why we do not select any word at random. For our practice we select only the suitable mantras of personal Gods. Such mantras fetch to us the grace of personal Gods and make us happier in every walk of life.

While making a reference to the Mantras in this manner. I feel like touching a very vital aspect of Sadhna, which things are blurred in the present atmosphere of too much talk of Vedanta.

Obviously enough there are two ways of life, the way of the Sanyasi and the way of life of a householder. One is quite opposed to the other. A Sanyasi renounces everything of the world, whereas a householder needs and accumulates everything. Shastras declare both ways of life to be the paths of emancipation. Both are said to be the "Moksha Marga" Nivarthi Marga and 'Privrithi Marga'. The one realises, through renunciation and detachment, while the other goes through all attachments and accumulation of all that is needed for physical life. We have two different sets of Mantras to suit the two ways of life. Mantras for the Sanyasis have the effect of increasing the sense of detachment and renunciation and also have the power of destroying the objects of worldly affections, if there should survive any such objects for him. Quite contrary to this are the Mantras suitable for the householder which have the efficacy of harmonising and enriching the material aspect of life also.

The Mantras of the Sanyasi have a destructive effect in the material field of life, whereas the Mantras suited to the householder envisage constructive values also.

"Om" is the Mantra for the Sanyasi. The Sanyasi repeats "Om" "Om" "Om". It is given to him at the time of 'Sanyas - Diksha', at the time when he has completely renounced attachment to the world. Renunciation and detachment increase with the repetition of 'Om'. 'Om' is chanted aloud by a Sanyasi to put on end to his desires. Desires are destroyed by loudly chanting the mantra 'Om'. And if there is any desire deeply rooted in the mind of a Sanyasi, the chanting of 'Om' will result in the destruction of the object of such desire in order to make the Sanyasi, wholly desireless. The Sanyasi thus attains Peace through the renunciation and destruction of desires, whereas the peace comes to the householder when his needs are satisfied, when his desires are fulfilled. The mantras for the householders have the effect of fulfilling the desires.

If unfortunately, the householder begins to repeat the pranava Mantra viz. 'Om', 'Om' 'Om' he experiences destructive effects in his material life. The effect starts with monetary loss and then goes on to destroy objects of affection, one by one. Such a man, when he finds loss of money and separation from the dear ones, he is reduced to utter peacelessness and frustration. Where is the chance of spiritual development or experience of Peace and happiness for such a dejected soul? The path of peacelessness and misery in the world, cannot lead to Eternal happiness. If the man is proceeding towards Eternal happiness every day he should feel the increase of peace and happiness, and this alone will assure him that he is proceeding towards abiding peace and eternal happiness. If you walk towards the light you should be able to feel the increase of light at every step. If you are spending some time in devotion to God, you should feel peace and happiness in life. If you are not feeling peace and happiness you should be wise enough to doubt the correctness of your devotion, you should be wise enough to think that your method of devotion is wrong, that the Mantras that you are repeating do not suit you. The mantras that suit the Sanyasis can never suit the householders. Hundreds of God-loving and God-fearing families, have been ruined due to the destructive effects of Sanyasa Mantra viz. "Om". "Om" destroys desires and also destroys the objects of desires and therefore it produces calmness of mind and renunciation and detachment from material life only to Sanyasis when they repeat Om; to them it brings the experience of peace of mind and from this experience they generally recommend the chanting of 'Om' to their followers. But when a householder repeats 'Om', he experiences that as long as he is repeating 'Om' he feels peace of mind, but when he comes out to indulge in business or household work, he finds he finds that the air is against his desire and schemes. The silencing effect on the mind and destructive effects in material life, both are lived side by side. Some people say that we should ignore material life in regard to the devotional practices and Mantras. But this is a fool's ideology. Can you possibly ignore the considerations of material life, when the Mantras do affect it? Select a path which will make you happier in your material life also. Do not live in a fool's paradise. Do not think that your sufferings and miseries of today will work as reservations in the galleries of heaven for tomorrow. Be peaceful and happy in the present and try to make this state permanent. This is the path of Deliverance in Life Jeevan-Mukti, the most exalted state in human existence, the state of abiding Peace and Eternal Bliss. And this you are entitled to have through correct and suitable Sadhana. And because the Mantras play an important role in the field of Sadhana, you must be very very careful in the selection of the Mantra. The theory of Mantras is the theory of sound. It is most scientific and natural. Ladies should never repeat any Mantra beginning with Om. The pronunciation of Om is like fire to the ladies. This is the practical experience of many devoted ladies who repeated 'Om Namah Shivaya' or 'Om Namonarayanaya' or 'Om Namo Bhagawate Vasudevaya' or any such mantra beginning with Om. It cannot be God's wish that you should suffer in your devotion to him. Do not cling to the unhelpful Mantras. The moment you find you have got into the wrong train, it is wise to get down from it as soon as possible. It is foolish to stick on to the wrong train and go wherever it takes you.

I hold that the devotees of the Almighty God should not suffer at all. That is the fundamental condition of the path to Eternal Bliss. I hold that bliss or happiness should increase at every step till we get into the realm of eternal happiness. I hold that the devotees of the god should enjoy peace and happiness at every stage, because he is the fountain head of all peace and happiness. It cannot be that our march towards the light should at any stage increase the darkness before us. The march towards the Anant Anandam must give the experience of increase of Anandam at every step and in every walk of life.

The devotee of the Almighty cannot suffer. If he is found to suffer, he cannot be said to be a devotee of God. It pains me when I find people suffering in the name of God and devotion. I offer an open invitation to such aspirants and seekers of God. I invite them to come out of their miserable devotion, and step into the peaceful blissful chambers of Sadhana, blessed and illuminated by the divine radiance of Shri Guru Deva. I invite them to put an end to their sufferings and peacelessness and crown their day to day life with success peace and joy. Do not waste time and life. Life is to enjoy. So come on to the field of all joy. The gates of all glories of life are open for you. "Make hay when the sun shines". Avail the opportunity in hand and enjoy life to the fullest.'

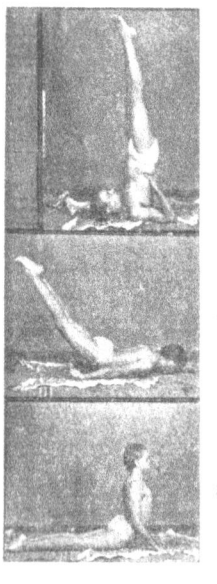
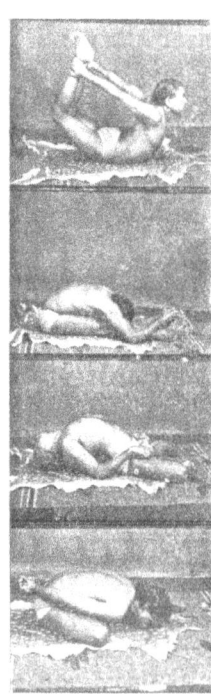

**Demonstration of *hatha yoga asanas*
Mahasammelan, Cochin, October 1955**

On Day 3, the discourse of the 'Revered Maharshi Bala Brahmachari Mahesh Yogi Maharaj' was not titled, but instead captioned; "Here is no empty promise of Heaven after death. Here is the positive experience of heavenly Bliss during life time. Come on who desires for it.":-

जय श्री गुरुदेव ।

[*JAY SHREE GURUDEVA.*]

'Today is Nava-Ratri, the most auspicious and holy-day of the Divine Mother. From the very early morning today we had been feeling the thrills of the divine vibrations of Lalita - Laksha - Archana. We had been feeling the joy and great delight of the universal mother just as a child feels on the lap of his dear mother, when mother is happy. How much the Mother Divine is pleased with the Kerala Maha Sammelan. There was the programme of only two Laksha Archana today but Laksha Archanas were simultaneously performed this morning. This is nothing but the sure and positive indication of the great pleasure and satisfaction of the Divine Mother who so kindly and profusely blessed her children of Kerala. (Clappings) Blessed you are my dear good souls. Fortunate you are. You have been blessed by Vishnu, Shiva and Shakti in the Divine presence of Guru Deva. (Clappings and rings of Jai Shri Guru Deva from delegates).

Today, as if on the happy lap of the Divine Mother we have assembled here to discuss and finalise the scheme of peace and happiness in life. We have been discussing this matter for the last two days and I think today we shall be able to complete it.

Yesterday I had remarked that according to my methods of Sadhana even a busy house-holder can enjoy all the benefits of mind control and peace in daily life and can very well experience Atmananandam and that renunciation is not at all necessary for it. Today one learned man wanted me to clarify how my statement reconciles with the teachings of the Upanishads which declare that Atmananda can not be had unless everything has been renounced.

"Yawat Sarwam Na Santyaktam Tawat-Atma Na Labhyate" and "Tyage Naike Amritatwam Anshuh"[116]

I hold that the teachings of the Upanishads are the bare truths of Existence and the Eternal Laws of Nature. Every Shruti is perfectly all right, in its correct sense. It is bare fact that Atmananda cannot be experienced unless every thing has been renounced, i.e. unless the mind is free from everything of the objective field. This teaching of the Upanishads is one truth of life, and another truth of life is that the householder can enjoy Atmananda remaining in his family affairs and without renouncing the world. Now we have to see how both of these apparently opposed truths are not really conflicting. We have to see in other words, how they are the same.

The emphasis of the Shruti on the necessity of Tyaga for Realisation has got to be scrutinised to see how this requirement is fulfilled in the life of a householder whose life apparently is full of Raga as opposed to Tyaga.

For a clear understanding we shall analyse the state of mind of a Tyagi. If some monetary or golden offerings are made to a man who professes to be a Tyagi, he says "remove this from here." Now analyse the condition of the mind of this Tyagi. When gold is brought before him, he sees it as gold and the impression of its value is carried on to his mind. When the mind recognises the value of gold, obviously the gold has occupied a seat in the mind. Once the gold finds a place in the mind, clearly enough, it becomes the abode of gold and this is nothing but acceptance of gold and not its renunciation or Tyaga. All of us know that a wealthy man never carries wealth on his head. All the wealth remains in the bank, and only the impression of its value is carried in the mind. Thus possession of wealth is nothing but an idea of wealth in the mind, and therefore, when the idea of wealth of gold has come to the mind, i.e. when the gold has occupied a seat in the mind, then it can only be "possession" of gold and not "renunciation" (Tyaga) of it, irrespective of whether the gold remains near or far.

Thus we find Tyaga, in its true sense, has little to do with the objects remaining near or far. Tyaga therefore, has to be defined as giving up or foregoing the mental impressions of objects perceived. In other words, Tyaga is keeping the mind free from the impressions of values and natures of the objects perceived by the senses: or Tyaga is, not allowing the objects of senses to leave the impressions of their qualities in the mind.

This is the essential meaning of Tyaga mentioned in the Shruti referred above. This ideology of perfect Tyaga has to be lived by all those who want to realise the Atman or Brahman. Since realisation is the ultimate aim of both the ways of life, it goes without saying that both the house-holder and Sanyasi have to attain this ideology of Tyaga, and then alone will it be possible for them to realise the Truth. We shall analyse and see in what manner it is possible for a 'Pravrithi Margi Grihastha' (House-holder) to fulfil this requirement of Shruti through his own way or life which is obviously full of "Raga" (attachment).

By nature, a house holder is a "Ragi". Raga as opposed to Tyaga, is embedded deep down in the nature of a house-holder. Wife, children, friends, relatives, money, name and fame, for example, are seven points of attachment (Raga) for a house-holder. He is always devoted to these points of attachment. To these seven points of Raga, he adds one more point and begins to devote himself to this eighth point of Raga also, as he has been devoting to the seven others. This eighth point of Raga is his "ISHTAM" - his personal God - his beloved Deity - Almighty. "SAT-CHIT-ANANDAM". Gradually, he experiences that the eighth point of Raga is capable of giving him more Peace and Happiness in life than the others. When he devotes himself and meditates on the name and form (NAMA AND RUPA) of the LORD, he begins to experience some ANANDAM and also the Grace of the Lord in every walk of life. This experience of Peace and Anandam is Sadhana. And Sadhana naturally increases his devotion to God and makes him more and more attached to Him. Thus he develops intensity of Raga for the ISHTAM. Gradually, this final Raga goes on increasing and this increase of Raga and Love for the ISHTAM enables the Grihastha to feel the presence of his 'ISHTAM' always with him, in all his ways of life, in all his thought, speech and action. The man, although acting on the world as before, experiences that throughout all his actions the idea of his personal deity predominates in his mind and the actions and experiences of the senses fail to engage his mind with that great intensity with which they used to do before. Thus the objects of the senses fail to leave any enduring impression of their values in his mind, and this is the state of mind of a real Tyagi as explained above. This is how through the virtue of Raga, a householder - a full-fledged Ragi finds his way to place himself on the plane where he is essentially a Tyagi also. And this is how a householder is able to establish himself in a position to meet the requirement of the said Shruti for Realisation. And this is how, through his own quality of "Raga" a householder can very well establish himself on the plane of human perfection, the plane of Jeevan-Mukti, the most exalted state of existence, the state of Perpetual Peace and Bliss Eternal.

Thus we have seen that it is not at all necessary for the householder to go for a direct practice of "Tyaga" or "Vairagya" (Renunciation) for realisation. That practice is unnatural for him, antagonistic to his nature and opposed to his way of life. If a householder begins to practice detachment in his life, he finds himself in a plane where he is not able to reconcile the mental attitude of detachment with his physical tendencies in life viz. one of all-attachment. He need march only through the quality of Raga which is rooted deep down in his nature and is the essential quality of his heart and mind. He needs only to increase his Raga (Attachment) for his Ishtam or God. And to increase Raga for Ishtam (attachment for God) it is not at all necessary to practice Vairagya (detachment from or renunciation of the world). To love one child more than others, it is not necessary that all others should be ignored or kept away. If you have seven children you maintain your love for all but if you come to know of some brilliant qualities of a particular child, you begin to pay more attention to him without ignoring the others. Maintaining your love for all, you begin to love him more than others. Decrease of love for others is not all necessary for increase of love for one. The motivation is the knowledge of his superior or better qualities. In the same way, it is not at all necessary to renounce the world for the sake of increasing the Love of God. What is necessary is that the Sat-Chit-Anandam - quality of God should come to the limelight of personal knowledge or experience. Once you begin to experience Anandam through the Nama-Japa or Rupa-Dhyanam of the Lord. He is bound to attract you more than any other object of attraction in the world, because that joy is much greater than the joy received through any worldly means of joy. And this is the reason why I say that renunciation is not at all an essential requisite for God Realisation. According to my methods of Sadhana, a householder can very well experience that great joy, unbounded, and can very well realise God without any direct practice of Renunciation whatsoever. Methods of Sadhana, which I am advocating these days, are simple and easy to practice. Everybody can easily practice in the most comfortable posture for half an hour or one hour in the morning and evening daily and soon experience the great advantages of it. Normally it does not take more than one or two weeks for a man to experience the great unbounded joy - called Samadhi or Atmanandam and it does not take more than about seven days to experience calmness of mind or peace in day-to-day life. However peaceless or worried a man may be feeling, if he but starts the Sadhana, he is sure to feel some calmness and lightness in the mind from the very first or second day of Sadhana and he is sure to feel completely peaceful and happy within about seven days. This looks to be a miracle, but it is so.

And the truth of this statement has been supported by the personal experiences of those who have seriously taken to the practice and have narrated their experiences before you on this platform.

All these attainments are only due to the blessings of Shri Guru Deva. I am glad that hundreds of respectable families and thousands of people in Kerala have taken good advantage of my stay in these parts and they are enjoying 'Heavenly Bliss' as some of them have called it, in their own earthly homes; the 'Peace of the Himalayas' in the midst of all business and their householder affairs. Gates of Heavens are now open for them in their life on earth. This is the greatness of Shri Guru Deva's Blessings. Here is the positive experience of 'Heavenly Bliss' during life time. Come on who desires for it, is all the word of value that I can give out to you now towards the end of your Kerala Maha Sammelan.

JAI SHRI GURU DEVA
(Rings of Jai Guru Deva from the audience numbering not less than ten thousand).

....

In Praise of the Guru

Within the *'The Beacon Light of the Himalayas'* booklet, accompanying the transcript of each lecture given by 'Maharishi Bal Brahmachari Mahesh Yogi', there are images of verses in Devanagari script, all related to praising the *guru*, 'Guru Dev' Swami BrahmanandaSaraswati.

Preceding the transcript of Maharishi's discourse on Day 1, is the following:-

MAHARSHI'S DISCOURSE
"TIME IS AT HAND
Under the universal benevolence of Shri Guru Dev enjoy
all glories of Life Material and Divine"

Thus spoke Maharshi Bala Brahmachari Mahesh Yogi Maharaj
during His inspired exhortation on the first day of the
Mahasmmelan. In its essential features the discourse is
summarised by the verse.

वन्दे बोधमयं नित्यं गुरुं शंकररूपिणम् ।
यमाश्रितो हि वक्रोऽपि चन्द्रः सर्वत्र वन्द्यते ॥
अज्ञानतिमिरान्धस्य ज्ञानाञ्जनशलाकया ।
चक्षुरुन्मीलितं येन तस्मै श्री गुरवे नमः ॥
यद्द्वारे निखिला निलिम्पपरिषत्
    सिद्धिं विधत्तेऽनिशम्
श्रीमत्श्रीलसितं जगद्गुरुपदं
    नत्वात्मतृप्तिं गताः ।
लोकाज्ञानपयोदपाटनधुरं
    श्रीशंकरं शर्मदं
ब्रह्मानन्दसरस्वतिं गुरुवरं
    ध्यायामि ज्योतिर्मयम् ॥

vande bodhamayan nityan gurun shankara ruupishaam.
yamaashrito hi vakroapi chandrassarvatra vandyate..
agyaanatimiraandhasya gyaanaanjanashalaakayaa.
chakshurunmilitam yena tasmai shri guruvenamah..
yadadvaare nikhilaa nilimpaparishat siddhim vidhatteanisham
shrimat shrilasitam jagadgurupadam natvaatmatriptim gataah.
lokaagyaanapayodapaatanadhuram shrishankararam sharmadam
brahmaanandasarasvatim guruvaram dhyaayaami jyotirmayam..

The first two lines are taken from *'Shri Ramacharitamanasa'* the story of Lord Rama told in verse:-

vande bodhamayan nityan gurun shankara ruupinam.
yamaashrito hi vakroapi chandrah sarvatra vandyate..[117]

'I make obeisance to the eternal preceptor in the form of Lord Shankara, who is all wisdom, and resting on whose brow the crescent moon, though crooked in shape, is universally adored.'

The next two lines can be sourced variously, to *'Guru Stotram'*, *'Aarti'* and *'Guru Gita'*:-

agyaanatimiraandhasya gyaanaanjanashalaakayaa.
chakshurunmilitam yena tasmai shri guruvenamah.. [118]

'He who applies the collyrium of knowledge with a sharp pencil, to open the eyes blinded by darkness of ignorance, to the blessed Guru I bow down.'

The last four lines of Sanskrit are verses written in praise of Swami BrahmanandaSaraswati:-

yadvaare nikhilaa nilimpaparishatsiddhim vidhatteanisham
shrimat shrilasitam jagadgurupadam natvaaatmatriptim gataah.
lokaagyaanapayoda paatanadhuram shrishankaram sharmadam
brahmaanandasaraswatim guruvaram dhyaayaami jyotirmayam..

'At whose door the whole galaxy of gods pray for perfection

day and night. Adorned by immeasurable glory, preceptor of the whole world, having bowed down at His feet, we gain fulfilment. Skilled in dispelling the cloud of ignorance of the people, the gentle emancipator, Brahmananda Saraswati, the supreme teacher, full of brilliance, on Him we meditate.'

On Day 2 of the *'Maha Samellan'*, the 'Great Congress'; Maharishi's discourse was entitled 'Theory of Spiritual Development, and was preceded by these Sanskrit verses:-

नारायण समारम्भां श्री शुकाचार्यं मध्यमाम् ।
शङ्कराचार्यं पर्यन्तां वन्दे गुरुपरम्पराम् ॥
अज्ञानगाढान्धतमोपहाभ्याम्
विवेकविद्याविनयप्रदाभ्याम् ।
विश्वेशतत्त्वप्रतिबोधिकाभ्याम्
नमो नमः श्री गुरुपादुकाभ्याम् ॥
वर्णाश्रमाचार प्रचारिकाभ्याम्
सर्वस्य राष्ट्रस्य सुखावहाभ्याम् ।
क्लेशैः समस्तैः परिवर्जिताभ्याम्
नमो नमः श्री गुरुपादुकाभ्याम् ॥
ऐंकार ह्रींकार रहस्ययुक्त
श्रींकार गूढार्थ महाविभूत्या ।
अूंकार मर्म प्रतिपादिनीभ्याम्
नमो नमः श्री गुरुपादुकाभ्याम् ॥

naaraayana samaarambhaam shri shukaachaarya madhyamaam.
shankaraachaarya paryantaam vande guruparamparaam..
agyaanagaadaandhatamopahaabhyaam
vivekavidyaavinayapradaabhyaam.
vishveshatatvapratibodhikaabhyaam
namo namah shri gurupaadukaabhyaam..
varnaashramaachaara prachaarikaabhyaam
sarvasya raashtrasya sukhaavahaabhyaam.
kleshaih samastaih parivarjitaabhyaam
namo namah shri gurupaadukaabhyaam..
AIN-kaara HREEN-kaara rahasyayukta

SHREEN-kaara guudaartha mahaavibhuutyaa.
OM-kaara marma pratipaadinibhyaam
namo namah shri gurupaadukaabhyaam..

'I bow down to the Tradition of Masters starting from Lord Narayana, with Shri Shukacharya in the middle, and extending to Bhagavan Shankaracharya.[119]

Salutations again and again to Shri Guru's sandals, which remove the darkness of those who are blind due to strong ignorance, which bestow the education leading to the knowledge of discrimination, and which awaken the reality of the ruler of the universe.

Salutations again and again to Shri Guru's sandals, which establish the rules of conduct for the castes and stages of life, which create happiness in the whole country, and which are devoid of all afflictions.

'ऐ *AI-N*' practice & 'ह्रीं *HREE-N*' practice, along with 'श्रीं *SHREE-N*' practice has hidden meaning, mystery & great power, communicating the vital point of 'ॐ *OM*' practice, I bow down again and again to the sandals of the blessed *guru*.'

ऐं ह्रीं श्रीं ॐ

This last verse is of particular interest as it contains reference to several sounds used in meditation practices, syllables known as *bija mantras*, - '*bij*', '*bija*' or '*beeja*' means 'seed'. Such *bij mantras* are known as '*nirguna*', 'without a quality, or form' in that they are not necessarily associated with deities, whereas there are also '*saguna mantras*', e.g. '*namah mantras*', which are 'with a quality, or form', and these relate to specific deities. Sometimes *mantras* are chosen according to one's *ashrama* (life stage). According to Kashmiri Shaivism, and other *tantra* traditions, there are both Shiva and Shakti *mantras*.

On Day 3 of the Congress, five Sanskrit verses of *'Guru Paduka Stotram'*, in praise of the *'guru's* sandals', precede the transcript of Maharishi's discourse:-

सुरसरित्करुणार्णवहंसिके
मुनिमनःकुमुदाकरचन्द्रिके ।
सकलमानवमानसपद्मिके
निवसतां हृदि मे गुरुपादुके ॥

अनन्तशोभासमलंकृताभ्याम्
असीमपुण्यप्रचयप्रदाभ्याम् ।
दुर्वासनोन्मूलनतत्पराभ्याम्
नमो नमः श्रीगुरुपादुकाभ्याम् ॥

अघौघविध्वंसनमुद्गराभ्याम्
तापत्रयोन्मूलनसंगराभ्याम् ।
त्रिकर्मणां बन्धविमोचकाभ्याम्
नमो नमः श्रीगुरुपादुकाभ्याम् ॥

ग्रन्थित्रयास्याशु विदारिकाभ्याम्
षट्चक्रतः पारमुपागताभ्याम् ।
मनोमलस्यापि विशोधिकाभ्याम्
नमो नमः श्रीगुरुपादुकाभ्याम् ॥

दुःखार्णवे जगति येन हितया नृणाम्
प्रेम्णाश्रिता निखिलधर्ममतिर्निनान्तम् ।
जेजीयमानमथयं विमलैस्तपोभि-
र्दीप्यमानमतिनौमि गुरु भुवस्ताम् ॥

जय श्री गुरुदेव ।

surasaritkarunaarnavahamsike
munimanahkumudaakarachandrike.
sakalamaanavamaanasapadhmike
nivasataam hridi me gurupaaduke..

anantashobhaasamalamkritaabhyaam
asimapunyaprachayapradaabhyaam.
durvaasanonmuulanatatparaabhyaam
namo namah shrigurupaadukaabhyaam..

aghaughavidhvamsanamudhgaraabhyaam
taapatrayonmuulanasamgaraabhyaam.
trikarmanaam bandhavimochakaabhyaam
namo namah shrigurupaadukaabhyaam..

granthitrayaasyaashu vidaarikaabhyaam
shathchakratah paaramupaagataabhyaam.
manomalasyaapi vishodhikaabhyaam
namo namah shrigurupaadukaambhyaam..

duhkhaarnave jagati yena hitaaya nrinaam
premnaashritaa nikhiladharmatarirnitaantam.
jejiyamaanamathatam
vimalaistapobhirdedipyamaanamatinaumi guru bhuvastaam..

'May the Guru's sandals which are like swans on the river Ganga resembling waves of compassion, which illuminate the mind of saints as moonlight illuminates plenty of water-lilies, and which resemble the lotus in the heart of all men, dwell in my heart!

Salutations again and again to Shri Guru's sandals, which are well adorned with infinite splendour, which give unlimited accumulations of *punya* (merits), and which are eagerly engaged in destroying bad inclinations.

Salutations again and again to Shri Guru's sandals, which agree together to destroy the three afflictions, which are hammers destroying a whole mass of sins, and which give release from the bondage of the three duties.

Salutations again and again to Shri Guru's sandals, which quickly untie the three knots (*granthi*), which entered into the state beyond the six *chakras*, and which are washing away the impurities of the mind.

By whom the boat of the entire *dharma*, which moves on an agitated ocean of sorrow and pain in this world, is guided with love for the benefit of men, this always victorious Guru shining intensely through spotless spiritual practices, I praise extensively.'

Spiritual Regeneration Movement

In 1956 Maharishi continued to travel about South India, holding meditation camps at Trichur and elsewhere. When he returned to Madanapalle, he is said to have been accompanied by a large entourage of over a dozen people, all of whom stayed at Brindaban Lodge. In total, Maharishi spent several months in Madanapalle, and it is claimed that during one visit there, he taught about 200 people to meditate.

Maharishi in Kashmir, 1956

Maharishi also took his teachings to various other provinces of India, where 'spiritual development' camps were convened; at Hardwar (in the North West, not so very far from Uttar Kashi), and Pahalgam, in Kashmir, the latter lasting two months. Spiritual development camps were also arranged in cities, such as Calcutta (Kolkata), Bangalore, Bombay (Mumbai), Ahmedabad and Ujjain. Maharishi is said to have travelled to some of these destinations using domestic aeroplane flights.

Many, many people turned out to hear his lectures about meditation (it is even said that mass 'initiations' were not uncommon), and the desire to contact ever-greater numbers of people steered him to ever-greater success.

Maharishi visited Madras (Chennai) in South India, and on 30th November 1957 attended the 15th Session of the World Vegetarian Congress, where he spoke on "Vegetarianism and All Isms Through Spiritual 'Ism'":-

'My own Self as Representative of East and West:

We are here today to find a solution for a complicated problem of existence, confronting the whole humanity of the civilised world - the problem of safety of life, of love, protection, peace and happiness: not only of individuals but of the whole creation and of nature too. All the creatures are sprung from God. Man is probably the polished son of God. And so unto him the great responsibility. Man must be sensible enough to look to the protection of life on earth, the precious property of the Great Father.

Vegetarianism is a direct means to this, is the claim of this World Vegetarian Congress. True it is. Accepted that Vegetarianism leads man for all Good. Accepting all values of Vegetarianism, the question arises how we are going to establish it. How are we going to change the 'killing world' of today into a non-killing world of tomorrow? How are we going to change the spirit of killing, the spirit of aggression, the spirit of violence into the spirit of kindness and love - overflowing love for the whole creation? How are we going to change hardness and cruelty of heart to softness and overflowing love for everybody?

Through platform speaking? No, it is not possible. Through outer suggestions? No, it is not possible. Through singing the values and glories of Vegetarianism into the ears of the non-vegetarians? No, because their ears may receive the message but the hardness of their heart will repel it. How then are we going to establish Vegetarianism? Suggestive knowledge - suggestions from outside do not much change the man. You have heard on this platform the experience of the President of the World Vegetarian Congress. They have experienced, speaking does not go a long way to change a man. All the great religions of the world have been speaking for it from the time immemorial - Eternal Vedas have been speaking of it, Holy Bible has been speaking of it, Holy Koran has been speaking of it, yet the killer kills. The killer knows that he is killing and in return he will be killed. The sinner knows that he is committing a sin and that he will be punished for it. Not that he does not know. He knows it. But, with this information, the cruel is not afraid - his cruelty is hardened still. The killer declares his action is the role of a saviour, he kills in the name of life, he kills in the name of saving life, he kills in the name of maintaining life. He kills and murders ruthlessly in the name of protections and peace. In the name of world peace and protection have been waged the deadliest of wars. In the name of peace and protection are preparations being made for the murder of man and creation. Shame to the greatness of the human intelligence which fails to recognise the Judge Supreme!

Our task of the day is to find a cure for this major ill of humanity. The heart of man is be changed. The inner man has to be transformed. If we want to establish real and good vegetarianism in the world we have to rise with a practical formula to transform the inner man.

My experience says the inner man is instantaneously transformed by a flash of Divine Experience. A direct experience of the Blissful nature of Soul, the inner man is completely transformed. The mind experiencing the Great Bliss feels satisfaction and this satisfaction of the mind results in right understanding and virtuous action, kindness, love and compassion for all. And here in this great assemblage of the eminent people of the world I declare that the experience of the Blissful Nature of the soul is not at all difficult. It is easy of attainment by one and all irrespective of caste, creed, or nationality. Without much elaborating the glories of Divine experience I invite you all to my Spiritual Development Camp at Mylapore to have direct experience of the Divine through simple, easy and effective methods of meditation which directly lead the mind to the glorious realm of the Divine. And with this experience the life of every man is transformed for all good. Not only will virtues dawn in us, but also the increase of vigour, energy, courage and confidence in life will be experienced. You will begin to enjoy innumerable advantages of concentrations and control of mind and efficiency in the field of action which will go to glorify all aspects of life - material, mental and spiritual. And then your world will be a better world. And then vegetarianism, rationalism, materialism, and even socialism or any other 'isms' of life will prove to be a useful 'ism' will be useful and successful 'ism' of life. Therefore my message is that-

If we want to establish real and good vegetarianism and if we want to live successfully any 'ism' of life - individual, social or national or international - it is first necessary to rise to Spiritualism and through Spiritualism we can successfully rise to an 'ism' according to our taste. All the 'isms' of life are good. But they become bad with the bad minds. Spiritualism trains the mind for all good. And so through Spiritualism can be lived any ism for all success in life. May be that you have been hearing till now that there are many pre-requisites for a spiritual life but I convey to you the message of the holy tradition of the Great Maharishi of India, I convey to you in the name of the spiritual master of India, His Divinity Swami Brahmananda Saraswathi Maharaj, the Illustrious in the galaxy of the Jagad Guru Sankaracharyas of India that it is easy to live spiritual life in the midst of all the material glories of the world. It is really easy to experience the Blissful Nature of the Divine through simple techniques of 'taking a dive within.' Just half an hour sitting in the morning and evening daily is quite sufficient to raise you up to the high pedestal of spiritual glories and at the same time increase your capacity of action in daily life. So there is key to lay open the gateway of all glory of life. You have come to

India from far off countries with the message of vegetarianism. Now Mother India wants you to go with the joy of the Divine and the glorious message of Spiritualism, and that through spiritualism will be established real, good and lasting vegetarianism - which is the action of this World Congress.'[120]

* * *

Using the city of Madras as his base, Maharishi hatched plans for a great event in celebration of the late Swami Brahmananda. The Seminar of Spiritual Luminaries was to be held in Mylapore from 29th-31st December 1957, where 'eminent saints and philosophers of all countries' were exhorted to attend. The stated reason for calling together these people was 'to contribute their experience in finding out a practical formula of spiritual regeneration of the world'.

Perhaps Maharishi was hoping that devotees of Swami Brahmananda would attend, for it would it would make his endeavours that much more easy if followers of his late master endorsed this initiative.

Sri P. S. G. Rao unveils the portrait of Guru Deva on the occasion of the inauguration of the Seminar.

On 29th December 1957, Sri P. S. G. Rao unveiled a portrait of Swami Brahmananda and recalled the *guru*:-
'I only want to bring home to you that although I had the good

fortune of his *darsan*, and of his elevating contact during the last Kumbh Mela at Allahabad, I know how great he was, how holy and divine. He was a real Jagad Guru, who felt for every body on earth and planned for the elevation of every soul everywhere, in every corner of the earth. I feel happy to reflect on one important aspect - his holy plan to spiritually rejuvenate the world and elevate the life of every one from the abyss of worries, troubles, miseries, distractions, and distortions to the high pedestal of permanent peace, bliss, and fulness of spiritual glory. As Shankaracharya, he was the head of the Hindu Religion and as such was under certain restrictions regarding his plan to elevate humanity. For 12 years he worked out his plans as Shankaracharya and at the age of 84 retired. The manifest merged into the unmanifest. Now his universal spirit has begun to work for the elevation of suffering humanity through his Brahmachari disciple, present with us, the blessed Maharishi Bala Brahmachari Mahesh Yogi, who has come out of the fastness of the Himalayas to shower the blessings of the Guru Deva in his Spiritual Development Camps. It is under his divine guidance that the 89th birthday of the Holy Master is being celebrated and under his effulgence is being held the Seminar of Spiritual Luminaries also, for the spiritual regeneration of the world.'[121]

It is said that the Seminar of Luminaries was attended by over 10,000 people and as the event drew to a close Maharishi asked those assembled there: 'Why can't we spiritually regenerate the world through this technique?'

Apparently his question drew tumultuous applause, prompting him to arrange a day's extension to the festivities. The Seminar's invitation to find 'a practical formula of spiritual regeneration of the world' proved to be somewhat self-fulfilling for on Wednesday, 1 January 1958 Maharishi announced:-

Spiritual Regeneration Movement is the natural consequence of the growing worries, and miseries in daily life of man everywhere in every part of the world and in every walk of human life- individual, national and international. Lack of spiritual development in man has resulted in decadence of even the human qualities in him. The resultant mental chaos, corruptions and restlessness everywhere is the direct outcome of the lack of spiritual development in man. We hold that intellectualism has failed to improve this deplorable state of human life, and right approach to spiritualism alone will succeed in curing this abiding ill of human existence..

To diagnose the cause of human ills and suffering it is necessary to find where the fault lies – Whether modern man fails to rise to spirituality to glorify his life or whether the current mode of spiritualism has failed to rise to the modern man to glorify him.
It is generally held that modern man is too much engrossed with the material glories of life and is too profoundly enamoured of the glare of increased material comforts of this scientific age and that is why it has become rather difficult for him to take to renunciation and rise to the glory of the soul. I hold a different view. I differ entirely from the age-old common concept of spiritualism which pleads for detachment as an essential pre-requisite for spiritual development.

Achievements of material science, the glare of increased material comfort, and the joys of the material world are not responsible for the spiritual degeneration of man. The candle light cannot possibly stop the spreading of the bright sunlight. Material glories of a limited nature cannot possibly afford to evade the dawn of the unlimited glories of the Soul. If a man is inside a room lit by a candle with doors closed, can he say that the candle is holding the man from opening the door and letting in the bright sunlight? It is as meaningless as saying that the candle light has put out the sunlight. Behaving in the world and enjoying the comforts of material life, one can easily lay open the gates of spiritual glory within him. Materialism cannot evade the dawn of spiritual glory in man. So it is wrong to blame the growth of modern materialism for the spiritual degeneration of man.

The main cause for the spiritual degeneration of society is the wrong approach to spiritualism preached in plenitude by the pioneers and pleaders of spiritual glory. Needless stress has been laid on detachment and renunciation for the realisation of the Divine.

The path of spiritual development through renunciation does not reconcile itself with the natural life of the majority. Renunciation is foreign to the way of life of the majority of the people who are householders, men of action in the world, whose life is naturally a life of attachment – not detachment or renunciation. Spiritual development through renunciation and detachment is an ideology of the order of the recluse and its application should be restricted to that order alone. When it is brought to the field of the householder it creates confusion. He feels that he is not in a position to detach himself from the responsibilities of an active life and if renunciation is essential for realisation, then unfortunately – he is not meant for it. Such an attitude in the majority of the people has created a gulf between materialism and spiritualism, breaking the natural harmony of the inner and outer life and leading, consequently to the spiritual degeneration of the man; depriving the majority of the great gains that spiritual development lays open to them.

We owe all reverence and devotion to all those who renounced the world, experienced bliss, and out of kindness, came back to the world to awaken us from the deep slumber of ignorance to rise to the glories of God and glorify our life. Their message of the 'great treasure hidden within' was right and for that we owe all gratitude to them, but the path of renunciation they advocated was not suited for the busy man of the world.

This fear of detachment has barred the majority from attempting on the spiritual side of life and led the people to feel content with the gross forms of prayer and worship, which though full of values, fail to satisfy the needs of peace and bliss in life. No doubt, prayer and worship, of Almighty are needed for peace and bliss in this life and hereafter, but a connecting link is needed to link the mind with the glories of the Divine. That link seems to be missing when the mind flies away at the time of prayer and worship. That link has to be supplied – the means of concentration has to be provided for everybody everywhere in the world. It is fro this that the Spiritual Regeneration Movement has been started.

The old order of spiritualists who advocate the need for detachment and renunciation for the realisation and glorification of life, could only be accepted in a changed form and increased value. The modern world would accept spiritualists which does not run away from the glories of material life. It must have strength enough of life to increase their lustre by the light of the inner self.

If spiritualism is to help the man of the 20th Century it must appear in a new garb to attract the modern eye and not frighten material life. If a spiritual technique of living the elevated material life is evolved, the modern taste would go for it. If the glories of the soul could be lived and enjoyed in the midst of the material glories of life modern taste would love to have it. If by some technique of the revelation, the light of the Divine could strengthen the values of material comforts of life, modern man would rush for it. The Spiritual Regeneration Movement has been started to meet this need of the present day.

It is clear to the Divine will working out the plan for spiritual regeneration of the world that the mode of spiritualism which has amply propagated either the sense of detachment and renunciation or the gross form of ritualism for the blessings of the Almighty, has failed to serve man in his quest for peace and happiness. The Divine Nature has therefore now planned to bring about regeneration through regenerated spiritualism which has the capacity to synthesise the two vital aspects of life- material and spiritual practically harmonising the material and spiritual 'isms' of life, the regenerated spiritualism coming on to us through the universal benevolence of the great spiritual Master, the Supreme, the Sage the Seer, Vedanta Incarnate, His Divinity Sri Swami Brahmananda Saraswati Maharaj, the Illustrious in the galaxy of Jagatguru Shankaracharyas of India.

We are only tools in the hands of His Will, we are only to act as He dictates – as the Lord said in the Gita "NIMITTA MATRAM BHAVA SAVYA SAACHIN"[122]

I invite all the spiritual leaders of the day and all leaders of public life, of all countries, to extend their co-operation to this movement for spiritual regeneration of the world which is directly the work of the Divine. It is directly for the raising of the life of everyone from the abysss of cares and anxieties and the high pedestal of spiritual glory to enable man to enjoy the glories of life – material, mental and spiritual.

The one aim of the Spiritual Regeneration Movement is to provide a simple and easy method of concentration and infuse the system of meditation in the daily life of everybody everywhere on earth. To meet this end, this movement has been started to work for the construction of meditation centres, everywhere in every part of human habitation. These meditation centres will provide all facilities to those desirous of enjoying the benefits of the control of mind, experience peace and spiritual joy in their daily life and increase their energy to be able to work more, quantitively and qualitatively, in the field of thought and action and to those who want to live and enjoy all the glories of life, earthly and heavenly.

We believe men are in need of something that would develop their latent faculties, help them to rise above the cares and anxieties of life to high pedestal of peace and happiness and increased efficiency I the field of action. Such men do not belong to any one particular province or land and they are not the followers of any one religion or philosophy. They are the citizens of the universe and are scattered all over the world, following different religions. For them all, is meant this Spiritual Regeneration Movement.[121]

In the following months, in addition to the holding of several more spiritual development camps, including ones in Madanapalle, Anantapur and Mylapore, and created a total of twenty-five new meditation centres across India.

Hon'ble Sri M. Anantasayanam Iyengar and the Maharishi are seen enjoying the divine effulgence of Guru Deva.

But even though the Spiritual Regeneration Movement was gaining momentum, by the Spring of 1958 Maharishi wanted to accelerate its growth even further:-

"One fine morning I thoughtfully reviewed the work done and calculated how much time it will take for the whole world with this rate and I found out that it will take 200 years (laughter).

Then I said 'No, I must change my ways of work'; then I thought what to do. Then I thought: I must go to the most advanced country because I thought – the country is most advanced because the people of that country would try something new very readily.[123]

'When I met some people in the morning I said, 'I want to go to America,' and they said, 'All right'."[124]

Letters giving news of Maharishi's desire to travel abroad were quickly dispatched to followers in Bombay, Calcutta and Madras. Within a few days there came a response: 'Send him here, he will stay with us for two weeks, and we will make all arrangements.'[48]

Arrangements were made, but the trip was delayed whilst travel documents were obtained. It seems that Maharishi had concerns about how his appearance, which he shared with friend Narayana Iyer, about the suitability of his wearing a white *dhoti*, rather than a orange coloured robe of a *swami*, as worn by Vivekananda (1863-1902) who famously spread the message of Hinduism to Japan, USA and Europe. The simple *dhoti* was of course strongly associated with Mahatma Mohandas Gandhi (1869-1948), the pre-eminent leader of India's independence movement.

* * *

Maharishi Leaves India for the West

On Sunday, 27th April 1958 Maharishi boarded a plane at Calcutta Airport bound, not for the United States of America, but for the neighbouring country of Burma. The wandering *brahmachari* attracted attention there and several lecture dates were organized, attended by a large complement of local men, women and children. This was the first clear indication that Maharishi's teachings were capable of attracting people from outside the specifically Hindu world. In May 1958, after ten days of talks and initiations, Maharishi flew from Rangoon in Burma to Bangkok in Thailand and then on to the Malaysian island of Penang

On Thursday, 22th May 1958 the *Times of Malaya* carried an interview in which Maharishi declared:-
> 'My system of meditation is a golden link to connect and harmonize materialism and spirituality. It is a direct process to integrate man's life on earth. I invite everyone to take the maximum advantage of my stay in Penang.'

In Penang, he found many Indian expatriates eager to receive his message, and even gained appreciation from the Sikh community, who are traditionally wary of Hindu doctrines.

The touring continued and by 14th June 1958 he had settled in Singapore working on plans for the establishment of a meditation centre there, and news came that a broadcast he had recorded for Radio Malaya was shortly to be broadcast. It was transmitted at 9pm on Thursday, 24 July, and for five minutes the airwaves resounded to his high-pitched tones as millions listened to his message.

MAHARSHI MAHESH YOGI'S MESSAGE
(Broadcast from Radio Malaya Singapore, 24th July 58 at 9 p.m.)

'Almost everywhere in the world every man is suffering from cares and anxieties in daily life. Man feels not the peace of mind. Why? Because he is not able to meet with his wants. He is not able to satisfy his desires. He lacks in proper means to fulfill his wants in daily life. He begins to think more and more how to acquire them, and when he fails to find proper means, he begins to feel worried and miserable.

This will be the miserable condition of man as long as he is not in a position to get whatever his desires. And the man will always be desiring for more and more till he gets permanent happiness of greatest order. *To desire for more and more happiness is the legitimate desire of man.* Nobody can be blamed for his desire of greater happiness. Everyman on earth must enjoy the maximum in life. I invite everybody to enjoy the greatest happiness, heavenly bliss in life here and now.

When we think about the joys of the world and try to locate the permanent abode of greatest happiness, we find that through our senses we are experiencing the charm of gross nature and the charm of the subtler fields of nature are not being experienced by us because *our senses can experience only the gross objectivity*. For example, our eyes are able to see only the gross form; when the form becomes very minute, our eyes fail to see it and we need a microscope. So our eyes are able to give us only the joy of gross forms and not of the minute forms. Similarly our sense of smell, the nose is able to smell only the gross smell; when the smell becomes faint and subtle the nose fails to smell it. Similarly our sense of taste. The tongue is able to experience the gross variety of tastes. When the taste becomes very fine the tongue fails to experience it. We know when the sweetness is increased in a sugar particle and when it becomes a particle of saccharine, then the tongue declares it to be sour. It only means that the tongue has not the capacity to experiencing the sweet taste when it is raised to a high degree.

In this manner we find that all our senses are capable of experiencing only the gross field of objectivity and they have not the capacity of experiencing minute field of nature.

So long as the mind is experiencing things through the senses it can only enjoy the glories of gross nature. The glories of subtle fields of nature are much more charming than those of the gross field of nature.

Real joy of life lies in the field of subtle nature, behind the field of sense perception. It is the field of subtle form, subtle sound, subtle smell, subtle taste and subtle touch which the senses cannot appreciate but the mind can very well perceive. So we find that the gross field of nature being experienced by senses is not charming and fascinating as is the field of subtle nature which can be perceived directly by the mind and if our mind could go on experiencing subtler and subtler fields of nature, it would experience greater and greater charm as it advances towards the ultimate subtlety of nature and transcending the subtlest nature the mind would directly experience the nature of the Transcendental Reality which is BLISS, ETERNAL AND ABSOLUTE.

This is the path of experiencing greatest happiness, the BLISS OF THE ABSOLUTE.

All the joys of world whether they are pertaining to the field of gross nature or subtle field of nature, they are of relative character and so long as the mind experience the joys of relative order it would always be hankering for more and more. Unless the mind has experienced the greatest joy of relative field and unless it has transcended it to experience the Absolute Bliss, it will not be satisfied in a permanent manner. And unless the mind is satisfied and contented for its thirst of joy it cannot experience lasting peace. If man wants to live in peace permanently it is necessary for him to withdraw the mind from the gross filed of sense perception for some time and take a dive within, and directly experience the glories of subtle nature within himself, and finally experience the Absolute Bliss.

Having experienced the Bliss, the Mind would be contented and satisfied for its thirst of joy. This contentment of the mind will naturally keep it un-wavering and steady. The mind will not unnecessarily wander here and there and will naturally be established in lasting peace. Apart from experience of peace, thought force will increase and will be enjoyed all advantages of a controlled mind. This obviously adds to man's capacity and efficiency of work in his daily life. These are of course material gains of the spiritual experience.

Man should have a clear view of life and the true perspective of values in life. We should give all due importance to the material values of life, but should not overestimate them. We should be cautious that they are not overbalanced. Overestimating the values of material life has always had a danger of ignoring and missing the more charming glories of inner life and the experience of great happiness that is present in everybody's heart.

One must be able to live and enjoy all aspects of life, material, mental and spiritual. *My message is the message of a flower*, a flower invites everybody to enjoy the outer beauty of it and also to enjoy the honey within it. I invite everybody to enjoy all glories of material life and also to enjoy the inner glories of life through a simple process of meditation which directly leads the mind from the gross to the subtler fields of nature and ultimately leading it to the Blissful realm of the absolute. I have found this easy to take a dive within and experience the great happiness. And it is the experience of thousands of people coming in my contact that they begin to feel calmness of mind, more energy and happiness in their daily life within two or three sittings of meditation

I reject the idea of disciplining the mind for a long time in order to experience the Bliss. Why should a long discipline or long training to the mind be necessary for the experience of Bliss when the mind is already searching for more and more happiness?

I admit that man's mind wanders but the fact remains that it is wandering only in search of some great joy. *The mind is wandering only to settle down somewhere in Bliss.* So to lead the mind to Bliss, it is only necessary to change the phase of experience. It is only necessary to change the face of mind from outward to inward. And the very first step in the inward direction begins to feed the mind with greater charm. Then the mind is only enamoured to march on and on. Spontaneously it goes deep inside experiencing greater charm at every step. Every aspirant finds that the mind rushes on to inward Bliss from the very beginning of practice. Spirituality has long been considered in terms of utter difficulty, strenuous and long discipline and negation of material life, but in contradistinction to this approach I have found that through a proper method of meditation spirituality can be realised in a short time in an easy manner and man can find peace and happiness in a permanent manner right now in the present life. I hold that every man and woman has an innate capacity to enjoy the Bliss for the Blissful Divine Omnipresent exists in the heart of everybody.

For the last two years I have been giving out this easy system of meditation to the various types of people in India and I have found that it miraculously works for the people of all tastes, all varieties, of all ages and all circumstances in life. To give it a wide publicity for the benefit of all *I have started a Spiritual Regeneration Movement in India and in that connection I have come out for a world tour.* The main purpose is to infuse this simple and easy system of deep meditation in daily routine of man everywhere so that everybody may enjoy peace and happiness in his daily life and world may be re-generated into the values of spirit, into the values of morality and virtue, peace and happiness of lasting nature.

Out of India I have visited till now Rangoon, Bangkok, Penang, Kuala Lampur and Singapore. Everywhere I find great response and enthusiasm from the people for my practical message of peace and happiness. Everywhere people have felt that they had not heard and known before that peace and happiness in life could be had so easily and cheaply. *All glory to my Lord the Great Spiritual Master His Divinity, Swami Brahmananda Saraswathi the Head of Hindu Religion in India, Shree Jagath Guru Shankaracharya of Jyotir Mutt Badrikashram in the Himalayas*, at whose feet I have lived a life of complete surrender for thirteen years and whose grace I am showering on all.

In public lectures I always declare that peace and happiness n daily life is easy through my system of meditation. Control of mind is easy development of latent faculties is easy for everybody who can devote a few minutes in the morning and evening in deep meditation according to my practical guidance. It has been widely accepted by the people that *this easy system of deep meditation is a glorious link to connect and harmonise materialism and spiritualism in life*. It does not need a negation of any aspect of material life for success in spiritual experience.

On the other hand spiritual experience gained through this meditation directly goes to add all glories of material life. I have found *people of all religions and nationalities have been deriving equal advantage of this system of meditation* which is only a technique of living in peace and happiness, which is the key to open the gates of heaven in life of man on earth.

I am convinced that if this system of deep meditation is introduced in the educational system everywhere the coming generation will be very energetic and advancing, *all the disruptive forces will be eliminated once for all* and a new humanity will be born.

It is a boon for everybody. May the suffering humanity through this meditation take refuge in the Blissful nature of the DIVINE OMNIPRESENT.

JAI GURU DEV[125]

From Singapore Maharishi returned to Penang where he set about establishing another Spiritual Development Centre and training more Spiritual Guides to continue his work.

Back in India, devotees were kept abreast of news with handwritten epistles sent by Maharishi chronicling the movement's progress. The Madras mission took to publishing a newsletter, known as the *'Torch Divine'*, the first edition was produced in July 1958 whilst he was still in Singapore.

By mid-August 1958 the Singapore meditation centre was ready to be opened and the occasion was celebrated at the city's Victoria Memorial Hall. Of those who spoke at the opening on 17 August, the testimony of one speaker, a business magnate, is of particular note:-

> 'Within 3 or 4 days of the initiation, I was able to meditate without any obstacles or foreign ideas disturbing my mind, and sometimes I am forgetting myself in serene silence when I enjoy unspeakable happiness, calmness, and Peace. Now I always feel with full of spiritual vigour and happiness. Swamiji is grand like the Himalayas wherefrom he comes, but humble like a child, Great like Truth but simple like love.[126]

The next trip was to be his longest yet, for his destination lay in faraway Hong Kong, where he quickly set about forming a meditation centre, to be called the Happy Valley. Maharishi announced:-

> 'Salutations and prostrations to the hoary Greats of the universe appearing from time to time, from time immemorial to smoothen the path of Salvation: starting right from the Great Almighty Lord Narayana, Shiva, Rama, Krishna, Buddha, Christ, Mohammad, Guru Nanak Dev, Bhagwan Shankaracharya, Tulsi, Soor, Kabir and the Great Spiritual Master Shri Guru Deva Swami Brahmananda Saraswati Bhagwan and all the Spiritual Master of the past and present who have been shaping the spiritual destiny of man and have been the Guiding Lights of the world and who are directly responsible for the great inspiration of the present Spiritual

Regeneration Movement to bring happiness and all round development of man's life in every part of human civilization.'[127]

On 8th September Maharishi spoke at the Hindu Temple, regarding the responsibilities of the managing committees of temples.

"These managing bodies stand between the deity and the devotee, between man and God in the temples. They have a super human responsibility. They have to manage the affair in a way so that the spiritual power of the deity is maintained and devotees get maximum grace of the Lord. Spiritual power of the deity is maintained by proper modes of worship and devotees gain maximum grace if they are receptive to Divine Grace. What do I mean by receptivity of the devotees?

Supposing a man comes out of his shop or office and goes before the deity in the temple; his mind is full of worries and thoughts of the outside world. He prostrates and worships with a mind full of other thoughts. If the mind is wandering elsewhere, then where is the receptivity for the Divine Grace? The blessings of the Lord are not received. The divine current is reflected back and the devotee returns from the temple as he entered in – without any divine charge. This is not the correct manner of going to temples for divine grace. If you are going in a temple just for sightseeing, just for enjoying the decorations on the deity, then you may go anyway; but if you want to go before the deity for getting Divine Grace, then first sit quiet for a few minutes in some lonely place of the temple. Meditate for some time. Calm down your mind. Get rid of worldly thoughts. Let the mind, in peace, be raised to some degree to the Divine level. Then you become receptive to Divine Grace. In such a state of pure, calm and elevated mind, go before the deity, worship and prostrate. You will feel the divine thrill, you will experience a surcharge of divine power. Receive it and again quietly retire to a silent place nearby. Sit again in silence for a few minutes to assimilate the blessings. And then leave the temple to enjoy God's Grace in all walks of life.

For this it is very necessary that the temple management should provide the facility of meditation rooms. Just small meditation rooms, each for a man to sit in silence. In the absence of meditation rooms the devotees are not able to receive that much gain which can be achieved from the temples. This is the main reason why all these places of worship are being ignored by the modern trend. It is not the fault of the people to ignore a thing which does not prove worthy of its advertisement. Temples have been advertised from times immemorial as centres of Godhood on earth, the great reservoirs of divine energy; but when a devotee fails to receive it, his doubting is legitimate. Do not blame anybody for doubting. He is expressing to you his doubts only to remove them. Help him if you can. If the managing committee of the temples are really sincere and if they want to develop faith and devotion in the minds and hearts of the people, let them sincerely respond to this call of Spiritual Regeneration Movement and erect meditation rooms in their temples. This system of meditation rooms in the temples will safeguard their validity and increase their utility."[128]

A meditation centre was founded in Hong Kong and the inauguration was officiated by a local magistrate, Mr Hing Shing Lo. Maharishi then addressed the assembled crowd and confidently pointed out that 'everybody has the capacity for Deep Meditation'. Clarifying the role of the centre, he told its staff:

'It will be the sacred duty of the management to drum into the ears of the people that here is a place where everybody can get the key to all peace and happiness in life.'[129]

Whilst in Hong Kong, Maharishi wrote a message the editor of the *'Torch Divine'*:-

"Let it be known to all our Guru Bhaiis, new and old and to all the Devotees of our Lord that His 90th Birthday Anniversary is approaching fast with a great significance and purpose and has a special message to deliver to the world. I request every devotee everywhere to collectively celebrate this day in a grand manner and feel His Divine Grace and remind to the public of His great message of Love, Peace, Harmony and Bliss."[130]

On the 13th December 1958 Maharishi wrote a message for readers of the *'Torch Divine,* and in it he highlighted the importance of Swami Brahmananda, 'Guru Deva':-

"When I review the progress of one year of this great movement I find myself between gain and loss. In the beginning I thought, one year would be sufficient for the Light to spread in all countries but when I came out of India six months ago I found it was easy to give out a flash of the Divine Glory without loss of time, but to establish permanent Light Houses of that Great Effulgence needs more time in each place. So my movements were not as quick as originally planned. In six months I could only reach the Far East borders of Asia.

Guru Deva's wish to spiritually regenerate every place, is growing more intense as I move ahead. His message has so far spread satisfactorily out of India to the South East and Far East Asian Countries. Centres have been opened in many places to keep on guiding all the people all the time.

As I experienced in India, I am experiencing in these parts also. Even the 'hardest rocks are found melting under the great heat of the Rising Sun of Guru Deva's Grace. Materialistic hearts of iron are being transformed into spiritual hearts of gold. The Divine Grace is rising up like a high tide to envelope the various currents of the growing materialism. It is rising up as a typhoon in the atmosphere to have its own influence all around the people are feeling, the evil is suppressed by itself. Guru Deva's Grace is Great. We have only to realise it."[131]

At a farewell party arranged by the Hong Kong Meditation Centre, at the Hindu Temple in Happy Valley, Maharishi explained a little about the position that his master held:-

'Sri Guru Deva, His Divinity Swami Brahmananda Saraswati the Great Jagad Guru Bhagwan Shankaracharya, under whose universal Benevolence are being established such meditation centres everywhere in the world. It may be mentioned here that Jagadguru Shankaracharya is the title of the head of Hindu Religion as 'Pope' is in the Christianity. The easy system of successful meditation (for Divine Revelation and better material circumstances in life of everybody) which is being initiated in this Meditation Centre has come to us through the Grace of this Great Divine Personality and highest Authority on Religion and Spirituality in India.'[132]

Moving on from Hong Kong, Maharishi planned to spend to spend only two days in Honolulu but was prevailed upon to stay longer - one month longer as it happened. *Honolulu Star Bulletin* told its readers about this visitor:-

'He has no money; he asks for nothing. His worldly possessions can be carried in one hand. Maharishi Mahesh Yogi is on a world odyssey. He carries a message that he says will rid the world of unhappiness and discontent ...'[133]

MEDITATION

EASY SYSTEM PROPOUNDED BY
MAHARISHI MAHESH YOGI

INTERNATIONAL MEDITATION CENTRE
HONOLULU, HAWAII

Someone in Honolulu asked him 'How does meditation improve the fortune of a man?' Maharishi's answer was as follows:-

'Our system of meditation involves the All Mighty Power. We take the 'MANTRA' of some God according to our faith and meditate on that. The power of the 'MANTRA' brings to us the Almighty. When we proceed in meditation we find that our MANTRA becomes finer and finer. When the MANTRA becomes finer, the power of the MANTRA increases to fetch more blessings of the Almighty. With this increases the fortune of the devotee. In this manner our system of meditation improves the fortune of man. It is no exaggeration of facts. It is only the explanation of the experiences of aspirants and a logical answer of the 'HOW'.

This is the answer for those who believe in God, the Manifested Aspect of the Unmanifested, Omnipresent, Omnipotent, Divine Power. Now we shall see how this question is answered for those who do not believe in God, but who believe in their own efforts.

Good fortune is the result of our good deeds, and misfortune is the result of our bad deeds or sinful actions. Sins are burnt away in the fire of Divine Experience during meditation. Thus meditation destroys the very cause of misfortune and leaves the man to enjoy the results of good deeds alone. This is how meditation destroys the dark side of life and brings forth the bright side of all fortune in life.

Now I will answer this question in terms of modern scientific terminology:
According to the findings of the present material science, the ultimate reality is electronic and protonic energy - capable of being transformed into different objects. All the different objects are nothing but different modes of vibrations of the electronic energy. Every thing that is experienced is but a particular setup of vibrations of particular frequencies. Because the whole creation is nothing but vibration, everything is always being affected by every other thing in creation. Vibrations produced by thought, speech and action of everybody is influencing the whole nature.

Vibrations produced by any thought and action may be

classified by two types of effects - favourable and unfavourable. Good and virtuous thoughts and actions produce vibrations of favourable effects for the doer and for the whole creation. Bad and sinful thoughts and actions produce detrimental effects for the doer and for the whole creation. Mantras are special syllables whose vibrations are more powerful than those of the other syllables. There are various types of Mantras to produce various types of vibrations for different effects. Mantras suited for the life of a house-holder are different from the Mantras suited to the life of a SANYASI or a monk who has renounced all pleasures of the world.

Our system of meditation is mainly through the mantras properly suited to the way of life of the aspirant; for the house-holder our mantras have constructive values in all fields of life. These vibrations influence the whole field of creation, making all powers of nature favourable to the aspirant - making friends of enemies and influencing the whole atmosphere for all love and harmony and prosperity for all good.

This is the scientific explanation of how our system of meditation improves the fortune of man.[134]

The interest shown in Maharishi's philosophical thinking and in the practice of meditation he had been teaching during the nine months or so since he left India, further endorsed his firm belief in his mission:-

'In my childhood I thought I was hearing Americans are most advanced. Just with this thought, and I had one thing in mind - that I know something which is useful to every man; therefore no matter where I am people will find in me the commodity that they want. (laugh) With that confidence I left India and gradually I came to the States.'[135]

In the January 1959 issue of *'Torch Divine'*, a selection of quotations from Swami Brahmananda Saraswati were published:-

Drops of Nectar

(Sayings of Shree Guru Deva, "Vedanta Incarnate", His Divinity Swami Brahmananda Saraswathi Maharaj, the illustrious Jagadguru Shankaracharya, Jyotir Mutt, Badrikashramam.)

Having become a devotee of God one can never remain unhappy anywhere. This is our experience.

* * * *

People are unhappy because they do not have "ISHTA" (chosen Deity). Without 'Ishta' people are turning out to be orphans.

* * * *

It is only the 'ISHTA' that saves one from 'ANISHTA' (Untoward happenings).

* * * *

See your 'ISHTA' as all-pervading. That is 'ANANYATHA' (one pointed devotion).

* * * *

Among Vishnu, Shankara, Devi, Surya and Ganesha, none is greater or smaller. All of them are quite capable of bestowing on their devotees all that is good in its entirety.

* * * *

By repetition of the "Manthra" given to you by your Guru as per your qualifications, your sins shall be destroyed.

* * * *

Develop fully one 'ISHTA'; then no 'ANISHTA' can ever befall you.

* * * *

By doing Japa your sins shall be destroyed, JAPATO NASTI PATHAKAM.

* * * *

Of the five Deities Shankara, Vishnu, (Rama, Krishna), Surya, Ganesha and Devi, whosoever is more adorable to you the Manthra of that Deity should be repeated by you everyday.

* * * *

You must get to know the Manthra of your 'ISHTA' and the method of 'Dhyana' thereof, through an experienced 'SATGURU' and somehow or other devote some time every day for Japa of the 'Ishta Manthra' and Dhyana.

* * * *

Through Japa "SIDDHI" (Realisation) shall result. There is no doubt about this. "JAPAT SIDDHIR JAPAT SIDDHIR JAPAT SIDDHIR NASAMSAYAM".

* * * *

See your 'ISHTA' everywhere. There should be no place where your 'ISHTA' is not seen.

* * * *

It is absolutely difficult to get the vision of your 'ISHTA' until and unless you get one pointedness on your ISHTA. To cure a disease both "OUSHADA" (medicine) and "PATHYA" (Dietic Restriction) are necessary. To cure the disease of restlessness of the mind "ABHYASA" (Practice) is "OUSHADA" and 'VAIRAGYA' (Detachment) is PATHYA.

To apply your mind to your ISHTA is ABHYASA.

To constantly think of ISHTA, meditate on it, talk always about It and think always about It is ABHYASA.

When the mind is engrossed in the ISHTA, detachment automatically comes in. Therefore, we say you need become a "RAGI" (a person having attachment). That is to say there is need for the mind to develop attachment to the ISHTA.

* * * *

Let constant thinking of God be the main work for the mind and carrying on "VYAVAHARA" (worldly activities) only secondary. In that case you will have "LADDOOS", (sweets) in both hands.

* * * *

There is no need to apply your mind entirely in order to carry on "VYAVAHARA."

It is possible to carry on "VYAVAHARA" with only a little co-operation of the mind.

* * * *

Just like the Miser whose mind, even while attending to VYAVAHARA, mainly and constantly thinks of the money, you should be attending to VYAVAHARA while your mind mainly and constantly think of God.[136]

* * * *

More quotations of Swami Brahmananda were published in the following issue of *'Torch Divine'*:-

Having become a devotee of God one can never remain unhappy anywhere. This is our experience.

* * *

The "JIVA is going on doing its work from several births. Its tendency to work exists since times immemorial. Therefore if the work is just started with a little co-operation of the mind it shall continue to go on just like the Wagon moving a long way off, if it is just jerked and pushed by the Engine.

* * *

It is necessary to bifurcate the work of the mind as main and secondary. Thinking of God should be considered as main and giving a little co-operation to carry on VYAVAHARA also as secondary.

* * *

Apply your body and wealth mainly, and your mind secondarily, to run the VYAVAHARA.

* * *

When the Mind is mainly engaged in (Thinking of) God, you shall receive His grace. God is All-Powerful (SARVA SHAKTIMAN). Even a little of His Grace is capable of bestowing on the JIVA all that is good in its entirety.

* * *

The declaration of the Lord that is proved by the Vedic Scriptures is this: "WHOSOEVER THINKS OF ME WITH ONE-POINTED DEVOTION, I SHALL CONDUCT HIS NECESSARY VYAVAHARA ALSO". The experience of the BHAKTAS also goes to prove this declaration of the Lord.

* * *

Accumulate "ARTHA" (wealth); but in such a way that it is not against "PARAMATHA" (ultimate good). That which hinders 'PARAMARTHA' and results in accumulation of Sin is not 'ARTHA' but 'ANARTHA' (negation of wealth).

* * *

As is the cloth, so is the price. For carrying on the short-lived activities of 'VYAVAHARA,' employ your short-lived body and wealth. Mind is a permanent thing which remains with you always. Even in the other world it will continue to stay with you. Therefore connect it with a permanent thing. God, being the eternal existence both in animate and inanimate things, is the only permanent thing of the highest order. Connect your mind with Him.

* * *

If the mind is satisfied with wealth, wife or children, why does it go elsewhere? Because, it cannot stick on to anything. From this it is clear it is not satisfied with any thing of this mundane world. It runs after things taking them to be good and desirable but after a short while it leaves them.

Nobody wants your mind in this world and mind also is not satisfied with any thing of this world.

The mind is not fit for the world nor the world for the mind.

* * *

When the mind realises God, it is permanently established there and shall not desire for other things. From this we can understand that God alone is fit for the mind and nothing else.

Keep in mind, that your mind which is not wanted by any body in this world is useful to take you near God.

Therefore, in this market place of the World, carry on

VYAVAHARA with your body and wealth and allow your mind to go towards God.
Then your VYAVAHARA in this world will get on well and the path to PARAMARTHA will also be clear.[137]

H.H. Maharshi Mahesh Yogi—In Contemplation.

Reception accorded to His Holiness Maharishi Mahesh Yogi at the newly built temple of the Jen Sen Taoism Budhism Association of San Francisco—1

International Meditation Society (IMS)

On 29th January 1959 Maharishi left Hawaii, and upon his arrival in the USA, was booked himself into a hotel room in San Francisco. There he gave talks to visitors, and after several weeks was invited to take up residence in a local apartment. He also spoke regularly at the newly built temple of the 'Jen Sen Taoism Buddhism Association of San Francisco, 1340 Pacific Avenue':-

> 'I gave one lecture and there was a couple, couple, a lady and a man - her husband, and they knew that I was staying in some small hotel there which was organised by the people of Honolulu and they thought that in that place many people would not be able to meet me at all. They had some big apartment somewhere; they took me there and from that day I was speaking every day in one organisation in San Francisco, gave about 29 lectures and every evening the whole thing was full and ... because people found something which they thought can't be false; even though they didn't understand what transcendental meditation was, when they heard me and they asked questions they thought even if they don't understand - but the man seemed to be able to ... (loud laughter), so they were not afraid of me, and when they started to meditate, then they became the - they became propagandist about it. They spread it; quickly it spread.'[135]

During his stay in San Francisco Maharishi received his first press coverage in the USA and was rather surprised that the meditation had been dubbed a 'non-medicinal tranquilizer'. His comments are worth noting.

> 'Cruel ...! I feel like running away, back home. This seems to be a strange country. Values are different here.'[138]

Whilst there were undoubtedly many who would be attracted to the ideals of the Spiritual Regeneration Movement (SRM), others might be content with something less if it could offer the effects of a relaxant pill. Anyway, on 30th March 1959, Maharishi founded another organisation, one with a more neutral sounding name; the International Meditation Society (IMS).

On Wednesday 29th April 1959, after three months in San Francisco, Maharishi flew to Los Angeles Airport and promptly gave a press conference at the Ambassador Hotel, where he told the audience of his intention to spiritually regenerate the entire world and explained how this might be achieved:-

> 'I have brought from the Himalayas the fulfilment of every man's need in this fast tempo of modern living.'

> 'I have brought from the land of ancient sages to the modern man of this new world a simple technique of living in peace and happiness'[139]

Next morning, Duane Duzan of the *'Mirror News'* noted:-
> 'It is a system of ultrasonically induced deep meditation," said the Hindu, "whereby man can achieve inner peace and happiness and outer harmony in life'[140]

Apparently, the issue of tranquillisers had been raised, which had elicited this observation from Maharishi:-
> "They are a great misery on the whole world. Meditation is a non-medicinal tranquilizer, and it has no evil effects."[140]

The 'simple technique' was of course the 'system of ultrasonically induced deep meditation', which the *brahmachari* had been giving instruction in, since relocating to South India following the death of Swami Brahmananda Saraswati and the controversy over the contents of his Will.

The 'Herald Express' writer, Ted Hilgenstuhler, wrote:-
> 'Just a few magic sounds uttered from the mouth of His Holiness Maharishi Mahesh Yogi could change this often troubled world of ours into a heaven on earth for every human being.

Wars would cease. All psychosomatic illnesses would vanish. People would lead happier, longer, and more fruitful lives.'

"I will fill the world with love," he said.'[141]

The *'Los Angeles Examiner'* ran an article by Ted Thackrey entitled 'YOGI GIVES INSTANT MEDITATION':-

'Mystic East met Mystified West at the Ambassador Hotel yesterday.'

'Maharishi Mahesh Yogi, from Uttar-Kashi, India, sat on his deer skin and smiled affably while he tried to explain his 'Sputnik Method" of learning meditation in a hurry. It brings peace he said, with the first easy lesson.'

'Profusely bearded and clad in a white, flowing robe, the Yogi fingered one of the three strands of beads around his neck and listened to a rose – sniffed it sometimes, too – as he said:

"My life truly began 16 years ago at the feet of my Master when I learned the secret of swift and deep meditation, a secret I now impart to the world." ….. Thus far, he has established 50 meditation centres which teach his hurry-up contemplation method.

'His first in the Western world was dedicated last week in San Francisco. Now he has come to set up another one. He will live with a follower in Hollywood.'

"I do not worry about where the necessary money will come from," said he. Be assured that it will come when people learn how simple and swift – is my method of meditation. Americans like anything they can do in a hurry.'[141]

A few days later, the *Los Angeles Times* carried a small ad advising readers about a forthcoming series of talks to be held at an actors club in Hollywood:-

>Maharishi Mahesh Yogi
>Master from the Himalayas
>Valley of the Saints – Uttar Kashi
>Will speak at the Masquers Club
>May 1 to May 7 – Phone …

The first talk at the Masquers Club had a brief introduction by Richard Sedlecheck, Maharishi's host in Hollywood. Then, Maharishi sat for a while in silence before quietly intoning what sounded like a prayer:-

>*'vande bodhamayan nityan gurun shankara ruupinam.*
>*yamaashrito hi vakroapi chandrah sarvatra vandyate..*
>
>*andhasya gyaanaajana shalakayaa.*
>*chakshuruunmilitam yena tasmai shri gurave namah..*
>
>*naaraayanam padmabhavam vasishtham shaktim cha*
>*tatputraparaasharam cha.*
>*vyaasam shukam gaudapadam mahaantam*
>*govindayogindramathaasya shishyam..*
>
>*shri shankaraachaaryamathaasya padmapaadam cha*
>*hastaamalakam cha shishyam.*
>*tam trotakam vaarttikakaaramanyaan asmataguruun*
>*santatamaanatosmi.'*[142]

It is unlikely that anyone in the room could either hear or understand what he was saying. But had they been able to hear his words and have a very good grasp of Sanskrit they would have understood him to be reciting ancient verses in praise of the *guru*, which translated would read something like:-

'I make obeisance to the eternal preceptor in the form of Lord Shankara, who is all wisdom, and resting on whose brow the crescent moon, though crooked in shape, is universally adored.

He who applies the collyrium of knowledge with a sharp pencil to open the eyes blinded, to the blessed *guru* I bow down.

To Narayana, to lotus-born Brahma, to Vasishtha, to Shakti and his son, Parashara,
to Vyasa, to Shukadeva, to the great Gaudapada, to Govinda, to Yogindra, (ruler among *yogis*), and then his disciple.

To the lotus feet of Shri Shankaracharya (Adi Shankara), to his pure disciples Padmapada, Hastamalaka, to him Trotakacharya, to Sureshwara, to others, to our tradition of *gurus*, I bow down.'

Having finished his recitation of the Sanskrit prayer, Maharishi then spoke in English:-

'My salutations and prostrations to the holy greats of the universe coming on from time-to-time to smooth the path of salvation. My salutations to Lord Shankara, Lord Buddha, Lord Christ and all the great masters of all religions, who are the direct source of inspiration to the Spiritual Regeneration Movement, which is a timely call for the people of the world to rise to the highest pedestal of peace and happiness in their day-to-day life.'

'Through a simple process of meditation, meditation that unveils the latent faculties and brings to light the vital forces hidden in the inner personality of everybody. As Christ has said; "Kingdom of heaven is within me", the kingdom of heaven that dwells, that sphere which knows no misery. Heaven, peace and happiness of greatest order and of permanent nature in the kingdom of heaven. And that is the subtlest aspect of our own personality. As long as we are out of contact with that inner state of being which is bliss, pure bliss, happiness of greatest order and permanent nature. As long as we are out of contact, so long our life is incomplete. We are devoid of the best in life.

Obviously enough, ...'[142]

At that point Maharishi was interrupted by a man who asked the audience if they could all hear. There was a mixed response. So, after some adjustment to Maharishi's microphone, the talk continued:-

'As long as a millionaire is out of contact of the treasury, he is no longer a millionaire. You may think that the treasury is in his possession and he is a millionaire, but as long as the contact with the treasury is not made, no longer the joys of the millionaire. So, if we lose the contact with the treasures of the inner self the life is very incomplete.

We have the gross aspect of our life. We have the subtle aspect of our life. We have the transcendental aspect of our life, which is our option.'[142]

A local couple, Helena Olson and her husband, Roland, planned to attend a talk at the Masquers Club:-

'The thought of a Master from the Far East at the Hollywood actors club was exhilarating. I could hardly wait.'[143]

The Olsons enjoyed the talk and afterwards overheard someone saying that Maharishi was staying in an apartment but that what he needed was to stay in "a big, old house". Well, the Olsons lived in just such a place and after discussing the idea, invited Maharishi to come and live with them, an invitation he accepted.

They explained the situation to their 15-year-old daughter, Tina.
"'He is a yogi or Holy Man from the Himalayas. I am not much up on Holy Men, but I understand they are Hermits and know many things."

Tina thought it over for a moment.
"Then what in the world is he doing here and where is he staying now?"

"He is staying with a young man over in Hollywood, but it's noisy there and he needs a very quiet place for whatever it is he teaches.'"[144]

The evening after Maharishi arrived at the Olsons, he announced to them:-
"I will initiate you in the morning"[145]

Now, the Olsons were ordinary Americans without any specific knowledge about Hinduism or *yoga*, so how then would they react to Maharishi asking them about their *"Ishta-Devata"*, their chosen god or goddess, as he had asked Mr & Mrs Menon, in Ernakulum, several years before?

As it happens, Helena harboured doubts about the 'initiation':-
"'What do you suppose we are getting into?" I asked my husband as I looked through my closet to find a suitable white dress.

"I don't think it is anything we need to worry about. As far as I can make out from his lectures, he has to give us a certain word to repeat. When we say that word, our minds become quiet automatically and we can get to the Transcendental consciousness."

"If it's that simple, why doesn't he just whisper the word to us and not bother with initiation? I've had enough ceremony and rituals to last me a lifetime. I don't care about not having any more.'"[145]

The couple met with Maharishi in the hall and followed him to where they were to be initiated.
"'- - pungent incense, small lights, little dishes, candles, pictures of his Master, vases and vases of flowers.

No words were spoken and in the quiet as we stood with him, something of the world fell away. The essence of wisdom and serenity, and of purity filled the room. I could not help but think, 'This man speaks to us through silence.'

In the first few seconds I felt my entire being quicken, and then a penetrating sensation of warmth. A flood of delight, of love.

After some time, a soft voice whispered, "Open your eyes." Roland and I opened our eyes to look into each others'. I gasped at the sight of Roland's face. It was serene, yet glowing. All the drawn, serious lines seemed erased. His eyes were large and shining. I hoped mine were the same.

Maharishi had fulfilled his promise of Bliss.

We sat for a moment, then Roland said, "The word you gave me, -- does it mean anything at all?"

"No," said Maharishi. "It has no meaning. That is why it can carry you from the conscious level of thought. If you repeat innocently as a child, you will go within very deep. It is like a boat to carry the mind to Bliss."

"What sort of a 'Word is this, - - is it for Christians?"

Maharishi smiled. "These words were known many, many centuries before there were Christian words, and the effects of saying these words are well known. This is the ancient Vedic tradition that is passed down through our Masters. If you had a Christian word, you would associate thoughts and you would be trapped on the conscious level of thought. My words are just words. They do not belong to any religion. Do you feel happy?"

"Oh, yes, I certainly do. I want to thank you for coming to our home and giving us this blessing," said Roland.

To me, Maharishi said, "How do you feel?"

I laughed a high, little nervous laugh. He seemed puzzled. I wanted to say so much, but I simply could not formulate any questions or define my feelings. In answer, I whispered, "Thank you."

As I sat there holding the flower he gave me, I looked up to see a beautiful smile on his face.

"Do this a few minutes regularly morning and evening. We shall discuss it more in the lectures."'[146]

During Maharishi's stay at the Olsons' house at 433 Harvard Boulevard, Los Angeles, the place turned into a teaching centre and became very busy, with many people going there to hear Maharishi and to learn to meditate.

"Meditation is the non-medicinal tranquilizer," Maharishi would say, "but that is only one of the by-products. When we plant an apple tress, the main purpose is to have apples, but long before the apples are ready, we enjoy the shade of the tress. The shade is a by-product. Release of tension is a by-product of Meditation. It is just automatic."[147]

By mid-June it had been decided to establish an 'International Meditation Center' of the Spiritual Regeneration Movement. Helena Olsen asked Maharishi about this organisation:-

"It is a good thing," he said. "I am free to carry on the spiritual work. I am not for money and rules and things like that. A board of trustees can see to those things."[148]

The idea was for the organisation to deal with Maharishi's travel arrangements, raise funds, find suitable venues for lectures and get publicity materials published. The officers of the organisation were to be; Dr John Smith Hislop Ph.D., a businessman and former professor of English, would be President, Charlie Lutes, another businessman, who generally chauffeured Maharishi about, would be Vice-President, and Roland Olsen with his accounting background, would be Treasurer.

It had so far been assumed that those who learned meditation would be happy to make donations towards the various costs, and a basket was therefore placed outside Maharishi's room:-

'And I felt very ashamed with that basket on the door and people coming to myself. It was just like begging on the door and, it was, I, it was too odd to me to put a basket in front of my room. When the people are missed from… and the donations were coming something.'

'And about money I had never thought, and it was just out of my, out of my life completely. And then I said what we should do, and back and forth quite a lot of arguments and then I said, "Let us, let us fix".'[149]

Perhaps Maharishi was thinking of his master, who had a sign erected to warn visitors that no financial contributions were to be made to him. Perhaps, as Maharishi himself said, he just felt ashamed of appearing as a beggar, but instead of moving the basket elsewhere and staying with the idea of meditators making voluntary contributions he put forward an idea that was not only bold but shocking. Maharishi wondered whether a regulated pattern of financial support could be arranged, a fixed 'donation'. After a fair amount of discussion, the idea was agreed on and a figure was set, of one week's wages per family.

Traditionally, the idea of charging a pupil for learning to meditate seemed abhorrent. Guru Dev quoted Tulsidas:-

"harai shishya dhana shoka na harai.
so gura ghora naraka mahun parai."[150]

'He who takes the wealth of the disciple
but does not take away the sorrow,
that *guru* will be sent to a horrible hell.'

Guru Dev explained clearly why he never accepted donations himself:-

'When I accept any pupil, I make an effort so that he comes to knowledge of the Self or comes to see God. If, because of being unfit, he is unable to reach there, I will escape hell — with this thought in mind I never accept any kind of economic service from any pupil.'[151]

Whilst living at the Olsons' home Maharishi made full use of the house phone. One day he announced:-
"Soon my friends will be here from India".

"How very nice. On a little visit, are they?" asked Roland.

"Yes, a little visit."

"Tell us a little about your friends, Maharishi."

"Oh, very nice, - - devotees from India."

"Are they on a world tour?"

"Mainly they come to see if I am all right. In India, devotees have much devotion to the Master." He laughed a little. "They spend all their time caring for him and serving him."

"Are they all men, or a couple, or what? I asked.

"A young girl, her brother, and the president of one of the Centers in India."[152]

After taking stock of the situation, the Olsons figured that they had enough space for Maharishi's guests from India.

"Maharishi, I am so delighted that your friends are coming and that we have room."

His smile was worth more than all the extra burdens or discomforts.

"When may we expect them?"

"In two days."

"Two days!" Roland and I said together. After a two-minute silence, I capitulated with, "Oh, well."[153]

Sri T. Rama Rao, Lakshman & Mata-ji and Maharishi

The Indian visitors were 'Mata-ji', her brother, Lakshman, and Shri T. Rama Rao, the bank manager from Madanapalle.

After the guests had been a while at '433', Helena Olson asked Maharishi about Mata-ji, and he offered her this thumbnail sketch:-

"Mata-ji has married into one of the oldest, wealthiest families in Calcutta. They live according to the old traditions. All the families live together in a large apartment building and the elders rule. They are very strict. Mata-ji is not allowed to go on the street without her face covered. It is unusual that she would come here."

"Maharishi, Ram Rao told us Mata-ji is considered to be a saint in India. How do you define sainthood?"

"A saint is said to do no harm in the world."[154]

More formally known as Shrimati Sitadevi Saraf, Mataji had a long association with Maharishi:-

'Mataji was a very one-pointedly devoted soul. She met Shri Guru Dev when she was about 17 years old. At that time Guru Dev was only dealing with sannyases. And being himself a Sannyasi, he had no contact with ladies and so he did not even teach them. But Mataji Sita wanted to be initiated into the spiritual life by Guru Dev. When her request was turned down, she decided to fast til her wish was granted.

After several days witnessing the firm resolve of the daughter and her firm fasting, the family started to be concerned for her welfare and decided to report to Guru Dev and, if possible, persuade Him to fulfil her intention. Then Guru Dev consented and asked [them] to bring her to him. After some questioning she was asked to come next day for initiation.

In that way Mataji Sita became the first female disciple and among Maharishiji's close co-disciples of Shri Guru Dev.'[155]

For Mataji, the Olson's home in Los Angeles must have seemed like a world away from life in Calcutta. Indeed, her association with Maharishi stirred interest back in Benares, where the controversy over who should succeed Swami Brahmananda Saraswati as Shankaracharya of Jyotirmath was far from resolved.

Swami Swaroopanand was born Pothiram Upadhyay on September 2nd 1924 in the Jabalpur area of Madhya Pradesh. At the young age of 9 years old he left home to visit the holy places of India, including Varanasi where he eventually studied with Swami Karpatri (aka Hariharananda Saraswati), a disciple of

Swami Brahmananda Saraswati. At 19 years old he became a freedom fighter in the 'Quit India' movement (1942) and was known as 'Revolutionary Sadhu' (serving two prison sentences for same of 9 months & 6 months). In 1950 Guru Dev made him a *dandi sannyasi*:-

> 'I was the disciple of Gurudev and had been taken into his fold through a ceremony called *danda sannyas* which Mahesh Yogi could not get done as he was not a *brahmana*.'

> 'Before joining Gurudev's staff he was working as a clerk in Gun Carriage Factory for 30 rupees a month.'

> 'Also Mahesh was his secretary and he was not Gurudev's disciple in any way but was a part of the administrative staff.'

> 'Gurudev had reached Kashi (Benares) to abandon his body and take leave for his heavenly abode. When we learnt of it, all of us rushed to Kashi to take his final blessings. His health was deteriorating and people were wondering as to who would succeed him. At that time Mahesh asked him to go with him to Calcutta where there is better medication. We all opposed this move as any travelling would worsen the situation but an astrologer was brought in who predicted that he would live till he would be 125 years and hence he should travel. As soon as he reached Calcutta, he dies within four days!'

> 'Now Sita Saraf was in Calcutta when Gurudev passed away and she along with Mahesh played out a drama claiming that they asked Gurudev to accept their lives but Gurudev refused and passed away. It was also spread far and wide that when Gurudev's soul was leaving his body, Mahesh Yogi's soul was also exiting but Gurudev pushed his soul back because Mahesh had to complete Gurudev's incomplete work for which he had to go abroad!'

> 'Also as per the Will, that was revealed, it stated clearly that the order of succession was to be Shantanand, Dwarkaprasad Shastri, Vishnudevanand and Parmanand. However, all of them

passed away in exactly the reverse order! If Gurudev, who has the far sight to foresee such events, had written the Will, how could they all pass away in exactly the reverse order?'

'The Will named four people- Shantanand, DwarkaPrasad Shastri, Vishnudevanand and Parmanand. Now when the Will was opened for reading it turned out that Shantanand did not understand Sanskrit, he used to work for Geeta Press on the salary of 14 rupees per month and thus was not capable enough. Dwarkaprasad Shastri was a married man with family, Vishnudevanand was not educated enough, and Parmanand's big toe on the right leg was amputated and a disabled person is not given *sannyas*, thus he was nullified. Thus the four were rejected and Swami Krishnabodhashramji was made Shankaracharya, but Mahesh Yogi instigated Shanatanand to fight the court case.'

'Thus it was a Will that was tampered by Mahesh Yogi and his associates.'

'She who was Sita Saraf, that lady became ill, then she went to South India for a cure. There, in South India, hearing the name of Maharshi Ramana, he added 'Maharishi' to his name. This title was not given to Mahesh Yogi.'

'After Gurudev's death he left India, there was a lady called Sita Saraf who gave him money and he left for Singapore from where he left for America and started teaching *Bhavateet Yoga* there.'

'Mahesh Yogi was not a *brahmana* and hence did not have the right to give anybody any *mantras* hence he would place the Gurudev's picture so as to symbolise that the *mantra* was being given through Gurudev.'

'The tradition is such that the *mantra* is a very private and secretive conversation between a *guru* and a disciple.'[156]

In July, the '1st International Convention of the Spiritual Regeneration Movement' was held at Sequoia National Park, in California. There, Maharishi unveiled his hopes and plans for spiritually regenerating the world, and a 'Three-Year Plan' of action was formulated.

Afterwards, one particular topic continued to occupy his attention; the need for him to train others to teach meditation:-

"Since the technique for Deep Meditation must be handed down person to person, it will take a long time for me to spread my message. But I can train hundreds of Guides who can teach and check experiences. If we have Spiritual Guides initiating in all parts of the world, and Meditation Guides teaching the value of Deep Meditation, it will all go very fast, and the world can soon be entirely at peace."

Roland was quite interested.
"How will you put this in operation?"

"The best way is to establish a headquarter and then invite people to come to a training course for three months," said Maharishi.

"Possibly in India?" asked Roland. "Or why not Los Angeles."

Charlie Lutes, who had just returned for some papers, answered that question. "Can you imagine the shock if someone asks us where we received our training to teach Meditation, and we said, "Seventh and Broadway in Los Angeles!"

Maharishi laughed. "India would be best," he said.

We had been hearing from Lachsman, Mata-ji's brother, how inexpensive it was to build and how little food costs in India by comparison with Los Angeles.

Plans, or schemes, for the Meditation Academy began to gather momentum like a snowball rolling downhill. Every day when we came home they were bigger and bigger. An artist in the group made a drawing; an architect drew a set of plans; the site was to be in a high valley close to the Himalayas in Uttar Kashi. "Here," said Maharishi, "the air is pure, no one has lived here except wandering Sannyasi who meditate constantly. The source of the Ganges is close and the crystal clear stream flowing through this Valley becomes India's famous river. No smoking, no alcohol, no violence has ever been known there."[157]

An application form was created to be completed by all potential trainee teachers:-

Training of Spiritual Guides in the Himalayas

INSTRUCTIONS: Answer each of the following questions as fully as possible. Mail your answers to the application-form questions to "Chief Executive, Three-Year Plan, S.R.M. Foundation of America, 1803½ No. Van Ness Ave., Los Angeles 28, California." Applications as received will be forwarded at once to Maharishi Mahesh Yogi.

1. Do you feel for the sufferings of mankind?

2.(a) Do you seek for a practical formula to bring peace and happiness to people in their daily life?

  (b) What have you done so far in this connection?

  (c) Are you prepared to spend about four months time in the Himalayas to learn and master that formula in practice and theory?

3. Describe your religious training – if any. (State in detail the names of guides, institutions and duration of the training.)

4. Do you hold, or have you ever held leadership of any group,

or do you have aspirations of leadership? (State names and details.

5. Have you understood the ideology of the S.R.M. and the Three-Year Plan adopted by the 1st International Convention of the S.R.M. at Sequoia National Park, California, U.S.A. on the 26th of July, 1959?

6. What is your vocation, nature of work performed, and hours of duty?

7. How many members of your immediate family? (State relationships)

8. What is your age, birth date, and country of birth?

9. What is your nationality?

10. What are your educational qualifications?

11. What languages do you speak?

12. What countries have you visited, and what was the duration of your stay?

13. What was your purpose in visiting foreign countries? (State whether visit was for religious convention, pleasure, or business.)

14. Have you written any religious or other books or papers of public interest? (State title, publisher, and year of publication.)

15. Describe your condition of health.

16. Describe type of diet to which your system is accustomed.

17. State whether you can adjust yourself to a vegetarian diet in the Himalayas as only vegetarian foods are available there.

18. State the name of the great master of religion whom you adore most.

19. State the names of other masters of religion whom you favor.

20. Do you belong to any established sect of any religion? If so, which?

21. State whether you can afford your travel to and from the Himalayas and the expenses of your stay there.

22. State whether you can secure a donation of $500 for the construction of a meditation cave in the training center at Uttar-Kashi in the Valley Of Saints, Himalayas. (It is expected that each candidate will secure a donation of a sum sufficient to at least construct a cave for his own use, and preferably a donation of two or more caves to make training possible for others whose circumstances make a donation impossible.)

23. Which of the following sessions would you be best able to join?
    (1) December to March 1960.
    (2) March to June, 1960.
    (3) June to September, 1960

24. At the bottom of your answer sheet, please **print** your name, address, city, state, and country. Give your phone number. Date your application.

25. **Do Not** mail cheques or money orders to the Executive Director, Three-Year Plan. Donations from the United States should be mailed to : Treasurer, S.R.M. Foundation of America, c/o Mr. Roland Olson, 433, South Harvard Boulevard, Los Angeles, California.

Donations from other countries should be mailed to : Sita Devi Saraf, S.R.M. Foundation, India Office, 375/1, Upper Chitpur

Road, Calcutta-7, India.

In drawing up a budget for the training session at Uttar-Kashi, the applicant should consider the following items :-

(a) He (or she) will need to have a valid passport.

(b) A round-trip transportation ticket (from America, a round-world ticket.)

(c) Sufficient funds (preferably in travellers cheques) to pay living expenses. It is estimated that $400 would be the bare minimum.

(d) Special purchases of clothing should not be necessary. The December-January temperature will hover about the freezing point; cotton summer clothing should do for the balance of the year. The elevation of Uttar-Kashi is about 4,000 feet.[158]

Maharishi planned that in the first course in Uttar Kashi, 84 'Meditation Guides' would be trained, and they would establish 84 meditation centres. Naturally, it was planned there should be 84 meditation 'caves' built at Uttar Kashi.

* * *

Maharishi was to go to New York, but before leaving there was to be a party in Los Angeles. On Monday 20th July 1959 a 'Guru Purnima' service, in praise of the *guru*, was celebrated on the full moon day. Maharishi officiated at the *'puja'* giving a recitation of Sanskrit verses

'Now I'll begin invocation:-

> *naaraayanam padmabhavam vasishtham shaktim cha*
> *tatputraparaasharam cha.*
> *vyaasam shukam gaudapadam mahaantam*
> *govindayogindramathaasya shishyam..*
> *shri shankaraachaaryamathaasya padmapaadam cha*

hastaamalakam cha shishyam.
tam trotakam vaarttikakaaramanyaan asmataguruun
santatamaanatosmi..

shankaram shankaraachaarya keshavam baadaraayanam.
suutrabhaashyakritau vande bhagavantau punah punah..

ishwaro gururathmethi moorthibethavibaagine
vyomavarthavyaapthehaya dakshinamurtheye namah:

agyaanagaadaandhatamopahaabhyaam
vivekavidyaavinayapradaabhyaam.
vishveshatatvapratibodhikaabhyaam
namo namah shri gurupaadukaabhyaam..

AIN-kaara HREEN-kaara rahasyayukta
SHREEN-kaara guudaartha mahaavibhuutyaa.
OM-kaara marma pratipaadinibhyaam
namo namah shri gurupaadukaabhyaam..

yadhdvaare nikhilaa nilimpaparishatsiddhim vidhatteanisham,
shrimachchrilasitam jagadhgurupadam natvaatmatriptim
gataah.
lokaagyaanapayodapaatanadhuram shrishankaram
sharmadam, brahmaanandasarasvatim guruvaram dhyaayaami
jyotirmayam..[159]

No translation of these Sanskrit verses was given, but, had there been, it would have run something like this:-

'To Narayana, to lotus-born Brahma, to Vasishtha, to Shakti and his son, Parashara, to Vyasa, to Shukadeva, to the great Gaudapada, to Govinda, to Yogindra, (ruler among *yogis*), and then his disciple.

To the lotus feet of Shri Shankaracharya (Adi Shankara), to his pure disciples Padmapada, Hastamalaka, to him Trotakacharya, to Sureshwara, to others, to our tradition of *gurus*, I bow down.

To Shankar Shankaracharya (Shiva), Keshava (Vishnu, Krishna), Badarayana (Veda Vyasa), to the commentator of the Suutrabhaashya (Brahma Sutras), at the feet of the lord I bow down again and again

Unto Him who is manifested in the different forms as Isvara, as the *guru* and the self; who is all-pervasive like space; unto Sri Dakshinamurthi- the effulgent form facing the south; Unto Him (Shiva) be this salutation!

Salutations again and again to Shri Guru's sandals, which remove the darkness of those who are blind due to strong ignorance, which bestow the education leading to the knowledge of discrimination, and which awaken the reality of the ruler of the universe.

'ऐं *AI-N*' practice & 'ह्रीं *HREE-N*' practice, along with 'श्री *SHREE-N*' practice has hidden meaning, mystery & great power, communicating the vital point of 'ॐ *OM*' practice, I bow down again and again to the sandals of the blessed *guru*.

At whose door the whole galaxy of gods pray for perfection day and night. Adorned by immeasurable glory, preceptor of the whole world, having bowed down at His feet, we gain fulfilment.

Skilled in dispelling the cloud of ignorance of the people, the gentle emancipator, Brahmananda Saraswati, the supreme teacher, full of brilliance, on Him we meditate.'

Maharishi then explained that he would speak the '108 names' of Swami Brahmananda Saraswati, advising celebrants:-
'When I say *"namah"* then one petal will be offered'[159]

Maharishi proceeded to utter the 'names', or rather Sanskrit titles, Sanskrit; the first being; '*Ananta Shri Ananta Shri Ananta Shri Vibhushitaye namah*', which means; 'To the one who is Adorned with Limitless Wealth, limitless wealth, limitless wealth, I bow down'.

Maharishi kept reciting names for about another ten minutes, the last three names being; '*Shri Jyotirmath Badarikashram Adhishvaraya namah*', 'To the one who is Blessed Supreme Lord of Shri Jyotirmath, Badarikashram, I bow down', then '*Sat-chit-anandaya namah*', 'To the one who is Absolute Bliss consciousness, I bow down', and lastly '*Shri Brahmanandaya namah*', 'To the one who is Blessed Absolute-Bliss, I bow down'.

Perhaps none present, other than Maharishi and Mataji, understood the significance of the names, but the event was enjoyed by those there, including Helena Olson:-

> 'Quietly, Maharishi started the Holy Names of God. We followed the examples of Mata-ji and Lois who threw a few petals at the pronouncement of each Name.
>
> During the last part, all the candles on the plates were lit representing the spark of the Soul within us. Hindu chants were given by Mata-ji and her brother, Lachsman.
>
> Maharishi asked for prayers to be said and nodded in our direction. Roland and I started the "Our Father". Everyone joined in. It was like the roar of the ocean and gave a deep feeling of satisfaction to all who had been trained in the Christian tradition.
>
> Afterwards, prayers of all types were said. Many men surprised us with simple, beautiful prayers. Some were "established" church prayers, some were from the heart and memories of childhood. The air was filled with love and devotion. God became Reality, and it was natural to open our hearts and express our sincerest and deepest thoughts.
>
> A long silence indicated the prayers were over.'

'All helped themselves to the refreshments. Mata-ji had brought many gold medals with enamelled pictures of Guru Dev on them. She asked Theresa to pass these out to anyone who wanted one.

Then she took from a bracelet on her arm an unusually beautiful medal of Guru Dev seated on a gold lotus and presented it to me. Maharishi told me later that the Maharanee of the province where Mata-ji lived had presented it to her and it was precious to her. Blessed Mata-ji! She proved the true value of Meditation to me every day, and her treasured gift has served to enshrine her in my heart.'[160]

Before Mata-ji, Lakshman and Rama Rao returned to India they joined Maharishi on many sightseeing trips; car rides around the Hollywood hills, a midnight drive along the beach, visits to Marineland and Chinatown, and even a visit to the world famous theme park, Disneyland.

In September Maharishi left Los Angeles for New York

Many of Maharishi's talks in the USA were recorded, and here is one which is particularly relevant to the topic of meditation, in that he attempts to explain the nature of the mind.

'The question is about mind. Of what matter the mind is made? What is the content of the mind and the range of the mind and right and wrong, and all that? It's just discussed this afternoon.

All these questions are very clearly answered in Ishari Upanishad, in one Upanishad. I'll say it to you. Listen!

> *"aanandaadhyeva khalvimaani bhuutaani jaayante.*
> *aanandena jaataani jivanti.*
> *aanandam prayantyabhisanvishantiti.*
> *saishaa bhaargavi vaaruni vidyaa.*
> *parame vyomanpratishthitaa"*[161]

There is a whole thing about…

"aanandaadhyeva khalvimaani bhuutaani jaayante."; "From *ananda* alone all these beings are born"

"*aanandena jaataani jivanti.*"; In the *ananda* – '*ananda*' is 'bliss', ocean of happiness.- "In *ananda* they live."

"*aanandam prayantyabhisanvishantiti.*"; "Unto *ananda* they dissolve, at the time of dissolution"

"*saishaa bhaargavi vaaruni vidyaa.*"; "This is the wisdom told by Bhrigu to his son Varun."[162]

Maharishi seems to be confusing the father and son relationship, for according to conventional lore, Bhrigu is the son of Varuna, and not the other way around.

'Bhrigu - Maharshi Bhrigu - revealed this wisdom to his son, Varun. And where is this found? This wisdom of *ananda*? That all this was *ananda*, is *ananda*, will be *ananda*, this wisdom of *ananda*, where it will be found?

"*parame vyoman*" – '*vyoman*' means *akasha* - and "*parame vyoman*" means, "the field lies, lies beyond *akasha*" [162]

This mention of the Vedic Sanskrit '*parame vyoman*' refers to a verse in a much older text, *Rig Veda* I.164.39. Actually, the *Rig Veda* is said to be the oldest record of human thought in existence, with '*param*' meaning either 'beyond' or 'transcendental', and '*vyoman*' sometimes meaning 'celestial'.

'There, this wisdom will be found."

What wisdom? That all the beings are born of *ananda*, they live in *ananda*, and unto *ananda* all these will be dissolved. One thing we note here at the outset, that, this wisdom of the ultimate reality of life, this wisdom, the supreme wisdom of life, was handed on from father to son. That means, this was the wisdom in the field of the household. This we get from this outset. Bhrigu told to his son, Varuna. The father is expected to give the wisdom of life to his son. He is not only responsible for giving food and water and clothes to the son. But the father has to give to the son, the way of life, the wisdom of life. So that his son does never fall short of anything, does never suffer in life. This is one thing at the outset that we get from this, *upanishadic* teaching.

If the people of the world have to keep on enjoying the wisdom of the absolute, generation after generation, then something has to be done so that this great wisdom gets imbibed into the family tradition. It's passed on from father to the son, from father to the son, like that, in a most natural way. Then only the world could become peaceful, happy and joyful, harmonious, without any struggle and strife and suffering.

Now the teaching of the *Upanishads* says:-

"aanandaadhyeva khalvimaani bhuutaani jaayante." – "From *ananda* all these creatures are born"

Your question about the origin of thought, here is the answer. From *ananda*, from the field of bliss, the thoughts arise, and as a thought rises up, it is this thought that gives individuality to cosmic existence. It is the thought, rising of a thought, from the ocean of bliss, as a wave in the ocean; this rising of a thought gives individuality to the cosmic existence. Just as the rising of a wave gives individuality to the ocean.

From your experience you know, this field is the field of Being. It is unmanifested *'OM'*, where the thought ends or from where the thought rises. During meditation, you know, this field is unmanifested Being. That is - yes, finish off - that is your experience in meditation. The *mantra* becomes faint and faint and faint, faint, faint, faint, faint. As if, the gross levels of, of sound and then subtle levels of sound, and very subtle levels of sound, and then the subtlest level of sound, and then no sound. Here, this is the level of the unmanifested, and unmanifested state is the State of Being. Just to Be. There is no creation. Being is just existence, intelligence, pure life energy. This field is absolute; it is ever the same, never changing.

All the changes start with the creation, subtle creation and gross creation and very gross creation. You have heard in one of those seven lectures that the creation comes out of the, mmm, the objective creation comes out of the five elements, *akasha* and then air element, and fire element, and water element, and the earth element, like that. Finest of all these five is the *akasha tattva*, *akasha tattva*. You have, you have heard in *The Bible* or somewhere, this huh, 'In the beginning was the word and word was with God'. 'In the beginning was the word'. That means; the word was the generator of creation, creation came out of a word, came out of the vibration. The word, or sound, or vibration, are where the *akasha tattva* is – *akasha tattva* is recognised by sound. Wherever there is vibration, there is *akasha tattva*. Where there is no vibration, there is no *akasha tattva*. The finest state of the *mantra* there is that *akasha tattva*. Transcending the finest state of the *mantra* we transcend *akasha tattva* and when we transcend *akasha tattva*, go beyond *akasha*, then we find the, a field of all bliss, as enunciated by the Upanishads.

We know, same vibrations which when they are gross we have sound and when we speak them become less and less, and sound ceases to be, then the same things gives rise to light, light vibrations are much finer than the sound vibrations. And then? Again in the field of light there could be innumerable degrees, gross light and subtle light and subtle light.

That means the vibrations go on becoming finer and finer and finer and finer. Eventually, all vibrations of life have come to an end, giving rise to that state which we can't actually say vibrations, but yet it has its relative existence, and that is *ananda*. By transcending the finest vibrations of light, which is glow, that glow, and the basis of that glow is that *ananda*.'

Q. 'So it belongs to *akasha*, the light?'

Very fine, very fine, very fine, and the finest *akasha tattva*, that is the finest vibration of light, finest glow, gone, and then pure *ananda*.

Q. 'But then in case thus, that allows many more *tattvas*?'

Not *tattvas*, this is, this *ananda* is the basis of all subjective and objective creation – *ananda*....

Q. 'But what can we be learning of other *tattvas*?'

Ladder of other *tattvas* starting from, from this field of light, from that glow, from which is the, which is the basis of, mmm, which is *akasha tattva*, being the basis of objective creation.

Q. 'And then, and then *mahatattva*?'

Just in that glow. In that glow, in that, in that *ananda*.

Q. 'There are different changes in that *ananda*?'

In that *ananda*, and as the glow starts, the light starts, starts the *akasha tattva*, starts the objective creation.

Q. 'Glow still the objective creation?'

Glow still the objective creation, the basis of objective creation, glow, glow, and then that glow becoming finer and finer and finer and finer. And then becoming *ananda*. There can't be any line of demarcation but also finer and finer and finer and finer and finer and finer and finer and finer and finest. Transcending the being. How many of you experienced, have this glow?

And then, in that glow, or apart from the glow, or in that glow – you can't possibly make a very fine distinction – but *ananda*, waves of happiness. How many have felt?

That is the, that is the degree of finest, ultimately coming to the source of creation. This field, this field, this field of the glow, and then to make a difference, to make a distinction, from this field of bliss, *ananda*. These are, these are the fields, at the basis of creation. This is, this the basis of subjective creation, and the same, manifesting more and more towards the gross, becomes the basis of objective creation and then comes on to this, then the objective creation, the thought, subtle thought and gross thought, speech and action, and all goes on.

The field of thought – in that glow, but not in the gross aspect of the glow, but in the subtlest aspect of the glow, glow, on the basis of *ananda*. This is called '*chit*', '*chit*', c-h-i-t, *chit* – *chit* is the storehouse of impressions, and this is called, the field of *ananda* is *chit akash* - *akash*a, *chit akash*, that is, the horizon of the *chit*, *chit* which is the storehouse of all the impressions. What impressions are, we'll deal now.

There is quite a lot to say, regarding this field. If you don't confuse yourselves then I could just go on. If you begin to confuse, forget about it, but better to listen it huh? Listen to it.[162]

Another recording from this time touches on elements, and is focussed on the topic of *mantras*. Maharishi is asked how he selects the *mantras* and his reply is candid as he refers to the Indian religious roots of the meditation, explaining that he selects them according to the initiate's favourite deity:-

Q. 'Maharishi, how may a person find, you know, which of the five materials are predominant in them?'

'They, they have their method of, uh, oh, from the tendencies they know, from the, from the cut of the face they know. From the tendency. From the tendency.

Q. 'Do you take that into consideration when you give the person a *mantra*?

'I don't go into all these vibrations, botherations. I ask him "Which god you like?" He says "Shiva" - Okay, Shiva!

[Maharishi laughs, very loudly]
Where is the time to go into complications and all that? Ask him directly "What he likes?" and that is it.
[more laughter].

And somebody comes, "Oh my, I don't have any liking for anybody", then I trace behind, And then, "When you were young?" and "Which temple you were going more?" and "What your father was worshipping?" and then he comes round.
[Maharishi resumes the laughter]

Q. How would you apply this to the Westerners?

MMY. Oh here we don't go into these minute details.
[more laughter]

We get the *mantra* direct and that does all good for him.
[yet more laughter]

Into, not into so much details.'[163]

So, it appears that for those who showed no favouritism for a particular god, Maharishi would ask questions which might show a tendency towards an elemental quality that the god / goddess is said to represent. According to Maharishi, the *panch devata*, the five 'presiding deities' of the '*tattwas*' (elements) are;

Vishnu	-	*Akasha* / Ether
Surya / Sun	-	Air
Devi / goddess	-	Fire
Shiva	-	Earth
Ganesh	-	Water [164]

For those who were not religious, it must have been uncomfortable to hear Maharishi state and re-state the religious connections of the meditation. Maharishi would also re-iterate his claim that the meditation he taught came from 'Guru Dev':-

'Some sound, some specific vibrations which will go to refine the quality of the man. I come from the Shankaracharya tradition. That is the tradition which is the cherished tradition from a long time past. They are supposed to be the custodians of the real knowledge of Vedanta and Yoga; the philosophy of unity; the direct path to Realization; to that blessed tradition I belong. So I know from the blessings of my Master certain specific vibrations which suit certain people, and those vibrations I give as a medium of meditation. Now, thereby, we get the advantages of the specific vibrations and the method of meditation is such that it enables the mind to experience subtler phases of those vibrations 'til the vibrations vanish, giving rise to the Source of all vibration.'[165]

Maharishi explained the basic theory of this TM meditation:-
'the value of the *mantra* lies in resonating with the existing impulse of a man'.[166]

"This meditation provides a missing link for every religion, such a universal principle of meditation. And what is that principle? The principle on which this meditation is based is nothing new, only a matter of knowing the viewpoint. That's all. And what is that viewpoint? Each mind has a natural inclination, a natural instinct, a natural faculty to go to a field of greater happiness.'[167]

"The technique of meditation that I give to the people is just how to turn the mind in the right direction. How to turn the mind just 180 degrees, and one step, in that direction. As I said, the intensity of light increases as you turn towards the light. One step in this direction and the mind finds increasing charm. This increasing charm attracts the mind by itself, not much needed to thrust the mind in that direction. No! Just a right turn and one step that way and the mind is found there already. Such is the simple principle of this meditation. It is based on the natural tendency of the human mind to go to a field of greater happiness. That is why it is declared to be easy, simple, everyone could do it. This is the message of the Spiritual Regeneration Movement. And this movement is such an innocent movement, it knows no frustration, it knows no friction from anyone whatsoever. It meets the individual on the individual level of man, not on the level of any culture, not on the level of any philosophy, not on a level of any faith, not on any level whatsoever. It meets the man on the level of man and transforms him to the Divine. The principle is simple. Practice is much simpler.[168]

Over the years, Maharishi made less and less mention of the religious origin of the technique, in fact Maharishi found himself deliberately choosing vocabulary that avoided association with religion:-

'It is I who gave it the present expression, but I learnt it from him (Swami Brahmanand) in the traditional way ... through very old expressions of religious order. Every religion has its own vocabulary; Hinduism has its own vocabulary; yoga has its own way of expression of the reality; Vedanta has its own approach. He taught me in the traditional way of yoga and Vedanta and Indian religious language. I gave it an expression in the universal way...'[169]

Maharishi attempted to explain to his followers why the TM teaching emerged in 1958 rather than say 1868 or 1768:- 'The extinction of the Age of Faith could be traced to about that time', and claimed; 'Faith has to be verified through experimentation'. He described the teaching of Transcendental Meditation as being 'old wine in a new bottle'.

It appeared that not only was Maharishi trying to disassociate the meditation from religion but also to dissociate himself from certain disciples of his master, which seems odd, since some of them had been disciples for decades and would surely have been privy to the same information about meditation as he had been! Not all of Swami Brahmananda's disciples seem to teach the same meditation techniques. This topic was touched upon in an interview with Cyril Dunn, a correspondent for the 'Observer' newspaper in Britain:-

'The Maharishi told me that the other disciples of Brahmanand - and there are thousands of them - 'do not tally with me now.' [170]

So, had the *guru* asked his *brahmachari* to spread the message of meditation?

'Oh he must have known! [audience laughter] He never, nnnmmmm, he never said to me. Otherwise quite a lot of time would have been wasted in planning. [audience laughter, slow at first, then uproarious] He saved us from that waste, [audience and Maharishi still laughing] waste of planning. It just blossomed and blossomed and blossomed and blossomed.'[171]

During the last years of the Shankaracharya's life, it appears that he initiated quite a number of people into the mysteries of spiritual development.

'For initiations it was unprecedented, for gathering to take initiations from him, there it was tremendous.'[45]

One of Maharishi's followers became intrigued as to whether 'Guru Dev' had taught the same techniques of meditation as his disciple:-

Male questioner - Maharshi?

Maharishi - Yes?

Male questioner - You have said in the latter years Guru Dev initiated quite a number of people. Was he using the, the **exact** technique that you are using?

Maharishi - [pause] Must be using **better** techniques than I am using [Maharishi laughing slightly].

Same male questioner - Was he still using the long *mantras* and all of that?

Female in audience - Huh!

Maharishi - [pauses] It's very difficult for me to find out what he was using. [laughter from audience] Because initiation is all in private ... [he pauses and audience laughs, Maharishi giggles and laughs too] ... And I was never interested who was given what *mantra*. I was interested in myself. [laughter and giggling]...

Full of divine radiance. People don't have to do the *mantra* and meditation in his presence. [male member laughs] Just ... the transformation was in his air, so full of life ... Out of that fullness I started to teach. [Maharishi pauses, slight audience laughter] At least by practice people could rise and raise themselves up.'[171]

On another occasion the topic of the specifics of Swami Brahmananda's methods of teaching was raised.

Questioner: Did Guru Dev give all the disciples the same?

Maharishi: From my observations I think he gave the basic technique and then the advanced techniques.[182]

Maharishi's approach, of not prying into the techniques of others who were taught by Swami Brahmananda, seems to be in harmony with the wishes of his master, for according to Umesh Srivastava, who met with the *guru* when he was young:-

'Pujya Shri Gurudeva has been always insisting upon his disciples that You should not be curious to know that how He has initiated others or what laurels he had won in his spiritual journey, rather he used to insist upon that WHATEVER HE HAD BEEN TELLING TO THEM EXTEMPORE (THEY SHOULD FOLLOW THE SAME IN TOTO).'

Allegedly, Umesh Srivastava's father, Jugal Kishore Srivastava, actually introduced Maharishi to Swami Brahmananda:-

'Late Shri Jugal Kishore Shrivastava of "Bai ka Bagicha" of Jabalpur was unconditional and elevated follower of Swami Brahmanand Saraswatiji. Mahesh Prasad Shrivastava, also a resident of "Bai ka Bagicha", was introduced to Guruji by Jugal Kishoreji, who then became the disciple of Guruji and later became famous as Maharishi Mahesh Yogi.'[172]

मनोवैज्ञानिक, दार्शनिक, राजकीय एवं सामयिक, सतेज विचारधारा से सम्बद्ध प्रश्नोतरों का आनंद लीजिये !

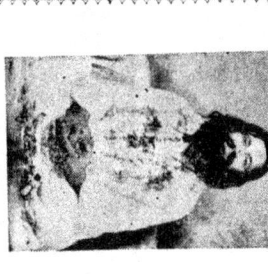

महर्षि योगी
(हिमालय)

विश्व के प्रायः प्रत्येक देश, विशेषतः अमेरिकन और यूरोपीय देशों के मुख्य सम्मेलन में इस ध्यान शैली की चर्चा प्रतिष्ठा हुई है ।

भारतीय दृष्टिकोण से यह राजसमागमों से इसका विरोध नहीं, दार्शनिक सिद्धान्तों द्वारा समर्थित भी है ।

किसी भी धर्म अथवा सम्प्रदाय से इसका विरोध नहीं । विश्वव्यापी काव्यात्मक दृष्टिकोण द्वारा समर्थित की यह सामाजिक क्रिया है जिससे संकीर्णता का लवलेश नहीं, केवल उदारता ही उदारता है ।

"द्वारपरिसरान्तु बहुमित्र कुटुम्बकम्"

इस आन्दोलन में खराबन नहीं, विचार नहीं, विरोध नहीं ।

इस आन्दोलन में किंचिदपि विषय नहीं व्यापक समन्वय है, लैरामाद्य द्रव नहीं, कराते प्रेम का सागर है, जटिलता नहीं सुरभता है ।

जिसका मन, मस्तिष्क-मन, जप-ध्यान, कल्पवन मन्त्र शान्ति करते समक्ष, स्थिर न रहता हो, जिनका, अधिकता परेशान रहती हो, जिसके मन में किसी कारण से या बाह्यता हो बरसाति का पड़ुमथ हुआ हो, जो सबसे सोमारिक व्यवहार करते हुए कोई सरल मार्ग हृदय की शान्ति का पढ़ुमथ प्राप्त करना चाहते हों, जो कुपना काव्यविरून्स हो बढ़े हों, जिनके जीवन में मन एवं बुद्धि के दो स्वर गठ हों, जो क्षणी मानसिक शान्ति का विकास मार्ग चाहते हों, लोक-परलोक की उलझनों से छुटकारा पाना चाहते हों जो जीवन में सदेव

सरल ध्यान प्रक्रिया द्वारा विश्वव्यापी आध्यात्मिक पुनरुत्थान आन्दोलन के प्रवर्तक

वशिष्ठब्रह्मचारी श्री महर्षि
महेश योगी
(हिमालय)

"आइयेपधारिये श्री इस युग के ऐसे ब्राह्मसम्राट की जो मोबिकबाद की छद्मसंगुन्धा का प्रचार करे सके और उसी छायानु निःसंग, कमाल, क्षप्रबुद्धा के समाधिन करे सके—क्षणमात्र मानव जीवन में मिल मुकित को दूर कर सके—वैज्ञान मुकित की मुद्द परिषाप को पूर्ण की चरिताय घासण कर सके।

आइयेधारिये ही विज्ञान का कार्य हुआ करती है—मिलित्व पर आही हुई ज्ञानित हो रहीं है तो क्षणायसाबाद की सुरम्य रिधियाँ !"

श्री महर्षि, कमाल श्री विशिष्ट जगद्गुरुक भगवान् शंकराचार्य ज्योतिगीठाधीश्वर ब्रह्मलीन श्री ब्रह्मानन्द सरस्वती महाराज के शिष्य हैं और श्री गुरुदेव के प्रसाद से कुछ वो सरल ध्यान-प्रक्रिया प्राप्त हुई है । इसके विभिन्न और शैप होने बाले तमके लाभकारी प्रभाव हैं, जिससे धर्म, जाति, देश इत्यादि के भेदभाव के विना सब लोग निःशुल्क लाभ उठा सकते हैं ।

वाल ब्रह्मचारी श्री महर्षि महेश योगी, जवलकाशी (हिमालय), लगभग तीन वर्ष विश्व भ्रमण करते के उपरान्त अभी हाल ही में भारत लौटे हैं । परिषदा, धर्मगिकाएँ तथा यूरोप के विभिन्न देशों में सहस्रवें २ नर-नारियों की जड़न एक आयेने सरल ध्यान प्रक्रिया से सहद बतलाई, जिसमें कुछ क्षणमात्र ही में परमानन्द का अनुभव हुआ और जगह जगह ध्यान केन्द्रों की स्थापना हुई ।

महर्षि की प्रणाम ध्यान की सुगम साधना पद्धति से होनेवाले, क्षणकालिक शारीरिक, मानसिक एवं क्षाणत्मिक सरसीभाव, व्यक्तिगत एवं सामाजिक प्रयाय लाभों के संबंध में सुविधेज और यदि किसी क्षेत्र में रोका उठे तो भागक्षाल में उपरिमत कीजिये ।

When Maharishi returned to India in February 1961, Jugal Kishore assisted him in getting his message across. Leaflets were printed promoting *'Adhyatmik Punarutthan'*, or 'Spiritual Revival', with an introduction to simple meditation by 'Balbrahmachari Shri Maharshi Mahesh Yogi', with two quotations from his master, 'Jagadguru Shankaracharya Brahmaleena Shri Brahmananda Saraswati Maharaj', reproduced and translated here:-

अशान्ति सूक्ष्म शरीर में – वह उपरी भौतिक उपचारों से दूर नहीं होगी ।

अशान्ति हटाने के लिये सूक्ष्म शरीर की चिकित्सा आवश्यक है । बिना आध्यात्मिक ज्ञान के शान्ति नहीं मिलेगी ।

'By treatment of the outer physical existence, the peacelessness in the *sukshma sharir* (subtle body) will not go away. For the purpose of removing *ashanti* (peacelessness) the healing of the subtle body is required. Without spiritual knowledge, you will not get peace.

अभ्यास करते चलो । मन भागे तो भागने दो तुम मत उसके पीछे भागो ।

जहाण् मन जाता है वहाण् यदि इसे कुछ रसास्वादन हु तो वहीं चिपक जाता है । भयवान् में लगाया जायगा और कभी भगवान् के दिव्य स्वरूप का रस मिल गया तो फिर वहीं चिपक जायगा । इसलिये मन को भगवत् भजन में लगाना चाहिये ।

हर हालत में परमात्मा में मन को लगा ।

सन्देह मत करो कि भगवान् का भजन कभी व्यर्थ जायगा ।

> 'Proceed with the practice [meditation]. If the mind runs away, let it run away, you do not run afterwards.
>
> Wherever the mind goes, if it becomes appreciative there, then right there it clings. If it will become attached to Bhagwan, and has sometimes got a taste of Bhagwan, then afterwards it will get stuck to that very place. Therefore you should apply the mind in worshipping the Lord. In all circumstances apply the mind to Paramatma. Make no mistake, no worship of Bhagwan will be futile.'

-

When asked directly the source of the meditation he taught, Maharishi would always credit his master. Interviewed by BBC Television presenter Robert Kee Maharishi explained how he came by his knowledge of this meditation:

> 'MMY – I would say a very systematic teaching of my Master in India.
>
> Kee – Who was your master?
>
> MMY – He was Jagad Guru Shankaracharya Swami Brahmananda Saraswati, a very great saint in the Himalayas, hailed by all the people.
>
> Kee – He is a Hindu saint?
>
> MMY – Yes, a Hindu saint, but what I think is the essence of every religion, is really the same – to enable every man to rise above conflicts and anxieties and sorrows and sufferings in life, and to live a peaceful and joyful and harmonious life.'[173]

Transcendental Meditation (TM)

After being known as both 'Meditation' and 'Deep Meditation' during the late 1950's and early 1960's, then the term 'Transcendental Deep Meditation' began to be used after Maharishi visited Great Britain and Europe, and by the mid-1960's this method of meditation became fixed as 'Transcendental Meditation'.

Since acronyms are very popular in the States, 'Transcendental Meditation' then became widely referred to as 'TM'.

> Marie-Louise Jureit – 'And transcendental meditation - is this the right translation from India to English?'
>
> MAHARISHI - 'Yes I gave it a name. I gave it a name - transcendental meditation. The transcendental has been used by philosophers in the past, but transcendental word was attributed to an abstract expression of reality. When I brought it with meditation then it became a systematically verifiable experience - transcendental meditation. Otherwise the word transcendental was just a metaphysical expression devoid of any concrete meaning - it was just an abstract expression, but when I put it with meditation then it became a systematically verifiable experience.'[169]

But if 'transcend' means 'to go beyond' everyday discursive thought, is TM the only meditation that could bring about transcendence of the mind? Maharishi himself explained that any system of meditation that can transcend itself could be called transcendental meditation. Here is how one TM teacher recollects him explaining:-

> "Maharishi, are there other meditations or techniques which transcends?"

"Yes!"

"Which one?"

"They are transcendental Meditation. Everything which transcends is transcendental Meditation!"[174]

So the question that remains is, as to what extent is the technique of TM identical with Swami Brahmananda's teaching? How much or how little has the method been adapted? Maharishi declared that he was passing on the system of meditation that he had himself learned from his master, and as mentioned previously, names the Shankaracharya tradition as having maintained this knowledge, in its purity. He said:-

'I come from the Shankaracharya tradition. That is the tradition which is the cherished tradition from a long time past. They are supposed to be the custodians of the real knowledge of Vedanta and Yoga; the philosophy of unity; the direct path to Realization; to that blessed tradition I belong. So I know from the blessings of my Master certain specific vibrations which suit certain people, and those vibrations I give as a medium of meditation. Now, thereby, we get the advantages of the specific vibrations and the method of meditation is such that it enables the mind to experience subtler phases of those vibrations 'til the vibrations vanish, giving rise to the Source of all vibration.

Vibrations which we set forth expand and influence the whole creation. When we speak, the words go, they strike against the pillar, against the ceiling, against everything. They must be producing some effect. The effect should be either for the life of that, or against the life of that. So every thought, speech and action of man, or of animal, or of nature sets up a vibration. Those vibrations spread against the whole of the universe, striking against all water, all fire, all sky, everything. When they strike against things, then they produce some effect, either good or bad. So, that's a great responsibility to man who could understand good and bad. Such vibrations which go to influence the quality of the vibrations of man are life-supporting vibrations, and when they strike against everything in creation, they produce life-supporting influence in the whole field of creation. That is a universal gain.

One man meditates through the right medium and he produce life-supporting influences through the whole of creation, by virtue of a right vibration. And as we know, if we hit this flower against someone, it might hurt, but if we could excite the atoms of the flower, the effect would be stronger. Greater power lies in the subtlety of creation. So, when we get to the subtle phases of these vibrations, the power increases. The power of these vibrations is power to purify, to increase, power to improve the quality, power to add to the values of life. This power of the vibrations is found increasing as we go towards the subtler and subtler fields of creation. Thereby, one dive we take into the Absolute, and a very powerful influence we create for supplementing the life of the whole creation.

So, the individual gains and the universe, as a whole, gains. This is how, by the great power of the subtle vibrations of this type which suit a particular man, we are neutralizing the great tensions in the atmosphere. The effect is found in the homely life where tensions prevail. Within two or three days people begin to feel much, much better; great harmony in the circle of friends here and there, and this happens automatically, without any effort, by virtue of the right vibrations and exploring the subtle ranges of those vibrations. The whole process of this meditation is so scientific, it's so logical, that is why it is able to satisfy all types of people. All emotionalism will be satisfied because of experience of great charm; the emotions and the heart are satisfied by direct experience of great happiness. This is something which satisfies the intellect; which improves the intellect to a great extent; this is something which satisfies the heart; improves the qualities of the heart to a great extent. So here is the heart and the head both developed. Very great gain.'[175]

Purity of the Teaching

Maharishi has emphasised that his trained teachers place great importance on the 'purity of the teaching' of TM, and to make sure that every aspect of the *puja* ceremony and the initiation proceeds according to their training. However, whether TM teachers care to admit it or not, the TM teaching has not remained static, with Maharishi constantly tinkering to improve both technique and teaching.

Over the years, Maharishi has reviewed and revised aspects of teaching of Transcendental Meditation. At one time the recommended posture was the traditional Indian crossed-legged straight-spine pose, but this soon gave way to permitting initiates to sit in chairs. The recommended length of time to meditate has been varied, with a short period of inactivity added post meditation and the overall duration of meditation shortened from an hour to 15-20 minutes. Also, the way that the meditation process is 'checked' has been refined, and a list of numbered 'checking points' has been created, to be learned by all trainee teachers to Maharishi's satisfaction. And of course, TM, after initially being free of charge became a compulsory donation, which has been varied from time to time, and from place to place.

The TM *puja* has changed too, both in content and in the way it is intoned, having now a tune and being melodious.

In response to feedback from meditators, Maharishi came up with innovations such as a series of advanced TM techniques, which like TM appear to be based on much older meditation Indian practices. But since it is emphasised that learning the basic TM technique is all that is necessary, there are not that many takers for the advanced varieties.

There have been very mixed responses to the more recent *'TM Sidhi'* course, with some TM meditators claiming great benefits of using the *sutras* whilst others voicing dissatisfaction or disapproval. The introduction of 'Yogic Flying' was a controversial move and has led many to re-evaluate their involvement in the teaching and practice of TM.

Probably the biggest issue holding back the spread of TM is the secrecy and double-talk over the *mantras*.

From time to time, meditators and former TM teachers divulge the *mantras* they were given, and the TM teachers sometimes reveal details about the way the *mantras* are to be chosen for any given individuals.

By comparing the various lists from the different teachers, it has been concluded that Maharishi varied which *mantras* he gave to his teachers, and the selection criteria by which they should be applied.

With the arrival of the Internet Age, it is now that much easier to network, discover and share secrets, including those of TM. Online resources give seekers to understand that a suitable *mantra* can be chosen on the basis of gender and age alone.

So, after reading such information about TM *mantras,* published in books, magazines and on the Internet, some people convince themselves that they know which *mantras* are used in TM, and how they are chosen.

So, if one uses such a chart to check or verify any *mantra* a particular individual has divulged, then by using the following criteria; of 'date taught', 'age at the time', and 'gender', one might expect to be able to arrive at the same *mantra* as the individual was given. But it turns out that this process doesn't always deliver the 'correct' *mantra*, thus suggesting the information is incomplete. Furthermore it also raises questions as to whether or not the selection process is an exact science, and how much a meditation teacher's intuition plays a part in the process.

Maharishi was asked by British broadcaster, Sir David Frost (1939-2013), to explain about the *mantras* used in TM:-

    David Frost - 'Is that the same sound that you give to each person?'

Maharishi - 'No. Each person gets different, but we don't have as many sounds as we have men in the world, so they are grouped together.'

David Frost - 'How many sounds are there?'

Maharishi - 'Oh there are lots of sounds.'

David Frost - 'I mean, hundreds, or thousands, or ...?'

Maharishi - 'You could say thousands.'[176]

Maharishi trained many, many teachers of meditation, but not all of them teach under the auspices of Maharishi's various organisations. This is understood. It is reported that at a press conference back on 14th May 2003 Maharishi talked about this issue:-

> 'What I have taught, because it has its eternal authenticity in the Vedic literature and you should know that, how many? 30 - 40 thousand teachers of TM I have trained and many of them have gone on there own and they may not call it Maharishi's TM but they are teaching it in some different name here and there. So there's a lot of these, artificial things are going on, doesn't matter, as long as the man is getting something useful to make his life better, we are satisfied.'[177]

It is clear from many, many statements Maharishi made whilst spreading the news about meditation internationally, that he always acknowledged that this technique of meditation is not new, and that he received knowledge of this meditation from his master, Swami Brahmananda Saraswati.

It seems also that many other *swamis* teach this form of meditation without calling it TM. Dana Sawyer is a professor of religion and philosophy who has specialised in studying the community of *dandi swamis* in India, and is very knowledgeable about the Shankaracharya tradition, and about TM. Professor Sawyer sees a great similarity in the teachings of various *dandi swamis* and the teaching of TM.

'I spent nearly three years in *dandi maths* all over India and was always given the same instructions on how to meditate as I, and you, had gained from Maharishi.'[178]

The teaching of TM meditation is usually given on a one-to-one basis, but Maharishi himself was apparently happy to perform mass initiations, as he did in 1974 in Nepal, initiating approximately 35,000 Nepalis at one event.

According to veteran TM teacher Hans Bruncken, Maharishi went about the mass initiations by seating the Nepali's in three groups, according to their preference of personal deity, and then he broadcast a *mantra* to each group collectively.

'During the 35,000 initiations, Maharish initiated according to the deities the Hindu people choose.'

'When he visited the military pilots in the Himalaya airfield, he initiated the bomber pilots with their family *mantras*. He was sitting with around 20 pilots in the room of command and asked them: "do you have family *mantras*?" Everyone had. They belonged to old families, which could trace their ancestry to one of the *rishis*. There was no need to replace thus old *mantra* the whole family is meditating. Maharishi showed them to transcend with their *mantras* and it worked.'

'Leaving the airfield in the car, one American member reminded Maharishi that he did no *puja* for the initiation.'

"Yes, you are right! Next time you are here you will do the *puja*!"[179]

So, perhaps the meditation teaching is effective, whether or not one performs the *puja*? Perhaps too, as some TM teachers suggest, that though it is thought necessary to have the correct *mantra*, it is just as important, and possibly even **more** important, for an initiate to be given the correct guidance on how to meditate.

The Story of the Pandit, the Brahmachari and the Guru

During his tenure as Shankaracharya of Jyotirmath, Swami Brahmananda was worshipped by devotees, who would perform a ceremony known as *shodashopachaara* (a *puja* with sixteen methods of offering worship). His praises were also set to verse, some of which survive, include the following, which are attributed to Ashu Kavi Pandit Veni Madhava Sastri.[180]

वन्देऽहं यतिराजराजरमणं योगीन्द्रचक्रायुधं
चातुर्वर्ग्य-फलप्रदं सुविहितं मोक्षच्छटाच्छादितम्।
योगानन्दतरंगतानतननं त्रैलोक्यनाथं शिवं
ब्रह्मानन्दसरस्वतीं गुरुवरं ज्योतिर्मठाधीश्वरम्॥१॥

vandeaham yatiraajaraajaramanam yogindrachakraayudham,
chaaturvargya-phalapradam suvihitam
mokshachchataachchaaditam.
yogaanandataramgataanatananam trailokyanaatham shivam,
brahmaanandasarasvatim guruvaram
jyotirmathaadhishvaram..1..

'I praise Brahmananda Saraswati, the most excellent among the *gurus*, the supreme lord of Jyotirmath who loves the king of the kings of ascetics, who has the *chakra* of the chief of the *yogis* as his weapon, who gives the fruits of the four classes, who is well known, who is covered with the lustre of liberation, who spreads the sounds of the waves of bliss arising from *yoga* who is the lord of the three worlds, who is gracious and kind.'..1..

साक्षाद्ब्रह्मपदार्विन्दयुगलं पैशल्यकल्लोलकम्
नैष्कर्म्यांद्यखिलेश्वरं कृतिमता मानन्दधारान्वितम्।
ध्यानज्योतिरखण्डखण्डवरणैरद्वैतमानन्त्यकम्
ज्योतिष्पीठमहेश्वरं गुरुवरं प्रत्यक्षदेवं भजे ॥२॥

*saakshaadbrahmapadaarvindayugalam paishalyakallolakam,
naishkarmyaadyakhileshvaram kritimataa
maanandadhaaraanvitam.
dhyaanajyotirakhandakhandavaranairadvaitamaanantyakam,
jyotishpithamaheshvaram guruvaram pratyakshadevam
bhaje..2..*

'I worship the great lord of Jyotishpeeth, the most excellent among the *gurus*, who is God present before the eyes, who with his two lotus feet appears to be Lord Brahma in person, who is a wave of tenderness, who is the universal lord, inactive in the beginning, who among the learned ones is endowed with streams of bliss, who in his meditation by going beyond the parts to the wholeness, to the light, is non-dual and infinite.'..2..

सर्वानन्दकरं महाप्रभुवरं साक्षाच्छिवं सात्विकं
लोकनामुपकारकं निगमतो मार्गप्रभोद्दीपकम्।
शान्तं दान्तमपीह सर्वजगतां तापत्रयोन्मूलनं
वन्दे तं गुरुदेवदेवसदनं ज्योतिर्मठाधीश्वरम् ॥३॥

*sarvaanandakaram mahaaprabhuvaram saakshaachchivam
saatvikam,
lokanaamupakaarakam nigamato maargaprabhoddipakam.
shaantam daantamapiha sarvajagataam taapatrayonmuulanam,
vande tam gurudevadevasadanam
jyotirmathaadhishvaram..3..*

'I praise him the Gurudeva who is the dwelling place of the *devas*, the supreme lord of Jyotirmath, who creates bliss for all people, who is the most excellent among the great Lords, who is Shiva in bodily form, who is endowed with the quality of *sattva*, who helps all people, who has the light to awaken the path described by the scriptures, who is peaceful and restrained and who destroys the three afflictions of all people.'..3..

शास्त्रे साधुकथासुधा सुललिता कैवल्यनैर्गुणियका
सर्वानन्दकरी सुरत्नरसनालावण्यलीलाम्बुधिः ।
राराजीति विशिष्टभावगहना यस्य प्रसादाद्भुवि
ब्रह्मानन्दसरस्वतीं गुरुवरं प्रत्यक्षदेवं भजे ॥४॥

*shaastre saadhukathaasudhaa sulalitaa kaivalyanairguniyakaa,
sarvaanandakari suratnarasanaalaavanyalilaambudhih.
raaraajiti vishishtabhaavagahanaa yasya prasaadaadbhuvi,
brahmaanandasarasvatim guruvaram
pratyakshadevam bhaje..4..*

'I worship Brahmananda Saraswati, the most excellent among the *gurus*, who is God present before the eyes, by whose grace the ocean of the *leela* with the best salty taste, which is the nectar of the stories of the saints found in the scriptures, very charming, transcendental, beyond the three *gunas*, an excellent state unfathomable creating bliss for all beings --- shines brilliantly in the world.'..4..

यद्द्वारे निखिला निलिम्पपरिपत्सिद्धिं विधत्तेनिशं
श्रीमच्छ्रीलसितं जगद्गुरुपदं नत्वात्मतृप्तिं गताः ।
लोकाज्ञानपयोदपाटनधुरं श्रीशंकरं शर्मदं
ब्रह्मानन्दसरस्वतीं गुरुवरं ध्यायामि ज्योतिर्मयं ॥५॥

yadhdvaare nikhilaa nilimpaparishatsiddhim vidhattenisham,
shrimachchrilasitam jagadhgurupadam natvaatmatriptim gataah.
lokaagyaanapayodapaatanadhuram shrishankaram sharmadam,
brahmaanandasarasvatim guruvaram dhyaayaami jyotirmayam..5..

'At whose door the whole galaxy of gods pray for perfection day and night.
Adorned by immeasurable glory, preceptor of the whole world, having bowed down at His feet, we gain fulfilment.
Skilled in dispelling the cloud of ignorance of the people, the gentle emancipator,
Brahmananda Saraswati, the supreme teacher, full of brilliance, on Him we meditate'...5..

Another verse in praise, possibly written by the same poet is this:-

मायावादनिराशराशिशिशरणं सत्कारणाधीश्वरम् ।सद्गुण्याद्यखिलप्रभावविभवं वेदैकवेद्यं विभुम् ।

ब्रह्मानन्द कदम्बपुष्पलसितं श्रीशङ्कराचार्यकम् ।

याचेऽहं सततं शरण्यममलं मुक्त्यैककल्पद्रुमम् ॥

"maayaavaadaniraasharaashisharanam satkaaranaadhishvaram.
sadgunyaadyakhilaprabhaavavibhavam vedaikavedyam vibhum.
brahmaananda kadambapushpalasitam shrishankaraachaaryakam.
yaacheaham satatam sharanyamamalam muktyaikakalpadrumam.."

> 'I always take refuge in Brahmananda, in Shri Shankaracharya who is shining like Kadamba flowers, who through the doctrine of Maya (Vedanta) gives shelter to the multitude of hopeless people, who is the true being, the cause of creation, the Supreme Lord, whose greatness consists in all powers beginning with the quality of goodness, who is to be known through Veda only, who is all-pervading, who is spotless and pure and the one wish-fulfilling tree for gaining liberation.'

One of these verses appears in the TM *puja*, and Maharishi Mahesh Yogi explained this part of the *puja*, glorifying Maharishi's master, was written by one of the *guru's pandits*. It is verse 5 of a *'praarthanaa'*, 'a prayer', included in an *ashram* publication of 1947.[180]

'This was done by us; I didn't compose those lines, because I am not a Sanskrit scholar, but this was done by a, very, very eminent Sanskrit poet of Banares, and he was such a mysterious man, the poet.

He used to live us, just like us, and a good *pandit*, and when some *pandits*, learned people, used to come to pay their respects to Guru Dev, and he would sit, like that. And generally it is traditional, that in the presence of Shankaracharya, *pandits* gather. *Pandits* mean the learned people, highly great intellectuals of the country. They sit together and they try to bring home to Shankaracharya, each one of them, that he is the greater *pandit* than the others. And these dialogues are so highly intellectual and so very interesting, because they, everyone wants to win the grace of Shankaracharya, apart from his spiritual development, for their material glorification, because a certificate from the Shankaracharya of the great learning of the *pandits*, will make him flourish in his area. So they, very beautiful, and this *pandit* he used to defeat everyone because he was a born poet. He would versify anything that he wants to say. In poetry he would speak. And when in poetry, and so fluent and so high-class, so high-class fluent Sanskrit poetry, and others would just sit and listen to him, what he says.

He was very dear, sweet *pandit*. He wrote lots of stanzas of Guru Dev, absolutely, and this was one of them.

What happened was... this is very interesting.... this great *pandit* in his flight of the poet, he wrote Guru Dev's life, and he didn't know Guru Dev's life. Because all the time was spent in loneliness in the jungles, and, nobody would know.

And he said to me, "I am going to write."

And I said "Yes, you write", and this was our agreement that I'll get it printed, and he wrote, and I enjoyed it so much, but someday it was to come to Guru Dev for sanction. So, Guru Dev, he enjoyed hearing the whole thing. It was highly scholarly and very great, and everything that a good poet could put in that, he put it.

And then, when it was finished Guru Dev said, "It's very good, yes." And when the *pandit* went out of the room he asked him to take it to the Ganges, tie it down with a big stone, heavy, put it in the Ganges.

And I, it was a shock to me, I said "But, but there are beautiful passages in it".

He said, "Don't talk!' He said, "Nobody should read it, tell him to take it", it is because he didn't know his life and he said "If you don't put it in the Ganges I'll ask someone else to do it."

I said, "I'll do it".

We would have used all those beautiful sen[tences]... poetry. These days you would have enjoyed all. But he wouldn't allow it to remain.

He was absolutely divine, simple, and great, very great, he was very great.'[181]

Reference Notes

1. *'Vedanta Incarnate'*, Jugal Kishore Shrivastava, 2009, p48

2. *'Thirty Years Around the World - Dawn of the Age of Enlightenment, vol. 1 1957-64'*, Maharishi Vedic University, 1986, p243

3. *'Torch Divine'* Vol 1 No. 4, April 1959, p64

4. *'Self-referral consciousness and Yogic Flying are the gifts of the Vedic Tradition of Masters'* https://www.youtube.com/watch?v=k1cwMc4Myvg

5. *'Beacon Light of the Himalayas'*, Maharishi Mahesh Yogi, p57, - Taittiriya Upanishad 3:6

6. *'Katha Upanishad'* 2:3:10-11

7. *'Bhagavad Gita'*, Chapter 6 verses 11-13

8. *'Bhagavad Gita'*, Chapter 6 verses 24-27

9. *'Yoga Darshanam'* - *'Patanjali's Yoga Sutras'* - verse 2

10. *'Yoga Darshanam'* - *'Patanjali's Yoga Sutras'* - verses 1-4

11. *'Shri Shankaracharya Upadeshamrit'*, translated by Paul Mason as the *'108 Discourses of Guru Dev: The Life and Teachings of Swami Brahmananda Saraswati, Shankaracharya of Jyotirmath (1941-53) - Volume I'*, Paul Mason - Premanand 2009, revised 2015, discourse, 61, p153

12. *'The Biography of Guru Dev: The Life and Teachings of Swami Brahmananda Saraswati, Shankaracharya of Jyotirmath (1941-53) - Volume II'*, Paul Mason - Premanand 2009, revised 2015, p117

13. *'Jyorimathasya Guruparampara'*, a publication of Jyotir Math

14. *'The Biography of Guru Dev: The Life and Teachings of Swami Brahmananda Saraswati, Shankaracharya of Jyotirmath (1941-53) - Volume II'*, Paul Mason - Premanand 2009, revised 2015, pp18-19

15. ibid., pp20-21

16. ibid., pp43-44

17. ibid., pp46-47

18. ibid., pp48-49

19. Author's transcript of Maharishi Mahesh Yogi speaking in California, USA, on July 27th 1961

20. *'The Biography of Guru Dev: The Life and Teachings of Swami*

Brahmananda Saraswati, Shankaracharya of Jyotirmath (1941-53) - Volume II', Paul Mason - Premanand 2009, revised 2015, p77

21. ibid., p84

22. ibid., pp90-91

23. ibid., p201

24. *'Shri Shankaracharya Upadeshamrit'*, translated by Paul Mason as the *'108 Discourses of Guru Dev: The Life and Teachings of Swami Brahmananda Saraswati, Shankaracharya of Jyotirmath (1941-53) - Volume I'*, Paul Mason - Premanand 2009, revised 2015, discourse, 45, p119

25. exerpts are taken from pages 257-260 of his autobiography *'Living With The Himalayan Masters'*, published by the Himalayan International Institute in 1978

26. *'The Biography of Guru Dev: The Life and Teachings of Swami Brahmananda Saraswati, Shankaracharya of Jyotirmath (1941-53) - Volume II'*, Paul Mason - Premanand 2009, revised 2015, p140

27. *'Meditations of Maharishi Mahesh Yogi'*, Bantam, 1968, pp39-40.

28. ibid., p61.

29. refer to *'Sociology: A Study of the Social Sphere'* by Yogesh Atal, Pearson, 2012, p242

30. *'MIU World'*, vol. 1, no. 2, 1991

31. The webpage was viewable from February 28th 2001 to April 4th 2007, http://www.alluniv.edu/hostels/gnjha/gnjha_alumni.htm

32. *'Vedanta Incarnate'*, Jugal Kishore Shrivastava 2009, p48

33. *'Thirty Years Around the World - Dawn of the Age of Enlightenment, vol. 1 1957-64'*, Maharishi Vedic University, 1986, p184

34. *'The Way to Maharishi's Himalayas'*, Elsa Dragemark, Stockholm, 1972, p257

35. Author's transcript of Maharishi speaking, on video of 4th September 1972

36. *'Vedanta Incarnate'*, Jugal Kishore Shrivastava 2009, p48

37. *'Thirty Years Around the World - Dawn of the Age of Enlightenment, vol. 1 1957-64'*, Maharishi Vedic University, 1986, p184

38. *'The Way to Maharishi's Himalayas'*, Elsa Dragemark, Stockholm, 1972, pp255-256

39. Raj Varma quotes found on Guru Dev file *'M2000005.pdf'*

40. *'Strange Facts about a Great Saint'* by Dr Raj R.P.Varma, Jabalpur, 1980, P67

41. ibid., P70-71

42. Raj Varma quotes found on Guru Dev file *'M2000005.pdf'*

43. *'The Biography of Guru Dev: The Life and Teachings of Swami Brahmananda Saraswati, Shankaracharya of Jyotirmath (1941-53) - Volume II'*, Paul Mason - Premanand 2009, revised 2015, pp176-180

44. *'Thirty Years Around the World - Dawn of the Age of Enlightenment, vol. 1 1957-64'*, Maharishi Vedic University, 1986, p184

45. Author's transcript of tape recording of Maharishi speaking c1961

46. *'International Times'*, 15 December 1967, p10

47. Author's transcript of Maharishi speaking at Amherst, USA, 8th July 1971

48. *'Vedanta Incarnate'*, Jugal Kishore Shrivastava 2009, p48

49. *'The Way to Maharishi's Himalayas'*, Elsa Dragemark, Stockholm, 1972, p259.

50. *'Thirty Years Around the World - Dawn of the Age of Enlightenment, vol. 1 1957-64'*, Maharishi Vedic University, 1986, p185.

51. Author's transcript of Maharishi speaking Amherst, USA, on 8th July 1971

52. http://tmbulletin.net/emails/purnima2012.htm

53. *'Thirty Years Around the World - Dawn of the Age of Enlightenment, vol. 1 1957-64'*, Maharishi Vedic University, 1986, pp185-6

54. Author's transcription of Maharishi speaking, on video entitled:- *'Invincibility to Every Nation Maharishi's Supreme Offer to the World Courses for all areas of society to structure invincibility for the nation - Core courses on invincibility -Theme Fifteen - Global unfoldment of the age of enlightenment: Improving the quality of world consciousness - Tape 1 - Maharishi Speaks on Guru Dev and the History of the Movement: Enlivening Supreme Silence to Raise World Consciousness'*.

55. *'Shri Shankaracharya Upadeshamrit'*, translated by Paul Mason as the *'108 Discourses of Guru Dev: The Life and Teachings of Swami Brahmananda Saraswati, Shankaracharya of Jyotirmath (1941-53) - Volume I'*, Paul Mason - Premanand 2009, revised 2015, discourse 71, pp189-90

56. ibid., discourse 93, p268

57. ibid., discourse 9, pp28-29

58. ibid., discourse 90, pp253-4

59. *'Godhana'* is an article by Shankaracharya Swami Brahmananda Saraswati, contained in the 1946 cow special, *'Go-Ankh'* edition, of the magazine *'Kalayana'*, Gita Press, Gorakhpur

60. Umesh Srivastava, of Raipur, India, born 4th August 1940

61. *'Vedanta Incarnate'*, Jugal Kishore Shrivastava, 2009, p58

62. *'Shri Shankaracharya Upadeshamrit'*, translated by Paul Mason as the *'108 Discourses of Guru Dev: The Life and Teachings of Swami Brahmananda Saraswati, Shankaracharya of Jyotirmath (1941-53) - Volume I'*, Paul Mason - Premanand 2009, revised 2015, discourse 35, pp89-91

63. ibid., discourse 23, p62

64. ibid., discourse 21, p58

65. ibid., discourse 38, p98

66. *'Shri Shankaracharya Vaksudha'*, 1947, translation by Premanand Paul Mason, 2009

67. *'Shri Shankaracharya Upadeshamrit'*, translated by Paul Mason as the *'108 Discourses of Guru Dev: The Life and Teachings of Swami Brahmananda Saraswati, Shankaracharya of Jyotirmath (1941-53) - Volume I'*, Paul Mason - Premanand 2009, revised 2015, discourse 78, pp216-8

68. *'Shri Shankaracharya Vaksudha'*, p47 - translation by Premanand Paul Mason, 2009, part 13, p96

69. Raj Varma quotes found on Guru Dev file *'M2000005.pdf'*

70. *'Beaconlight of the Himalayas'*, pii

71. *'Shri Shankaracharya Upadeshamrit'*, translated by Paul Mason as the *'108 Discourses of Guru Dev: The Life and Teachings of Swami Brahmananda Saraswati, Shankaracharya of Jyotirmath (1941-53) - Volume I'*, Paul Mason - Premanand 2009, revised 2015, discourse 80, p224

72. ibid., discourse 97, p288

73. ibid., discourse 74, p199

74. ibid., discourse 74, p200

75. ibid., discourse 77, p211

76. *'Amrita-Kana'*, translated by Paul Mason as *'Guru Dev as Presented by Maharishi Mahesh Yogi: The Life and Teachings of Swami Brahmananda Saraswati, Shankaracharya of Jyotirmath (1941-53) - Volume III'*, Paul Mason - Premanand 2009, revised 2015, p23

77. ibid., p32

78. ibid., p16

79. ibid., p49

80. ibid., p68

81. ibid., p36

82. ibid., p50

83. *'Droplets of Nectar'* booklet

84. *'Shri Shankaracharya Upadeshamrit'*, translated by Paul Mason as the *'108 Discourses of Guru Dev: The Life and Teachings of Swami Brahmananda Saraswati, Shankaracharya of Jyotirmath (1941-53) - Volume I'*, Paul Mason - Premanand 2009, revised 2015, discourse 73, pp195-197

85. *'Amrita-Kana'*, translated by Paul Mason as *'Guru Dev as Presented by Maharishi Mahesh Yogi: The Life and Teachings of Swami Brahmananda Saraswati, Shankaracharya of Jyotirmath (1941-53) - Volume III'*, Paul Mason - Premanand 2009, revised 2015, p49

86. *'Shri Shankaracharya Upadeshamrit'*, translated by Paul Mason as the *'108 Discourses of Guru Dev: The Life and Teachings of Swami Brahmananda Saraswati, Shankaracharya of Jyotirmath (1941-53) - Volume I'*, Paul Mason - Premanand 2009, revised 2015, discourse 48, p126

87. ibid., discourse 56, p142

88. *'Strange Facts about a Great Saint'* by Raj Varma, M/s Varma & Sons, 1980, P135

89. *'Talk 328'*, Ramana Maharshi, 17th January, 1937, http://bhagavan-ramana.org/ramana_maharshi/private/tw/tw328.html.

90. *'Japa Yoga'*, Swami Sivananda Saraswati, 1939, p4

91. *'Shri Shankaracharya Vaksudha'*, translated excerpt published in *'Knack of Meditation - The No Nonsense Guide to Meditation'*, Paul Mason, Premanand, 2013, p75

92. Exerpt of introductory biographical material in *'Amrit-Kana'*

93. Translation of exerpt of introductory biographical material in *'Amrit-Kana'*

94. *'The Biography of Guru Dev: The Life and Teachings of Swami Brahmananda Saraswati, Shankaracharya of Jyotirmath (1941-53) - Volume II'*, Paul Mason - Premanand 2009, revised 2015, pp297-299

95. *'Hamare Gurudeva'* by Swami Vasudevanand, Jyotishpeeth, 1983, translated by Rakesha Cheekalimane, revised 2015

96. ibid., pp307-8

97. Brahmachari Sattyanand was a brother monk of Maharishi's. As a young man he had been married when he had met Guru Dev. When his wife died young and since he was without children, he left the world of business, and joined Guru Dev's entourage in his monastic order. He was also known as 'Swami' Satyanand.

98. Published in the final issue of *'Shri Shankaracharya Upadesha'*, the newsletter of the Shankaracharya of Jyotishpeeth's *ashram*, published on 20th July 1953, pp20-23

99. *'Importance of Brahmacharya!',* by Sri Swami Sivananda http://www.yoga-age.com/modern/brahma.html

100. *'Hermit in the House',* Helena Olson, Los Angeles, 1967, p67

101. *'Text and Context in the Communication of a Social Movement's Charisma, Ideology, and Consciousness: TM for India and the West: SRM's Emergence: Arya Samaj - Vedic Revival'* by Jay Randolph Coplin, Doctor of Philosophy in Sociology, University of California, San Diego, 1990

102. *'Maharishi'* pdf - Swami Srikanta Bharathi, Sree Matha, Hariharapura

103. Author's transcript of recording of Maharishi speaking in Rishikesh, India, 9th February 1970

104. *'Guru Stotram'* v.11

105. On 21st October 2007 Maharishi recalled visiting Kerala, in South India, in 1955 and instituting the *puja* ceremony in order to teach meditation, transcript by author.

106. *'Beacon Light of the Himalayas'*, p50

107. ibid., p50-53

108. ibid., p27

109. Author's transcript of Maharishi speaking at Poland Spring, USA, on 12th July 1970

110. *'Beacon Light of the Himalayas'*, p36-8

111. ibid., p79

112. ibid., p28

113. ibid., p29

114. ibid., p11-12

115. *'Taittiriya Upanishad'* 3:6

116. Translation of Sanskrit verses; *'yaavat sarvam na santyaktam taavadaatmaa na labhyate | sarvavastu-parityaage sesha aatmeti kathyate ||* 'Until all is not renounced, the Self cannot be accomplished. When everything is renounced what survives as the residue is the Self. & *'na karmana, na prajaya, dhanena, tyage naike amritatvam aanasuh'*, 'Not by action, not by progeny, not by wealth; but by sacrifice alone can man attain immortality.'

117. *'Shri Ramacharitamanasa'* 1:3

118. *'Guru Stotram'*, *'Aarti'* and *'Guru Gita'* verse 34,

119. *'Inauguration of the Dawn of Enlightenment'*, 1975, p23

120. *'Torch Divine'* Vol 1 No. 1, July 1958, pp 8-9

121. *'Torch Divine'* Vol 1 No. 1 July 1958, pp 2-5

122. *'Bhagavad Gita'* 11:33, 'Only be a mere instrument, O ambidexterous one'

123. *'International Times'*, 15 December 1967, p10

124. *'Thirty Years Around the World - Dawn of the Age of Enlightenment, vol. 1 1957-64'*, Maharishi Vedic University, 1986, p211.

125. *'Torch Divine'* Vol 1 No. 2 October 1958, pp16-8

126. ibid., pp24-5

127. *'Torch Divine'* Vol 1 No. 3 January 1959, p42

128. *'Torch Divine'* Vol II No. 1 October 1959, January 1960, pp92-3

129. *'Thirty Years Around the World - Dawn of the Age of Enlightenment, vol. 1 1957-64'*, Maharishi Vedic University, 1986, p229.

130. *'Torch Divine'* Vol 1 No. 2 October 1958, p20

131. *'Torch Divine'* Vol 1 No. 3 January 1959, p38

132. ibid., pp51-2

133. *'Honolulu Star Bulletin'*, Wednesday, 31 December 1958

134. *'Meditation: easy system propounded by Maharishi Mahesh Yogi'*, International Meditation Centre, Honolulu, 1961, pp26-8

135. *'International Times'*, 15 December 1967, p10

136. *'Torch Divine'* Vol 1 No. 3 January 1959, pp40-1

137. *'Torch Divine'* Vol 1 No. 4 April-July 1959, pp54-5

138. *'Thirty Years Around the World - Dawn of the Age of Enlightenment, vol. 1 1957-64'*, Maharishi Vedic University, 1986, p242.

139. *'Torch Divine'* Vol 1 No. 4 April 1959, p62

140. ibid., p63

141. ibid., p64

142. Author's transcription of tape recording of Maharishi, Masquers Club, Hollywood, USA, 1st May 1959

143. *'Hermit in the House'*, Helena Olson, Los Angeles, 1967, p20

144. ibid., p31

145. ibid., p49

146. ibid., p50-1

147. ibid., p159

148. ibid., pp110-2

149. Author's transcript from a recording of Maharishi talking in Rishikesh India, March 1970

150. *'Shri Ramacharitmanasa'* - *'Uttarakand'* 99:3

151. *'Shri Shankaracharya Upadeshamrit'*, translated by Paul Mason as the *'108 Discourses of Guru Dev: The Life and Teachings of Swami Brahmananda Saraswati, Shankaracharya of Jyotirmath (1941-53) - Volume I'*, Paul Mason - Premanand 2009, revised 2015, discourse, 77, p212

152. *'Hermit in the House'* Helena Olson, Los Angeles, 1967, pp110-2

153. ibid., p113

154. ibid., pp182-3

155. aka Sita Agrawal, who latterly lived at Geeta Bhavan, Swargashram, Rishikesh, India, until her passing on 6th June 2009 – see:- http://sashas-india.blog.de/2009/06/07/mata-ji-followed-guru-dev-and-maharishi-6259790/

156. Transcript of interview between film maker David Sieveking and Swami Swaroopanand, Shankaracharya of Dwarka, 22nd May 2009

157. *'Hermit in the House,'* Helena Olson, Los Angeles, 1967, pp175-6

158. *'Torch Divine'* Vol II No. 1 October 1959 - January 1960, pp86-7

159. Author's transcription of tape recording of Maharishi, 20th July 1959

160. *'Hermit in the House'*, Helena Olson, Los Angeles, 1967, pp191-2

161. *'Taittiriya Upanishad'* 3:6

162. Author's transcription of tape recording of Maharishi in the USA, entitled *'Glow'* of c1959

163. Author's transcription of tape recording of Maharishi in the USA, entitled *'Mantra Selection'* c1959

164. Reference to various audio files of Maharishi speaking, from 1959-1970

165. *'Meditations of Maharishi Mahesh Yogi'*, Bantam, 1968, pp106-7,

166. Author's transcription of tape recording of Maharishi talking in Rishikesh, India, 12th March 1967

167. *'Meditations of Maharishi Mahesh Yogi'*, Bantam, 1968, pp89-90

168. ibid., pp91-92.

169. *'International Times'*, 15th December 1967, p13

170. Excerpt from an article entitled *'You don't know you're there, but you know you've been'* by Cyril Dunn in *'Observer'*, 14th January 1968

171. Author's transcription of tape recording of Maharishi in Rishikesh, February 1969

172. *'Vedanta Incarnate'*, Jugal Kishore Shrivastava, 2009, pp61-2

173. *'The Maharishi and the Abbot'*, International SRM Publications, 1964.

174. Email to author from Hans Bruncken, November 2014, in which Hans notes that Maharishi made this comment about transcending on a Teachers Training Course in Rishikesh, India, in 1970. The author himself has also heard a similar comment by Maharishi, on a recording from the early 1970's.

175. *'Meditations of Maharishi Mahesh Yogi'*, Bantam, 1968, pp106-110

176. - Exerpt of interview between David Frost and Maharishi Mahesh Yogi conducted at London Airport and included as part of the *'The Frost Programme'*, shown on British television on Friday 29th September 1967.

177. Author's transcription of recording of Maharishi speaking, 14th May 2003

178. Email from Professor Dana Sawyer, May 2015

179. Email to author from Hans Bruncken, November 2014, in which Hans recounts his experiences of accompanying Maharishi to Nepal in 1974

180. This verse, and the verses below, can to be found in the Hindi book on Shankaracharya Brahmananda Saraswati, entitled *'Sri Shankaracharya Vaksudha'*, published 1947

181. Author's transcript of Maharishi speaking at his *ashram* in Rishikesh in February / March 1969

182. Transcript of Maharishi speaking in Rishikesh, 1st April 1970

Glossary

abhyasa, practice, exercise, study, habit, meditation
achaarya, acharya, teacher
adharma, vice, sin
adhyaatma, spiritual contemplation
adhyatmik, spiritual
adi, first
advaita, adwaita, non-dualism
agni, fire
agyaana, ignorance
aham, 'I'-awareness, notion of ego, self-consciousness
ahamkaara, egotism, arrogance, conceit, empty pride, vanity
ahimsaa, non-violence, inoffensiveness, benevolence
akasha, ether, etheric element
akshara, permanent
amrita, nectar
ananda, aananda, joy, bliss
ananyatha, endless, infinite, unbounded
anartha, loss, misfortune
anishta, undesired, harm, evil, calamity; mishchief,
anoraniyan, minuter than an atom
antahkarana, conscience, inner self
apaurusheya, not of man
archana, worship
artha, wealth
arya, noble
ashaanti, unrest
ashirvad, blessing, benediction
ashram, hermitage
ashrama, stage of life
astika, aastika, religious, devout
Atharva Veda, see *Veda*
atma, aatmaa, atman, Soul
atmananda, bliss of the Supreme Soul

aushadha, oushadha, a herb, a drug, a medicine
avadhoot, ascetic
avataar, incarnation
aviveka, absence of discrimination
bal, bala, young boy
bal brahmachari, celibate since boyhood
Bhagavan, Bhagwan, *bhagavaana,* Supreme Being, God
Bhagavat, God
Bhagwan, Bhagavan, *bhagavaana,* Supreme Being, God
bhajan, hymn
bhakti, devotion
Bharat, Bhaarata, India
bhavaroga, birth-sickness
bhavasaagara, sea of experience
bhavateet, transcendental
bij, bija, beej, seed
Brahma, Hindu god of creation
brahmachari, celibate student
brahmacharya, celibacy
Brahmaleena, absorbed in Brahman, Self-absorbed
Brahman, Absolute Divine Truth,
brahmana, a Brahmin, of Hindu *varna* (caste), learned, priestly
Brahmanand, *brahmananda,* Absolute bliss
brahmanishtham, possessing knowledge of immortal self
brahmavidyaa, theology taught in the Upanishads
brahmin, brahmana, one of 4 *varnas* (castes), learned, priestly
chaitanya, consciousness
chakra, wheel, disk
charan, ray of sun or moon
charana, foot, feet
chela, disciple
chit, consciousness
chitta, faculty of reasoning
dakshina, southern
danda, stick, staff
dandi, carrying stick
darshan, darsan, darshana, Holy look, vision
dasanami, dashanami, ten names

deva, divine
devataa, god
devataon, gods/goddesses
dharma, righteous duty
dharmashaala, a dwelling house for pilgrims
dharmik, (virtuous, devout, religious, godly, upright, etc.)
dhoti, sheet
dhyana, dhyaan, dhyaana, meditation
diksha, initiation
duhkha, pain, suffering
Ganapati, Ganesha Hindu god with elephant trunk
Gandharvas, celestial musicians
Gandharva-Ved, Indian classical music
Gayatri, sacred Vedic *mantra* of 24 syllables
gita, geet, song
Govind, Govinda, Krishna
grihastha, householder
grihasthon, householders
guna, quality
gupha, cave
guru, teacher, master
gurudwara, Sikh temple
gyaani, learned
gyan, gyaan, gnan, jyaan knowledge
hansa, swan
hare, lord
hatha, force, obstinacy
havana, fire sacrifice
hawai, pertaining to the air
ishta, deity
Ishwar, Isvara, God
jaati, varna, caste - see *brahmin, kshatriya, vaishya, shudra*
jagadguru, world teacher, universal teacher
jai, jay, jaya, jaaya, hail, glory, victory
Jai Guru Dev, Victory to Gurudeva, Glory to Guru Dev
japa, repetition of *mantra*
Jay Gurudeva, Victory to Gurudeva, Glory to Guru Dev
jeevanmukti, liberated soul

ji, term of respect
jiva, the individual soul
jivanmukti, liberated soul
jyotir, light
jyotishi, Indian astrology
kaama, love
kalyaana, happiness, welfare, benediction, prosperity
kamandalu, wooden pot
karma, law of action and reaction
Kashi, Benares, Banaras, Varanasi
kaupeen, loincloth
kayastha, subcaste of *kshatriya* caste, scribe
       see also *varna, brahmin, kshatriya, vaishya, shudra*
kirtana, singing praise of God
kripa, grace, kindness, forgiveness, pity
Krishna, dark, name of principal character of *Mahabharata* poem
krodha, anger
kshatriya, one of the 4 main *varna* castes, warriors, administrators
kutiya, hut, cottage
laddoo, laddu, sweetmeat made of *ghi* (ghee)
leela, sport, play, pastime
lobha, greed
mada, intoxification
madyama, madhyama vaani, voice from the throat
maha, great
maharaja, king
maharishi, maharshi, great sage
maharishyon, sages
mahat, intellect, great
mahatma, mahaatma, great soul
Mahesh, name of Hindu god Shiva
mala, maalaa, rosary, necklace, garland
manasaa, manasik, in the mind
mandala, mandal, circle
mandir, temple
mantra, word or words of spiritual power
Manu Smriti, Manu Samhita, law book
marg, marga, way, road, path

maryaadaa, principled code of conduct
math, hermitage, monastery
matsara, matsarya, jealousy
mayaa, maaya, delusion, prosperity, Lakshmi
mishra, mixed, combined
moha, delusion
moksha, final liberation, beatitude, redemption, absolution, salvation, freedom
mukti, liberation
murti, image, shape, likeness, form, picture, statue
naam, nama, name
naastika, nastika, naistika, unbeliever
niraakaara, without form
nirguna, without qualities, Absolute
nirodha, stop, obtruct, restrain, hold
nivarthi, see *nivritti*
nivritti, path of renunciation
oushada, aushadha, a herb, a drug, a medicine
paapa, sinful
padma, lotus
pagri, turban
pandit, learned man
par, para vaani, voice from the navel
param, parama, highest, chief, best, supreme, ultimate, perfect
Paramahansa, ascetic of highest order, Supreme Soul
paramartha, parmath, the ultimate good, salvation
Paramatma, *paramaatmaa,* Supreme Spirit, Supersoul, God
parampara, succession
pashyanti, pashyanti vaani, voice from the heart
pathya, way, path, road, course, custom
peeth, seat of monastery
praana, breath
praanon, the five vital airs
praarthana, supplication, request, prayer
prakritti, nature, habit
prana, breath
pranaama, salutation

pranava, name of 'ॐ *OM*' *mantra*
prarabdha, already commenced *karma*
prasad, blessing
pravritti, tendency, inclination or perseverance of mind
puja, pooja, ceremony, ritual
pujana, worship
punya, meritous *karma*
purana, old
purna, poorna, perfect
purnima, poornima, full-moon night
purusha, male
purushartha, human wealth or purpose, work for fulfilment of life
raaga, raga, attachment
raaj, raja, royal, king
rajasic, energetic, passionate
Rama, Raama, Raam, name of hero of *Ramayana* poem
Rig Veda, see *Veda*
rishi, sage, wise man
Rudra, name of Hindu god Shiva
rupa, roop, form
saadhaka, sadhaka, one engaged in spiritual discipline
sachchidananda, satchitanand, Truth, Consciousness, Bliss
sadguru, genuine *guru*
sadhana, spiritual practice or discipline
sadhu, wandering holy man
saguna, having qualities, endowed with attributes
sakara, having form
Sama Veda, see *Veda*
samaadhi, samadhi, stillness of the mind
samagri, materials, articles, implements, paraphenalia
samardarshi, impartial, dispassionate
sammelan, meeting, assembly, gathering
sampradaaya, sect
samsaara, samsara, worldly existence, mortal transmigration
samsaari, worldly
samskaara, mental impressions
sankalpa, wish, intention
sannyas, vow of renunciation

sanyaasi, renunciate
Saraswati, name of Hindu goddess of learning, name of river
satchitanand, sachchidananda, Truth, Consciousness, Bliss
sattva, sattvic, satvik, pure
satya, truth
shabd, sound, voice, word
Shaivism, sect that reveres god Shiva, Lord of the Yogis
shakti, energy, strength
Shankar, name of Hindu god Shiva
Shankaracharya, one of the heads of Hindu religion
shanti, shaanti, peace
Shastras, shaastra, Hindu Scriptures
shikshaa, instruction
shishya, pupil
Shiva, name of Hindu god of destruction, lord of the *yogis*
shloka, verse
shraddha, faith, veneration, reverence
shravana, devotion
shri, shrii, blessed, 'श्री SHREE', Shri Lakshmi (goddess of wealth)
shrotriyan, well-versed in *Vedas*
shruti, information heard from the *Veda*
shubha, happy, auspicious
shudra, one of 4 main *varna* (castes), labourer
siddha, perfected being
siddhi, one who has acquired supernatural powers
smarana, remembrance
smriti, smritti, remembered, from the *Shastra.*
sthula sharira, gross body
stotra, hymns of praise
sudra, shudra, one of 4 main *varna* (castes), labourer
sukshma sharira, subtle body
svarg, svarga, swarg, heaven, paradise
swami, renunciate
swaroop, svarupa, swarupa, divine form, real self, true self
tantra, ancient scriptures, ancient rituals
tapasya, tapas, austerity
tattva, tatva, truth, essence, principle, reality, element

tilaka, tilak, mark of sandalwood paste applied to forehead, emblem of a sect
tyaagi, unattached renunciates
upaanshu, upanshu, whispering, whispered
upaasanaa, sitting near, devout meditation, worship, prayer
upadesha, upadesh, lecture, advice, instruction, discourse, sermon
Upanishad, texts on *yoga*, to sit near
uttari, northern
vaanaprastha, forest dweller
vaani, voice, speech, language
vaidya, physician
vaikhari, articulate speech, speech
vairagya, freedom from worldly desires
vaishya, one of 4 main *varna* (castes), a trader
vanaprasthas, forest dwellers
vandana, adoration, obeisance
varna, caste, see *brahmin, kshatriya, vaishya, shudra, kayastha*
vasiyat, testament, a Will, request, legacy
vayu, air, life breath
Veda, ancient religious texts, *Rig Veda, Sama Veda, Yajur Veda, Atharva Veda*
Vedanta, relating to *Upanishads, Bhagavad Gita* and *Brahma Sutras*
vidya, knowledge, science, learning
vikas, progress, development
Vishnu, Hindu god of preservation
vritti, flow of mental activity
vyavahara, worldly activities, business, behaviour
vyoman, celestial
yagya, yajna, yagna, ritual, religious sacrifice
Yajur Veda, see *Veda*
yantra, mystic diagram
yatra, yaatra, journey, tour, pilgrimage
yogadarshanam, Patanjali's *Yoga Sutras*
yoga-shaastra, yogadarshanam, Patanjali's *Yoga Sutras*
yuga, period of time

www.ingramcontent.com/pod-product-compliance
Lightning Source LLC
Chambersburg PA
CBHW050625300426

44112CB00012B/1665